Nationalism and
Communism in Romania

Nationalism and Communism in Romania

The Rise and Fall of Ceausescu's Personal Dictatorship

Trond Gilberg

Westview Press
BOULDER, SAN FRANCISCO, & OXFORD

Copyright © 1990 by Westview Press, Inc.

Published in 1990 in the United States of America by Westview Press, Inc., 5500 Central Avenue, Boulder, Colorado 80301, and in the United Kingdom by Westview Press, Inc., 36 Lonsdale Road, Summertown, Oxford, OX2 7EW

Library of Congress Cataloging-in-Publication Data
Gilberg, Trond, 1940–
    Nationalism and communism in Romania: The rise and fall of Ceausescu's Personal Dictatorship / Trond Gilberg.
        p.   cm.
    Includes bibliographical references.
    ISBN 0-8133-7497-9
    1. Nationalism and communism—Romania—History.   2. Romania—
Politics and government.   I. Title.
HX550.N3G55   1990
306.2'04498—dc20   89-25056
                                                                                                                CIP

Printed and bound in the United States of America

 The paper used in this publication meets the requirements
of the American National Standard for Permanence of Paper
for Printed Library Materials Z39.48-1984.

10   9   8   7   6   5   4   3   2

Contents

Tables

1

Religion, Ethnicity, and Nationalism in Southeastern Europe

The history of Southeastern Europe has been inextricably bound up with three major aspects of the human experience, namely, the power of religion; the importance of ethnicity and ultimately nationalism; and the establishment, maintenance, and decline of empires. In this respect, Southeastern Europe is not basically different from any other region in Eastern and Central Europe, where these three factors have also played crucial roles. However, the *configuration* of these elements in the southeastern part of the continent has been special, producing a unique blend that can be called the societal culture of the region. In particular, "political" culture is of fundamental importance in understanding any political system in this region at this time and indeed for the foreseeable future. More generally, an awareness of the area's culture and history is also essential because of the way in which the past influences the present and helps shape the policies that represent any political system's future.[1]

Religion, Consciousness, and Politics

Religion spans politics, social life, ethics, and morality; it is a fundamental force in the lives of human beings. Because it spreads not merely through its own force, but clearly as a result of the acts of empires and their leaders, religion is a political force of primary importance. In fact, religion is a fundamental glue for the political order itself because it helps establish and nurture the notions of self and collectivity. Thus, religion is a primary element in the development of nationalism and has been a crucial factor in political life throughout the world during the last two to three centuries, particularly in Southeastern, Central, and Northeastern Europe.[2]

The importance of religion in Southeastern Europe is compounded because it became an area of competing religious influences. After the acceptance of Christianity as the official religion of the Roman Empire in 323 A.D., the Romans became the chief propagators of the Christian faith as they extended their political and military reach in the region. Following the fall of Rome in 476 A.D, the Byzantine Empire continued support of Christianity in large areas of Southeastern Europe. But with the fall of Constantinople in 1453, the Ottoman Empire established Islam as a major religious factor in the region. Because the Ottoman rulers were relatively tolerant toward their subjects' religious preferences (as long as these carried no overtones of political or military disloyalty), there emerged a mosaic of great religious complexity that to this day characterizes Southeastern Europe. This complexity continued over a considerable period of time, nurtured by the political and military influences of other empires that professed to defend the religious rights of *their* brethren in the faith. Thus, the Habsburgs repeatedly intervened in the region on behalf of Catholicism; the Romanovs protected the interests of the Orthodox of the area (while helping their own political needs in the process); and the Ottomans, determined to defend Islam and their political and strategic interests, repeatedly answered the incursions of others into their territories with armed force. Religion became both a subject and an object of the broader political game played in this unstable region.[3]

Religion is many things to human beings. It is, first of all, a means of orienting oneself toward the hereafter. The focus on an afterlife has often been used by political leaders as a substitute for the search for the good life here on earth, thereby reducing the likelihood of rebellion by the poor and disenfranchised who have always constituted the majority of mankind. As such, religion became a major factor in the efforts by all leaders of this volatile region to maintain their regimes. Even today, as Southeastern Europe remains under communist rule, religion continues to be a most important political factor in this region.

Religion is a powerful cementing agent for humans organizing their lives in society. It is also a perennial source of enduring hatred and conflict. All religions teach a measure of tolerance, compassion, and love toward those of the same faith; quite a few also preach hostility and intolerance for those labeled "infidels" or believers in competing religions. Religion provides something to believe in, and something to fight against. And it teaches ethics and morality, thereby establishing behavioral rules and taboos so that human existence is molded into societally acceptable forms. The role of religion in establishing some of the most important prescriptions and proscriptions of human life is particularly important in an area of mixed religions, because it creates separate societies whose rules frequently conflict, thereby fostering controversy, violence, and, occasionally, wars.[4]

Religion teaches the rules of interaction among individuals and the collectivities they form and ultimately establishes behavior towards authority, both secular and spiritual. In some cases, the thrust of "the word" is submission; in others, it is individualism and, if need be, rebellion against any secular authority perceived as detrimental, sinful, or immoral. The religions that prevailed in Southeastern Europe varied greatly in this regard. Orthodoxy preached submission to the secular order. Catholicism had a hierarchy of its own—individuals with clear political ambitions and capabilities who occasionally acted as counterelites to those in charge in the secular realm. Islam, although fundamentally a warrior's religion, allowed other religions to survive on territory it controlled, permitting a relative level of autonomy that was intimately tied to local self-government and the existence of the millet system.

Because of this heterogeneity of religions, those aspects of religious life and doctrine that had political overtones (e.g., the perceptions of self and the relationship between the individual and the collectivity) helped produce dramatically different political cultures in this region. Subsequently, when the multinational empires broke down after World War I, the new political entities that rose from the ashes inherited many subcultures, which would cause great problems in nation-building. In many ways, today's communist regimes in the region are still engaged in the quest for fully integrated nations, this time on the basis of a "socialist" culture.[5]

Religion can also provide a means to withdraw from the political reality in which an individual finds himself. Thus, the individual whose integration into civil and political society is inadequate may continue to exist in that society; he becomes "out of reach" of the political leaders who may control him and his outward activities but cannot reach his inner sanctum of values, attitudes, and emotions. Consequently, religion, one of the most powerful instruments for political integration, may also cause political alienation by establishing and maintaining a chasm between the ruler and the ruled. Throughout Southeastern Europe, religion *did* play this role during many centuries of foreign rule. And in the case of the Romanians, it can be argued that faith was a crucial element both in the maintenance of ethnic identity and in the national revival that occurred in the eighteenth and nineteenth centuries.[6]

Religious faith preceded nationalism, as we now define it, by many centuries. It may also have preceded ethnicity, or it may have been coterminous with it, one element nurturing the other. Certainly it preceded the formation of formal, national political structures, institutions, and procedures. In this way, it became a force for the formation and maintenance of political values and attitudes, a crucial element in joining individuals and their groups into a recognizable political entity, and a determining factor in establishing who was "in" and who was "out" in the society. Religion as a *state* manifestation became an indispensable part of regime maintenance and enhancement and was a primary cause of war between the political entities that emerged in Southeastern Europe. And, as the regimes became exploitative, decadent, and corrupt, religion provided a mechanism for withdrawal from politics and for the defense of group values against foreign rulers, as well as a maintenance mechanism for the group itself under adverse circumstances. It is no wonder, then, that the communist regimes of the region have been unsuccessful in rooting out religion; forty years is inadequate to influence such a fundamental political element in any significant way.

Ethnicity and the Importance of Group Affiliation

"Ethnicity" is a concept used widely in contemporary social science to define and explain a major political force in the modern world. It is the sense of belonging to some collectivity shared by individuals of the same racial stock, who speak the same language and possess a collective memory of myths, heroes, and villains, as well as shared values and attitudes on many topics. Primary among these is the idea that the group is important, better than others, and worthy of membership. Tee shirts inscribed with "Polish Power" or "Italian Power" connote pride and a sense of belonging, of many things shared. This sense is often strengthened by symbols, rituals, and behavior patterns. And it is carried from generation to generation through one of the most successful examples of political socialization in history.[7]

Thus, ethnicity is a condition in part transmitted by birth, through ascribed characteristics. It is also in part an acquired condition, because values, attitudes, language, and other key elements of ethnicity are learned. The combined force of ascribed and acquired characteristics makes ethnicity a major political factor, in many respects similar to religion. The most important thing about ethnicity is its ability to integrate individuals who meet all the criteria to the exclusion of those who do not, for internal cohesion means boundaries against others. This is clearly a recipe for conflict in a region that includes a great many social groups. Southeastern Europe was just such a region, and it has remained so to a much greater extent than Central and Northwestern Europe.

Like religion, ethnicity cuts across dividing lines established by class, residence, education, and occupation. It is therefore a much more integrative force than an ideology or movement based on any one of these criteria. In retrospect, it seems clear that Marxism (and its various deviations) could not possibly supplant religion and ethnicity in the collective psyche of the peoples in Southeastern Europe. The emergence of "national communism" as a distinct political manifestation in the contemporary era was therefore predictable. Today, it is the dominant political phenomenon in the region and likely will remain so for the foreseeable future. It is possible that communism can survive *only* as a "national" phenomenon in this region.[8]

Ethnic consciousness and the rituals and other manifestations of group togetherness based on ethnicity also served as powerful protective mechanisms against the many invaders, rulers, and tax collectors that descended upon this region during the centuries between the fall of the Roman Empire and the emergence of sovereign states in the second half of the nineteenth century. For most of the peoples here, the rulers were always foreign—Turks (or their tax collectors, the Phanariot Greeks), Austrians, Hungarians, Russians, or Poles. And even after sovereign states were established in the region, the regimes were still controlled by individuals perceived as "ethnic others" by many minorities, who felt just as alienated from these Romanian, Serb, and Bulgarian leaders as they had from the representatives of the Byzantine, Ottoman, Habsburg, or Romanov empires. Therefore, ethnicity was a mechanism of defense against all these foreign and greedy rulers. Perhaps one of the most interesting examples of this can be found in Romania. The Romanians lived under foreign rule from the Roman abandonment of the province of Dacia in the third century B.C. until the establishment of political autonomy for the principalities of Moldavia and Wallachia in the 1850s. However, they maintained an ethnic consciousness and the basis of a distinct language during sixteen centuries. There are a number of other examples of the remarkable staying power of ethnicity as a group defense mechanism in this region.[9]

Today, ethnicity is recognized as a crucial political element even in communist systems. It has become an essential ingredient in the emerging national communism of a region where ethnicity has survived all attempts to destroy or weaken it. This is so because ethnicity is a vital part of *nationalism*, the third of the primary factors that have determined politics and history in Southeastern Europe.

Nationalism, Integration, and Conflict

Much literature on nationalism argues that it is a relatively late phenomenon in the history of mankind. It was not until the eighteenth century that an effective *political* nationalism evolved, creating institutions, structures, and procedures to maintain and expand the existing regime. And only during the last two-and-a-half centuries was a conscious effort made to set up a center for *all* societal activity and concentrate power in "the state," which existed independently of individuals, groups, and communities throughout the territory claimed by "the state" and its rulers. But the relatively recent appearance of nationalism on the world's political map does not mean that it is insignificant; in fact, it is probable that nationalism is the most important political phenomenon in the modern world.

In the communist-ruled systems of Southeastern Europe, the internationalism of Marxism has been abandoned as a guide to policy formulation and execution, clearly superseded by various forms of nationalism and localism. In fact, the political systems of this region are moving toward a new political form that may be called "national communism." ("National socialism," though more appropriate as a conceptual notion, carries unfortunate overtones that may well distort the meaning of the concept significantly.)[10]

Although nationalism is a powerful force for political and societal integration, it also has a disintegrative and disruptive flip side that can produce substantial problems. For example, in multiethnic societies, the nationalism of one group may lead to discrimination against other groups. Furthermore, clashing nationalisms may cause direct conflict among the states of a region such as Southeastern Europe. The history of the region certainly proves this: the Serbs, Bulgarians, Romanians, Greeks, and Turks repeatedly battled each other, in various configurations, during the centuries after the dissolution of the Roman and Byzantine empires. Even today, there are muted conflicts in the area—based upon nationalism, chauvinism, and discrimination—as exemplified by the verbal jousting between the Hungarians and the Romanians over the treatment of Magyars in Transylvania. Other conflicts also simmer just below the surface, most notably the old problem of Bessarabia, which continues to influence Soviet-Romanian relations.[11]

These three elements—religion, ethnicity, and nationalism—are enduring political phenomena in Southeastern Europe, and each continues to affect the behavior of masses and elites alike, even after forty years of communist rule. Each alone is a powerful force and may be considered an independent variable in value formation and political and socioeconomic behavior. When taken together, these elements produce a much more powerful combination, spawning ethno-national and religious subcultures. These subcultures, always important in Southeastern Europe, now dominate the political landscape to an extent that no leader could have predicted four decades ago, when communist elites established their systems and proceeded to "construct socialism."

Ethno-national and Religious Subcultures

Many scholars have recognized the vital link between religion and ethnicity, which in Southeastern Europe was further strengthened by the addition of nationalism as a political phenomenon centuries later. Briefly put, religion has often become the hallmark of ethnicity, and ethnicity tends to determine an individual's religion. Thus, the Romanians were Orthodox, but the Hungarians living among them were either Catholic or Protestant, as were the Germans of Transylvania and elsewhere in the Principalities. In the area that is now Yugoslavia, ethnicity and religion also went hand in hand—Orthodox Serbs, Catholic Slovenes, heavy Catholic preference among the Croatians—and throughout the region, the Turks were predominantly Moslems. Such religious heterogeneity worked as long as the leaders of the multinational empires were tolerant on this crucial issue. But once nationalism emerged as a *political* expression of ethnic and religious particularism, *subcultures*, based on religious, ethnic, and political preferences, evolved to further the interests of individual groups in competition with others. Under such circumstances, these three powerful elements were fervently supported by the masses and became powerful mechanisms of legitimacy and authority for the political leaders of each subculture. They also provided equally powerful incentives for conflict *among* subcultures. The combination enhanced the interests of a nation through forceful action; by the same token, it helped each nation defend itself from others, either actively (sometimes with weapons in hand) or passively (by maintaining ethnic identity, religion, and perhaps also language even while suffering discrimination or outright oppression by more powerful nations).[12]

The Hierarchy of Subcultures

Each subculture developed its own political and cultural mythology over time, for the purposes of integration and national maintenance. A hierarchy of subcultures also developed—a pecking order of "good" and "bad" nations, of hard workers and slovenly types. The value system of this hierarchy then affected personal and political behavior. For example, intermarriage between two groups that valued each other was relatively common, but marriage to someone from a "lower" group was not. Similarly, political, cultural, and socio-economic contacts developed according to the mythology of hierarchies (at least until two powerful groups came into conflict with each other, in which case the hierarchy would be changed for the duration of the conflict or, perhaps, permanently).

The development of such ethno-national subcultures was encouraged by the powerful religious preferences, hatreds, and prejudices that naturally existed in an area of such heterogeneity. The addition of religion to the ethno-cultural subcultures of the region yielded a most powerful combination for integration and disintegration, cohesion and division. This combination made Southeastern Europe a perennial conflict area, where warfare occurred with some regularity and relations between states remained tense even between military encounters. Economic blockade, political controversies, and harassment of the local minorities became routine elements of daily political life in this region. And when Eastern Europe was once again caught in the struggles between two major powerblocs in World War I and World War II, the states of the region lined up in different camps and fought each other with great ferocity. More importantly, internal struggle in those states that were multiethnic (and most of them were) resembled civil war, pitting ethno-national and religious subcultures against each other with considerable passion, hatred, and cruelty. Thus, the advent of communist power in this region came against a backdrop of deep-seated animosities, and the new regimes, consequently, carried enormous liabilities with them through the formative years and into the contemporary era. It is clear that these problems have not been solved and will persist as fundamental sources of political instability and potential conflict for the foreseeable future.[13]

Nation-building and Value Formation

Given the extraordinarily complex interplay of religion, ethnicity, and nationalism in Southeastern Europe, nation-building was a difficult proposition at best, and perhaps an impossible task in the worst of circumstances. In Bulgaria, Romania, and Yugoslavia, which constitute most of Southeastern Europe, nation-building primarily meant the establishment of structures and institutions that reflected the political needs and wishes of the ethnic majority, as well as the promotion of its myths, values, and attitudes. The minorities, however, experienced various forms of political discrimination, occasionally combined with religious and socio-economic discrimination, as well. But some minorities fared quite well under these circumstances. For example, the Germans occupied important administrative and economic positions in Romania and, to some extent, in the other countries of the region, and the Jews fared much better in terms of social mobilization (such as education, urban residence, and even occupation) than any other ethnic group, including the politically dominant majority. In fact, in all three countries, the vast majority of the dominant ethnic groups were peasants, and many of the minorities lived and worked in the cities. This created a peculiar cleavage between city and countryside that solidified the image of the urban areas as both "foreign" and corrupt, representing values and behaviors that were somehow detrimental to the national interest and values. Therefore, the modernizing communist regimes that descended upon the region faced problems beyond those usually encountered by a revolutionary new order. They not only had to deal with the transformation of the socio-economic system but also with the value systems and the ethnic and religious animosities associated with them for centuries—intractable remnants of the past in Southeastern Europe.[14]

Political Values and Attitude Formation: The Case of the Detached Individual

The complex interaction of religion, ethnicity, and nationalism, together with the development of ethno-national subcultures and hierarchies, produced enduring political values and attitudes in Southeastern Europe. Among the most prevalent are:

Widespread Parochialism, Apathy, and Cynicism About Politics

Since most of the peoples of this region experienced politics primarily as the activities of rapacious leaders and their underlings perpetrated *against* the masses, their attitudes naturally reflected cynicism about politics, and they rejected any kind of political involvement by the average individual. Indeed, parochialism became a survival mechanism for individuals and groups facing hostile foreign occupation. Thus, the Romanians isolated themselves in the forests and mountains to preserve their culture, believing that political elites were, ipso facto, exploitative and unworthy of allegience or emulation. Instead, they concentrated on their local community and developed a strong sense of loyalty, personal honor, and commitment towards their peers and fellow villagers, and disdain for outsiders. They were also quite willing to repay the exploitative central authorities through subversive or illegal activities that, presumably, matched the immorality of these elites and their representatives. Authorities were always considered corrupt, and the Romanians soon developed clever strategies and tactics of the "bakshish"—approach to power—because this was considered crucial to personal and group survival and, occasionally, even prosperity. Similar attitudes developed throughout the rest of Southeastern Europe. After all, this territory was first ruled by the Byzantine Empire, and, subsequently, by the Ottomans for several hundred years; both systems gradually deteriorated and became corrupt and weak, and in the process the practice of "bakshish" and the "deal" was institutionalized. This behavior pattern persists to this

day and is made more relevant than ever by the incompetence, malfeasance, and slovenliness of Romania's contemporary leaders.[15]

Open Challenge to Political Authority

In the mountains of the area now known as Yugoslavia, a second
tradition developed that must be understood to grasp some of the
fundamental aspects of the region today, namely, the heritage of brigandage and open defiance of outside authority. This was made possible
by the area's difficult topography and the inability of empirical power
to extend into the remote reaches of this far-flung empire. The heroes
of this tradition were the freebooters who hid in the mountains and
sallied forth to destroy Ottoman outposts and rob the representatives
of the Sultan, then disappeared back into the uninhabited areas, there
to preserve the national heritage until a better day. This tradition survives
to the present time, both in folklore and in the popular perception of
real heroics.[16]

"Bakshish" and brigandage were, of course, detrimental to the establishment and maintenance of political power. In addition, there was
little positive apathy among the masses; instead, the sullen multitudes
vigorously applauded the raids of the "bandits" and considered *them*
the heroes of national preservation and liberation. The villagers gave
the outlaws food and shelter and frequently provided recruits. They also
refused to cooperate with representatives of the established order who
came to search for the malfeasants. The resemblance between this situation
and contemporary wars of national liberation is strong. And combined
with the masses' tendency to withdraw from political activity, this
proclivity produced political cultures noted for their lack of instrumental
or institutional legitimacy.

The Lack of "Noblesse Oblige"

The masses in Southeastern Europe tended to reject political activity,
opting, instead, to retreat into their own world of ethno-national and
religious consciousness. And the political and socio-economic elites did
little to bridge the gap between themselves and the masses that widened
to an abyss over time. Most political leaders of this region, after achieving
national independence, regarded the societies they ruled as a source of
personal enhancement; they had no sense of shared circumstances or
"being in the same boat" as the ruled. The notions of autocracy, of
ruling *over* the people, became integral to elite attitudes and leadership
style throughout the entire region (albeit in varying degrees). Such
attitudes and behavior precluded the development of a sense of "noblesse
oblige," in which the elites consider themselves the spokesmen of the

people and feel an obligation towards the masses. The history of Southeastern Europe simply has too many examples of leaders who enriched themselves while neglecting the socio-economic, cultural, and educational needs of their populations. Thus, the negative attitudes and values of the masses that had evolved during centuries of foreign rule were reinforced by the behavior of native leaders. It is no wonder that many simply assumed that *all* politics, *all* elites were to be distrusted.[17]

Consequently, there was no real concept of citizenship as it is commonly known in the West, denoting a sense of rights and obligations on the part of both the ruler and the ruled. It also implies that the rulers have limited power and that individuals have political rights by virtue of birth, not merely as a gift from the leaders of the system. None of this is intrinsic to the political cultures of Southeastern Europe. There, individual rights are granted, not inherent. Participation by the masses may or may not be allowed, and the results of such participation may or may not be respected by the political leaders. The state does not exist to serve the public good through a process of give and take or consensus building, but rather to maintain the elite, extend their privileges, and widen executive power. Southeastern Europe is characterized by an etatism that reduces the average individual to subject status and denies any real sense of political influence to the man and woman in the street. This is a distinct liability for any regime that hopes to increase participation and political mobilization.[18]

The Quest for Legitimacy: Non-instrumental Sources

Etatism and the lack of "noblesse oblige" meant the rulers of Southeastern Europe had to establish their legitimacy on other bases, especially charisma, symbolism, and ideology. Thus, a tradition of leadership style developed that emphasized the need for a strong ruler, a Vozhd who could lead the unenlightened masses forward in the name of Christianity, nationalism, and a mystical populism that stressed the generic and organic link between the peasant, the soil, and his God, aligned against the "others," be they internal minorities or nations across the border. The quest for organic government in a population of cynics and political parochials precluded the development of any kind of civil society, of "unity in diversity," that is essential to a democratic system. Under these circumstances, there was no real prospect for political pluralism in Southeastern Europe in the decades prior to the imposition of communist rule. Furthermore, with the economic development that occurred under the etatist political order, no entrepreneurial middle class evolved; thus, the social stratum that carried the movement for liberal democracy in the western part of Europe, in Scandinavia, and in Great

Britain was missing in Romania. However, the autocratic tradition that emerged was well suited to communist-style autocracy, though particularly inappropriate for the kinds of semi-participatory communism now advocated by the Soviet leadership and some of the political elites throughout Eastern Europe.[19]

The Lack of Economic Prowess and the Absence of Instrumental Legitimacy

Even if the political system remains authoritarian and the public remains politically apathetic and parochial, legitimacy may be established on the basis of economic or administrative performance. This is certainly the case in the German Democratic Republic, where the Prussian tradition of administrative performance and the work ethic prevail in a system that is structurally very similar to those in the modern states of Southeastern Europe. But, just as emphatically, this is *not* the case in the southeastern part of the continent, where the work ethic is less pronounced and economic development lags significantly behind the other nations and, indeed, the rest of communist-ruled Europe. Legitimacy based on performance is therefore unlikely in this area. Thus, the problems faced by rulers and ruled alike are compounded: autocratic views and etatism among the political elites, parochialism and apathy (often negative) among the masses, and inadequate performance and insufficient incentives for performance in the administrative and economic arena. The picture is, therefore, quite bleak. Nonetheless, the systems and regimes of the region do not appear to be in imminent danger of collapse.[20]

The System-supportive Role of Nationalism in Contemporary Southeastern Europe

The enduring importance of nationalism is nowhere more marked than in today's communist-ruled systems of Southeastern Europe. Here, nationalism was quickly incorporated into the systems' mythologies as an integral part of the ideological justification for the communist rule practiced in Romania, Yugoslavia, Albania, and Bulgaria. In Yugoslavia, nationalism among the ethnic groups of that heterogeneous country always played a divisive role at the national level, except for a brief period during the height of Stalinist pressures on Tito after the expulsion of Belgrade from the Cominform in 1948. In the face of such adversity, a form of *Yugoslav* nationalism developed. However, this was a rather shallow form of nationalism, produced by circumstances, and it did not survive the relative reconciliation between Tito and the post-Stalin leadership. But the autonomy that Belgrade achieved as a result of this rift became an important factor in both domestic and foreign policy, adding to the meager fund of legitimacy at Tito's disposal (apart from his own charisma and unquestionable personal authority in wide segments of the Yugoslav population).[21]

In Albania, Hoxha's national liberation regime rid the country of fascists without the aid of Soviet troops. Much of the leadership's subsequent policy can be described as a quest for national communism in the local setting, with an emphasis on economic autarky and ideological purity. This emphasis was readily apparent during the long years of the Sino-Soviet dispute, in which Albania actively participated. The quest for autonomism in all areas was a primary factor in the subsequent break between Tirana and Peking, as Albania accused the Chinese of ideological revisionism and other sins against orthodoxy. It is not clear to what extent this national focus has helped establish or solidify the regime's legitimacy in the masses of the population or key societal elites. But it is likely that such a policy, despite the hardships it may have inflicted upon the population, produced a measure of pride in wide segments of the Albanian masses, and thus had a legitimizing effect for the regime.[22]

Romanian nationalism, indeed its ethno-chauvinism, has been an important political manifestation and a support mechanism for the regimes of Gheorghe Gheorghiu-Dej and Nicolae Ceausescu. Especially during the last fifteen to twenty years, Ceausescu has relied heavily on nationalistic slogans and the myth of Romanian cultural superiority to offset the dismal performance record of his planners, bureaucrats, and managers. The chauvinistic policies of the regime may have generated support at an earlier stage (notably during the invasion of Czechoslovakia in 1968), but that is a long time past, both in years and in political experience; in the interim, the masses have only seen increased repression, corruption, and economic dislocation. Romanian ethno-nationalism is now seen for what it really is—a fig leaf for continued dominance by a small clan and a steady deterioration of the standard of living. Thus, nationalism may have lost its capability to act as a regime-supportive mechanism in contemporary Romania. That would indeed be a bad omen for the Ceausescus.[23]

Notes

1. Numerous volumes may be cited to support this general proposition. I have relied heavily on *Cambridge Ancient History* (Cambridge, England: Cambridge University Press, 1923–1939), 12 vols. For a more specific backdrop, see, Chester G. Starr, *A History of the Ancient World* (New York, NY: Oxford University Press, 1965), esp. parts V, VI, VII, VIII, IX, and X.

2. The best book on this subject is John A. Armstrong, *Nations Before Nationalism* (Chapel Hill, NC: The University of North Carolina Press, 1982), esp. ch. 7 (pp. 201–241).

3. E.g. Robert Lee Wolff, *The Balkans in Our Time* (rev. ed.), (Cambridge, MA: Harvard University Press, 1974), esp. ch. 4 (pp. 50–69). The impact of Byzantium is discussed in André Guillou, *La Civilisation Byzantine* (Paris: Arthaud, 1974). For a study of the Ottomans, I recommend Nicolae Jorga, *Geschichte Des Osmanischen Reiches* (Gotha, Germany: Friedrich Andras Pertes Aktiengesellschaft, 1908), 5 vols.

4. Armstrong, *Nations Before Nationalism*, ch. 7.

5. On political culture in communist-ruled systems, see Ivan Volgyes, *Politics in Eastern Europe* (Chicago, IL: The Dorsey Press, 1986), esp. ch. 12 (pp. 282–311). Religion in communist systems is discussed in Pedro Ramet (ed.), *Religion and Nationalism in Soviet and East European Politics* (Durham, NC: Duke University Press, 1984), esp. ch. 1 by Ramet, pp. 3–31.

6. The best history of Romania is still R. W. Seton-Watson, *A History of the Roumanians* (Cambridge, England: Cambridge University Press, 1934), esp. pp. 111–114 and 175–182.

7. E.g. G. Carter Bentley, *Ethnicity and Nationality: A Bibliographic Guide* (Seattle, WA: University of Washington Press, 1981), esp. "Introduction" (pp. xi–xxi).

8. The concept of "national communism" is not a new one. For a recent definition, see Peter Zwick, *National Communism* (Boulder, CO: Westview Press, 1983), ch. 1 (pp. 1–15).

9. Seton-Watson, *A History of the Roumanians*, esp. ch. I and II (pp. 1–50).

10. The classical definition of "nationalism" can be found in Hans Kohn, *The Idea of Nationalism: Its Origins and Background* (New York, NY: Macmillan Company, 1944).

11. E.g. Seton-Watson, *A History of the Roumanians*, esp. ch. I and II (pp. 1–50).

12. I have summarized a great deal of literature here. One of the best discussions of this topic is Peter F. Sugar and Ivo J. Lederer (eds.), *Nationalism in Eastern Europe* (Seattle, WA: University of Washington Press, 1969), esp. Sugar's piece on "External and Domestic Roots of Eastern European Nationalism."

13. An example of this is the current conflict between Hungary and Romania regarding Bucharest's treatment of the Magyars in Transylvania. See "Lupta Intregului Popor," in *Revista Romana de Istorie Militara* (Bucharest) Vol. 4, No. 4 (1987) for the Romanian response to Hungarian charges of discrimination against Transylvanian Magyars.

14. Armstrong, *Nations Before Nationalism*, esp. ch. 1 (pp. 3–14). See also Norbert Elias, *Über Den Process Der Zivilization: Soziogenetische und Psychogenetische Untersuchungen* (Basel, Switzerland: Haus Zun Falken, 1939).

15. In Romania, such attitudes were certainly present during the long centuries of Ottoman domination. See Miron Constantinescu et al., *Istoria Romaniei* (Bucharest: Editura Didactica si Pedagogca, 1970), pp. 107–254 ("Epoca Medie—Feudala" by Stefan Pascu). See also Seton-Watson, *A History of the Roumanians*, ch. III (pp. 50–101).

16. This kind of hero is important in Romanian history, too; an example is Tudor Vladimirescu. For a discussion of Tudor and his times, see Andrei Otetea (ed.), *Istoria Poporului Roman* (Bucharest: Biblioteca de Istorie, 1970), pp. 327–344.

17. I have discussed this phenomenon in a number of publications, e.g. my *Modernization in Romania Since World War II* (New York, NY: Praeger Publishers, 1975), pp. 3–15.

18. E.g. Constantinescu, *Istoria Romaniei*, pp. 393–409.

19. On the traditions of Romanian socio-economic development, see Otetea, *Istoria Poporului Roman*, esp. pp. 414–422, 435–445, and 464–470.

20. I have discussed this phenomenon in a paper on "leadership drift," presented at the annual convention of the American Association for the Advancement of Slavic Studies, Boston, MA, November 1987.

21. E.g. Volgyes, *Politics in Eastern Europe*, pp. 193–195 and 353–355.

22. The post-Hoxha leadership emphasizes this national tradition despite the changes that have occurred since the old leader's death; see, for example, Louis Zanga, "Ramiz Alia Talks About Continuity in Albania Despite Change," *Rad Background Report/172 (Albania)*, September 24, 1987.

23. Surprisingly outspoken criticism of Ceausescu was voiced by Ion Iliescu, a former "rising star" in the Romanian party, in *Romania Literara*, September 3, 1987.

2

Romania and History:
The Enduring Legacy

For residents of Romania as well as for scholars studying the country, history is part of the everyday experience, of life and consciousness. The Romanian regime's leaders blare their historical analyses from the balconies of power. The press is full of allegations and direct claims to historical traditions and "Romania Mare," Greater Romania. Much scholarship in history, anthropology, and even linguistics is devoted to proving, time and again, that the Romanians are representatives of a glorious past, which is reflected in the greatness of the contemporary era. Much of this official propaganda is discounted by a cynical and dispirited public, but every Romanian feels the organic link with the past through values and attitudes that have been handed down from generation to generation. History colors the perceptions of all Romanians as they look at their reality, their surroundings, and the outside world.

Indeed, history is an integral component of the collective mythology that all nations create about themselves. Mythologies and perceptions influence behavior; hence, the past is integrally tied to the way in which citizens order their lives as individuals and as members of a collective political entity, regardless of the nature of that collectivity. And in a society like that of Romania with significant minorities whose histories are very different from the mainstream Romanian experience, the clash of different collective mythologies and behaviors causes tension and occasionally conflict.[1]

Ethnographers, linguists, and historians differ on the origins of the Romanians as an ethnic entity; furthermore, there are significant differences between official Romanian scholarship on this issue and the findings of others. During the last fifteen to twenty years, Romanian historians and anthropologists have produced a voluminous literature on the origins of their people, tracing back beyond the birth of Christ. They claim that the Romanians are, in fact, the descendants of the Geto-

17

Dacians, who occupied much of the territory of contemporary Romania before the arrival of the Romans in the first century B.C. According to this analysis, modern Romanians are products of the ethnogenesis of Geto-Dacians and the Roman officials and legionnaires who settled in the province of Dacia Felix. In the early years of the Ceausescu era, the emphasis in this analysis was on the "Romanity" of the ethnic mix, but more recently there has been a subtle but important change in emphasis towards the Geto-Dacian roots of the contemporary population.[2] During the last few years, official historiography from Bucharest has stressed the cultural equality or even superiority of the indigenous Geto-Dacians, thus minimizing the mission of the Romans in the dawn of Romanian history. All of this must be seen in the context of Nicolae Ceausescu's efforts to rewrite history and show that the cradle of European civilization actually stood on Romanian soil. This is an interesting political claim, but it adds little to the scientific knowledge about the Romanian past.[3]

More serious scholarship describes the emergence of the Romanian nation as a complex mix of interactions among a number of ethnic groups, including the Dacians (who were vanquished by Emperor Trajan in the first century B.C.), the Romans (particularly the soldiers who settled in the province of Dacia Felix after completing their service obligations), and various tribes (including the Avars and others that swept down from the north and eventually pushed the Romans back across the Danube River). Subsequently, other groups added to the ethnic mix on the soil of contemporary Romania, especially the many invaders that marched across this territory for centuries. There was probably a certain amount of intermingling with Gypsy elements over time, but, due to various taboos of interaction, this was likely limited. By the same token, the invading armies probably had little interaction with the conquered helots, who became known as "Vlachs" and were often looked down upon. Nonetheless, there was *some* interaction, as can be expected whenever armies occupy territory and dominant settlers establish them-selves among the conquered.[4]

All these events eventually produced a very heterogeneous ethnic mix in Romania. Today, there are few, if any, specifically Romanian physical characteristics. Individuals of this nationality range from tall and blond to short and dark, with many variations in between. The commonality of being Romanian is, therefore, largely a learned characteristic, stemming from political and ethnic socialization and shared habits and behavior patterns. But these shared characteristics have considerable staying power, as Romanian history has demonstrated. Furthermore, they have been acquired in stages and in response to different challenges. All these factors have contributed to a strong sense of nationality, nationhood, and, in a political sense, nationalism.[5]

The Genesis of the Romanian Nation

There is considerable evidence about the society that existed on Romanian soil prior to the arrival of the Roman armies. The society of Decebal and Burebista (the two pre-eminent kings of the Dacian era) was relatively highly developed, with considerable social stratification. There was a strong tradition of warfare, with a system of skilled commanders and strict discipline among the troops, as evidenced by the Dacians' fierce resistance when Emperor Trajan launched his invasion in 101 A.D. In fact, the intensity and duration of the fighting indicated mass support for the regime, its leaders, its gods, and its institutions and rituals. Thus, the Dacian kingdom clearly had the fundamental elements of a political system, as well as the basic aspects of commonality—a sense of belonging—among the masses.[6]

Details on developments after the Roman conquest are murky and controversial. The Romans established their own administrative, political, and economic infrastructure in Dacia Felix, but it is unclear how much they mixed with the local inhabitants. Earlier official Romanian historiography claimed that the Roman influence helped raise the cultural level of the Dacian inhabitants. In fact, the Latinity and Romanity of the Romanian tradition were hailed as the major manifestations of Romanian nationalism, setting this society apart from the Slavs surrounding them. This argument permeated the historical and political discourse emanating from Bucharest during the entire period of independence, through the establishment of communist power, and well into the Ceausescu era. It was abandoned during the heights of Stalinist subservience to Moscow from 1948 to 1952, but resurfaced even before the death of Stalin and became, once again, a point of official policy during the reign of Gheorghe Gheorghiu-Dej. In fact, the reappearance of this historical theme may indeed mark the beginning of national communist inclinations in Romania.[7]

Sometime in the early 1970s, official history and anthropology from the presses of Romania began to reevaluate this historical record. It was now argued that the intermingling during the Roman era led the Romans to assimilate into the culture of the indigenous population, resulting in a higher cultural level for the *Romans;* in other words, the Dacian (or Geto-Dacian) indigenous culture was superior to that brought by the conquerors from the outside. This "domestication" of the assimilation process was clearly "discovered" by official historians who had been so instructed by the political leadership, to further the main themes of nationalism propounded by an increasingly assertive, even chauvinistic, Nicolae Ceausescu. These themes emphasized that indigenous Romanian (i.e. Geto-Dacian) cultural, socio-economic, and political forms were superior to all others. Archaeological treatises produced during the last fifteen years have bolstered this claim by discussing several finds that place ancient civilizations on Romanian soil at an earlier time and at a more advanced level than elsewhere. In fact, some of these books and articles claim that early cultures here rivaled those of Mesopotamia and other areas in the Middle East in terms of order of appearance and level of development. During the last few years, this argument has become so strident that it has lost much of its credibility among impartial scholars.[8]

Scholars outside Romania differ considerably on the issue of what happened to the Romanians after the Roman conquest. It is generally accepted that there was some intermingling among the Romans and the indigenous population, but the extent of it is in dispute. Some scholars believe the provincial administration of Dacia Felix maintained rather strict segregation, using the locals primarily for manual work and reserving important positions for Romans. Intermarriage was discouraged. Other scholars contend there was a certain amount of upward social mobility for the Dacians, but argue that this process was limited and based upon individual arrangements and opportunities, not a conscious policy of group enhancement. In any case, there is general agreement that the assimilation process, regardless of scope, represented an opportunity for the less developed Dacians to reap the benefits of association with the most advanced civilization of their world.[9]

Romanians After the Romans

The historical record becomes even more confused after the Romans abandoned the province of Dacia Felix to the frequent and ferocious onslaughts of tribes from the north. Most scholars agree that the Romans simply left, taking their administrative apparatus, their records, and their soldiers with them across the Danube River and resettling on the right bank in what is now Bulgaria. But what about the Romanized segments of the Dacians? Did they leave with their masters? If they stayed, what happened to them? And, above all, what happened to the local population? Were they decimated by the conquerors, reduced to slavery and helotry? Was there an assimilation process at work, and if so, who assimilated to whom? This particular question is interesting from historical, ethno-national, and linguistic points of view, but it also has clear political ramifications, especially in regard to Romanian settlement in Transylvania.[10]

Again, there is a difference between the official scholarship sponsored by Bucharest and non-Romanian research. The latter is, in turn, further divided, with an aggressive Hungarian branch arguing a particular development with considerable vehemence, superseding other lines of reasoning. Yet, in all this research, there still is no definitive answer to the question of what happened to the Romanians during the centuries between the Roman abandonment of Dacia Felix and the reappearance of the "Vlachs" in medieval times.

The Romanians have produced two theories on this question. The first contends that the local population stayed in occupied territory and gradually provided a measure of culture to the conquerors, whose military skills and ferocity exceeded their knowledge and sophistication. Due to the severity of the occupation, however, the Romanians were ultimately forced to retreat to the forests and the mountains and isolate themselves from the rest of society. Maintaining an internal solidarity, they were committed to the preservation of their language (which had become the vernacular Latin of the Roman legions) and their culture and traditions. According to this theory, the bulk of the Romanians retreated to the Carpathian Mountains and settled in the less accessible regions of the forests and even "beyond the forests" (Transylvania). This is clearly a most important point, because it suggests that the very core of Romanian nationality was preserved in *Transylvania*. Furthermore, it suggests that there always was a Romanian presence in the mountains; therefore, the Magyars and the Saxons, who arrived in the eleventh century, were the newcomers to this strategic area.[11]

The second theory of Romanian historians is that the local inhabitants remained throughout the entire territory of the conquered land, but that the most important centers of Romanian civilization and culture gradually shifted to the less accessible regions, where foreign intrusions were less likely. Other Romanians, severely repressed by foreign occupiers, were gradually reduced to conditions akin to slavery, but still maintained their sense of commonality, their language, and their customs and culture.[12]

Official Romanian doctrine glorifies the staying power of the culture, habits, and language of the inhabitants abandoned by the Romans in 271 A.D. To maintain the characteristics necessary for group survival under the extremely disadvantageous conditions imposed upon the Geto-Dacian Romanians required fortitude, leadership, and commitment. According to the official rhetoric, the survival of group cohesion and the essentials of nationhood proved the superiority of the Romanians in comparison with their neighbors and conquerors—after all, only a superior culture could maintain itself and eventually prevail, regardless of the severity and duration of subjugation. Thus, the absence of the Romanians from the chronicles of Southeast European history for such an extended period of time is seen as an indication of strength and staying power, not weakness and cultural disenfranchisement.[13]

There are chauvinistic overtones to this official Romanian argument, but also elements of validity. There *is* a Romanian language that is, basically, the vernacular Latin of the Roman legions; despite the fact that perhaps a third of the vocabulary is of Turkish, Russian, or Greek origin, two-thirds can be traced directly to a Latin heritage. In addition, behavior patterns, folklore, music, traditions, and costumes set the Romanians apart from other peoples in this region. The folklore and the traditions emphasize the life and mythology of the forest, meadows, and mountains, lending considerable credence to the notion that the Romanians were basically a rural, forest people during the long centuries of foreign rule. These indicators suggest a continuity of group existence, albeit in relative isolation. This isolation is also conducive to the development of genetic ethnicity, even though this argument is hard to sustain given the variety of genetic types found in the contemporary Romanian population.[14]

The Hungarians propose a different scenario of Romanian ethnic survival. Much Hungarian historiography on this point argues that the Romanians either disappeared from Transylvania or never arrived there in the first place, so that the mountains were largely uninhabited when the Magyars and the invited Saxons arrived. This, again, is an argument of considerable political importance but somewhat dubious archaeological and historical validity. More moderate works admit that some Romanians existed in the area, but contend that they were scattered, unorganized, and involved in subsistence agriculture—a hunting and fishing culture of uneducated woodsmen. The Romanians remained in the steppes and agricultural areas of the Wallachian and Moldavian plains and were subjected to severe repression, thereby becoming gradually "deculturized," except at the local level—in native dress, folklore, and the customs of village life, which were allowed by the ruling elites as long as they carried no political or military overtones. The allegedly low (and declining) level of culture enabled the Romanians to maintain their basic group identity, because the rulers discouraged integration and assimilation and felt no real threat from such a group, however numerous.[15]

It may be argued that the Hungarian view is tainted by ethno-chauvinism, designed to belittle the importance of the Romanians, particularly in Transylvania, just as the spokesmen of Bucharest are guilty of overstating the Romanians' role. Some presumably neutral scholars in the West have examined the question from a different vantage point and have drawn conclusions that embody elements of both the Romanian and Hungarian theories. In summary, these scholars argue as follows:

First, Romanian group identity, including language, customs, folklore, and perhaps even dress, was preserved despite the repression meted out by countless conquerors and rulers, thereby demonstrating considerable staying power even in the face of great adversity.[16]

Second, this group identity was not dependent upon territory or the inclusiveness of the group, but on an ability to establish boundaries against others; that is, Romanians were quite capable of distinguishing "others" from "us," regardless of territorial lines. Therefore, their ethnic group could survive even in the midst of such "others," be they Magyars, Turks, Jews, Armenians, or Greeks. The repressive policies of the ruling "others" intensified this sense of boundary and helped strengthen ethnic identity among the Romanians, rather than weaken it.[17]

Third, ethnic identity became solidified over time because the group's symbols, myths, nostalgia, and boundary markers (such as dress and rituals) became part and parcel of its existence, whether the group lived together on common territory or was spread out among others. Thus, it should not be surprising that ethnicity survived centuries of repression, as long as that repression did not destroy the group's boundary markers and symbols of togetherness.[18]

The contrasting theories on the development of Romanian ethnic identity are further compounded by the issue of religion and *its* effect upon this group's national consciousness. Christianity was introduced into the area that is now Romania in the fourth century, and the Romanians have been Orthodox ever since. There is little doubt that religion, with its symbols and rituals, enhanced group identity among the Romanian masses. However, scholars differ on the matter of sequence: did religion "occur" first, becoming a key building block for ethnic cohesion, or had such cohesion already occurred, thus smoothing the path for religious conversion among like-minded individuals? One's view of this issue may depend upon where one kneels, so to speak. The Hungarians, who maintain that Romanian ethnic identity was weak in the centuries after the departure of the Romans, are apt to argue that religion became the primary vehicle for the awakening of group identity among the "Vlachs." The Romanians, on the other hand, claiming that ethnic cohesion and cultural superiority existed for centuries, consider religion just another (albeit powerful) element of group cohesion and defense against others.[19]

It is not necessary to settle this controversy to understand that ethnicity and religion worked together in a forceful combination for a number of groups, the Romanians among them. Religion was yet another element of outward and inward commitment to "us" and a corresponding boundary against "them." It was a part of group cohesion even prior to the introduction of Christianity. But this momentous event in the history of Southeastern Europe provided structure and organization to religious beliefs, thus adding to the political or administrative aspects of ethnicity. Religion was no longer just a set of attitudes and values; instead, individuals could now join together in a structure, listen to the words of a leader in rich vestments, and stand together in prayer—a powerful manifestation of the splendor and might of this institution. Thus, ethnicity became more organized and purposeful after the introduction of Christianity.[20]

Counterelites and Nationalism

The introduction of organized religion encouraged the establishment of a *counterelite* among the Romanians. The importance of the counterelite has been brilliantly discussed by John Armstrong in his monumental *Nations Before Nationalism*. Briefly put, counterelites are necessary for any group to begin to act in its own interests, because only they can represent the group politically and begin discourse and bargaining with the ruling elites. This is particularly crucial when the group is subjugated by others, as the Romanians were for centuries.[21]

The development of counterelites can only occur in a few narrow circumstances. The social pyramid of specialization and stratification must be sufficiently developed to produce its own elites, with the skills and the time necessary to act on behalf of the other strata. Counterelites may develop in a relatively unstratified group through other means, such as religion, which produces its own elite with multiple functions. This is particularly pertinent to the Romanians, because this group remained basically pastoral, relatively undifferentiated, and severely repressed for centuries, thus reducing the chances for the development of secular counterelites. Therefore, the village priest became the local counterelite for his flock, and through his inspiration, bright and ambitious young individuals could be taught and motivated to become group leaders. Then, as time passed, the new leaders from the community became increasingly important as counterelites, and a trend towards the secularization of elite formation was begun, wherein the priest functioned less as a leader and more as a "talent spotter" in the local community. As the process of elite development became self-sustaining, the stage was set for greater ethnic group activity and assertiveness.[22]

The close association between religion, religious structures, and the development of ethnic political leadership ensured that those elites that did emerge would claim to speak for God *and* the group. This was a most powerful combination that included both internal symbols of cohesion and clear boundary markers against others. For example, the group now had *its* leaders, *its* structures, *its* symbols and rituals. These aspects of commonality stood in sharp contrast to others and *their* symbols and signs of cohesion. Furthermore, the group leaders claimed to represent God against heathens, Christianity against infidels. The wars fought against the Turks by Stephen the Great and Michael the Brave were manifestations of the combined force of ethnic identity and religious fervor. This dynamic combination contributed significantly to the consolidation of ethnic identity among the Romanians and ensured that these monumental battles were fought with enthusiasm and ferocity over extended periods of time.[23]

By the fourteenth century, the confluence of ethnic identity, religion, and political and military structures was firmly established in Moldavia and Wallachia, and nationalism had become a political force in these two entities. This is not to say that there was at that point a full-fledged *Romanian* nationalism in the two principalities; the sense of unity across the borders of the two political units was insufficient for that. But the boundary markers against *others* were similar in both areas, and the elites of Moldavia and Wallachia (and those among the masses who were politically conscious) had more in common with each other than with outsiders. From that point in history, the movement toward *integrative* nationalism was only a question of time and effort. It could hardly be arrested.[24]

Throughout the centuries before national independence was achieved in 1876, Romanian ethnic conscience continued to develop despite repression by others in the three major parts of "Romania Mare"—Moldavia, Wallachia, and Transylvania. Throughout these areas, representatives of the foreign rulers controlled the administrative structure, the economic system, and the educational institutions of the country, ensuring the continuation and aggravation of the conditions suffered by the Romanians. Nonetheless, the Romanians' social structure remained relatively intact, social organization proceeded apace, and the processes of leadership development continued and expanded. Other factors also hastened this development. For example, as Russia gained strength and influence, Moscow became increasingly assertive as the protector of its Orthodox brethren in the Balkans. This emphasis on Christian solidarity against Islam was in part genuine; it was also a convenient excuse for Russian intervention in an area of vital strategic importance. Whatever the motivations, though, this protector role enhanced the status of the leaders of Moscow among the Romanians and helped deepen the Romanian sense of commonality through the vehicle of religion and the perception of being different from the Turkish overlords, the Greek tax collectors, the Armenian traders, and the German craftsmen who also inhabited this territory. As time progressed, the Russians repeatedly intervened to expand their influence, and each time, the Porte was left a little less powerful in the Principalities, thereby allowing more national activities among the Romanians. By the nineteenth century, such activities were sufficiently widespread and varied that one could speak of a real national movement in both Principalities, directed, first, toward independence and, second, toward unification and formation of a Romanian national state.[25]

The situation in Transylvania was rather different, as a number of scholars have pointed out. The Romanian population lived in poverty and subjugation under the political dominance of the Magyars and in relative economic subordination to the Saxons. The Magyars became increasingly assertive during the eighteenth century and again after the Ausgleich with Austria. The policies emanating from Budapest emphasized both the isolation of and control over the Romanians. But it also permitted the assimilation of upwardly mobile Romanians in an effort to co-opt such obvious leadership talent rather than allow it to become a catalyst for national aspirations. After the Ausgleich, there was also a concerted effort of Magyarization through the schools and by government control of language instruction, publications, and the means of communication. Under these circumstances, the development and strengthening of ethnic consciousness and national cohesion among the Romanians proceeded slowly and with great difficulty. The differentiation and stratification of the social system were hampered by the economic subjugation of this group; political development was strictly controlled; and cultural life, while allowed, was scrutinized for overtones that might threaten the power and privilege of the Magyars. Thus, the social pyramid was slow to materialize, and secular elites who could act as spokesmen for the masses of fellow Romanians were few. It therefore fell to religious leaders to spur national consciousness and nurture political talent until the process could become self-sustaining. The two Orthodox bishops, Andrei Saguna and Andrei Sulutiu, became powerful spokesmen for Romanian interests. They helped spread literacy by printing and disseminating Bibles in the Romanian language. They wrote passionately about the rights of the downtrodden. They campaigned abroad for support for the Romanian cause and even attempted to play Vienna against Budapest, occasionally with a measure of success.[26]

The importance of religious leadership in the development of Romanian ethnic consciousness and nationalism in Transylvania cannot be overestimated. During the nineteenth century, and especially after the wave of national "awakenings" and independence movements of the 1830s and 1840s, developments in the Principalities also influenced trends in Transylvania. Some of the emerging secular leaders of the Romanian movement "beyond the forests" travelled to Bucharest and Iasi and were inspired by developments there. Romanian nationalists from the south crossed the border and spent time in Habsburg territory, spreading the word of national consciousness, glory, and unification into historic Greater Romania. Ethnicity, nationalism, religion, and historic nostalgia were inspiring themes for the downtrodden Romanian masses, who now began to envision a better future—one that would be more suited to their glorious past, whether it was historical reality or mythology. And implicit in this message was the clear delineation between Romanians and the others, especially the Magyars, who were seen as both different and inferior.[27]

After 1848, unsettled political conditions throughout much of Europe caused increasing maneuvering among the major powers. The Habsburg Empire, long the dominant German state, was challenged by Prussia and eventually eclipsed by the Brandenburg leaders. This triggered further developments in the Balkans, traditionally an area of considerable influence for Vienna. Meanwhile, the Ottoman Empire was in a steady decline and faced more assertive policies by the Romanovs in their quest for influence in the Black Sea and freer access to the Mediterranean through the Bosporus and the Hellespont. France was also emerging as an important player in the Balkans, as Paris sought to extend *its* influence in an unsettled region where traditional imperial power clearly was on the wane. Britain, by contrast, continued to support the Sublime Porte, not because of Whitehall's love for Turkish policies in their occupied territories but because the Sultan still represented a useful counterweight to other players in the region.[28]

This complicated maneuvering by the major European powers in the Balkans gave the Romanian nationalist leaders in the Principalities ample opportunities for coalition-building. During the decades between the nationalist fervor of the 1820s and the achievement of political autonomy for Moldavia and Wallachia in the 1850s, the nationalists in Bucharest and Iasi courted the French political leaders on the basis of their common Latinity, encouraging them to undertake a civilizing mission. This approach had the distinct benefit of establishing outside "protection" while enhancing important domestic symbols of commonality, such as the Latin heritage and the difference between the perceived superiority of that heritage and the allegedly low level of life among the Romanians' Slavic neighbors (as illustrated by the saying "an island of Latin culture in a sea of Slavic barbarism"). The external and internal elements of national consciousness strengthened each other significantly.[29]

Elite, Masses, and Nationalism

During the nineteenth century, then, all the basic aspects of national consciousness and political nationalism coalesced, first in the Principalities and then in Transylvania. Socio-economic development had proceeded to the point where an indigenous elite had emerged (substantially different from the comprador elite, which had always served the foreign occupiers of the country). The religious infrastructure had also developed further, providing both leadership and a framework in which nationalism could be nurtured and expressed. And at the international level, external allies were ready to provide support in the councils of power. Moldavia and Wallachia thus possessed the necessary ingredients for the successful expression of national interests as defined by the elites and, presumably, understood and accepted by the masses.

The values of the masses, themselves, were also partly conducive to such nationalistic expression. The ethnic consciousness of the Romanians had not only survived invasions and deprivations but expanded, largely due to the efforts of both religious and secular leaders. However, it was a rather undifferentiated form of nationalism, emphasizing a few symbols and goals but generally lacking in the more sophisticated aspects, such as a *political* infrastructure to safeguard the fruits of liberation, if and when it came. Consequently, the nationalism of the masses could be manipulated with relative ease, because it was emotional and primarily concerned with simple, emotive symbols such as a national flag and a sovereign leader. Before Moldavia and Wallachia achieved autonomy within the Ottoman Empire, such demands had a great deal of mass appeal that obscured flaws in the administrative and political structures of both principalities, as well as deficiencies in the political and administrative cultures of the national elite.[30]

There are a number of well-known milestones on the path to full Romanian independence, most notably the rise of the national movement in the 1820s, the impact of the revolutionary year 1848, and the protracted and difficult negotiations that led to the granting of autonomy in 1856 and full independence and unification of the two Principalities twenty years later. During this period, Romania's secular and religious leaders gained considerable political skill in the domestic negotiating process. They also showed remarkable prowess in turning the interests of the great powers to their own advantage. In particular, they exploited French and Russian patronage and the rivalry between the Kremlin and the Porte in the Balkans to hasten the achievement of national sovereignty. And as long as it remained an issue of independence, the flaws of the leadership and of the system itself were hidden or ignored. But once sovereignty was proclaimed and duly accepted by the international community, these flaws resurfaced and produced massive problems for independent Romania.[31]

What were these basic flaws? At the elite level, the Romanian leaders were boyars, members of the landed aristocracy or the emerging commercial and entrepreneurial elites of the cities who had no experience in or inclination toward political pluralism or even limited democracy. Worse still, they considered the masses as utilitarian objects to achieve goals (such as independence) but failed to consider them as partners in the new political order. As stated in Chapter 1, there was no concept of noblesse oblige among these boyars; rather, they believed in personal and class enrichment at everybody else's expense. Thus, no sooner had the masses experienced the euphoria of winning their independence, weapons in hand, than they discovered that *their own* leaders were as lacking in compassion as the predecessors, even though they were fellow countrymen. Thus, the gap that had existed between the Romanian masses and the representatives of political power under foreign rule was reproduced under native leaders. As a result, the cynicism and apathy that traditionally permeated the Romanian political culture were only strengthened during the decades between independence and World War I.[32]

The economic and social policies of the new Romanian government tended to perpetuate the gap between the masses and the elites. A relatively rapid industrialization in some areas of the country produced its own dislocations, including urban slums and poverty, while the infrastructure of roads, hospitals, and housing lagged far behind. For much of the country, *rural* poverty remained a fact of life, and the landless day laborers and smallholders fell further behind the economically elite absentee landlords who ran their latifundia through exploitative middlemen. Economic development profited very few (who became very rich). The gulf between rich and poor increased considerably, and the masses remained steeped in backwardness, illiteracy, and ignorance. They continued to be afflicted by problems such as high infant mortality and low life expectancy and had few prospects for change. Periodic attempts at local reform amounted to little until World War I. And when change finally came in 1924, it was perceived as too little, too late.

Romania erupted in the greatest peasant rebellion of modern European history in 1907—a bloody protest against the poverty and injustices of the countryside.[33] The uprising was a graphic illustration of the alienation of the rural masses, stemming from the desperate economic situation many of them still endured after thirty years of national independence and mismanagement by national elites. The brutality of the repression meted out to the rebels also illustrated the attitudes of the leaders, who were unsympathetic to the arguments of the peasant spokesmen. Both sides learned some very important truths about each other, chief of which was that no one could be trusted and everyone was out for parochial interests. This mutual distrust was to continue, indeed to grow, in the years preceding World War II and the establishment of communist power in Romania.

Political repression, poverty, economic dislocation, and the cultural and educational misery of the Romanian countryside during the decades of independence produced a distinct political culture that was, in part, a reaffirmation of values that had been established over generations of foreign rule.

First, there was widespread distrust of central authority. The representatives of the center only came into the countryside to collect taxes, induct peasant sons into the military, or enforce rules and regulations that seemed meaningless to most and economically harmful to all. Central authority was also seen as morally corrupt and a threat to peasant values such as honor, trustworthiness, loyalty to kin, and solidarity with one's neighbor. Furthermore, the peasants believed that little attention was paid to God in the city, which was the site of immorality, loose living, and other behaviors not tolerated in the village.[34]

The city was further handicapped as far as the peasant was concerned, for it was the dwelling place of foreigners, especially Jews, who were admired, despised, and resented on economic, social, and religious grounds. Thus, the city was foreign in several important ways, and contact with it was to be avoided; only occasional trips on festive days or when official business called were acceptable. Most Romanians lived their entire lives in a small area, never visiting any of the major cities, including the national capital. For the peasantry, then, Romanian nationalism existed *without* attachment to the central authorities and the capital city.[35]

The parochialism of the peasantry was further enhanced by the second major trait of this mass, namely, *negative* apathy. Central authorities were to be avoided not only because they represented the city and all that it stood for but because they had nothing good to offer the average individual. Negative apathy is a most dangerous political condition because it rejects authority and produces no sense of legitimacy for the rulers. The negatively apathetic individual accepts the fact that there are kings and presidents and bureaucrats, generals and tax collectors, because they somehow have the *power* to rule; they do not, however, necessarily have the *right* to rule. Therefore, the political system must operate on force and submission, not delegated authority or positive apathy, where individuals do not care about politics but have left that arena to "authorities" whom they consider competent, moral, and capable of doing a good job without the involvement of the masses.[36]

The Romanian regime also lacked mass support in the cities. A substantial part of the urban population was made up of ethnic minorities who resented the rule of the Romanians. And even among the non-minorities, only those who profited from political power in an immediate and personal way supported the regime. The numerous political parties that developed after 1876 reflected the highly personalized nature of Romanian politics—many of them were coteries of local notables and lacked the requisite organizational infrastructure or systematic political platform. Consequently, political power was obtained and lost on the basis of acquaintances, ad hoc deals, and personal gain. Coalitions were formed and dissolved with dizzying speed; today's partners would be tomorrow's enemies. Support for the coalition would depend upon the potential for personal gain of each party's oligarchic leadership. The kind of political support that a regime needs to implement long-range societal goals could not be established under these circumstances.[37]

Another aspect of Romanian politics further alienated most of the public during the decades between independence and World War II— the time-honored approach to political recruiting known as nepotism. Political leadership in Romania tended to promote friends and relatives to positions of power, and regular, established procedures were ignored or simply non-existent. The musical chairs of coalition-building and the blatantly nepotistic approach of most political elites convinced those who had any interest at all that politics was, indeed, a dirty game. And those with no interest were apathetic for much the same reason: Politics was an unworthy activity that one should avoid in any form.[38]

Throughout much of the period 1876–1939, then, the Romanian scene reflected the venal nature its politics. Most political leaders were personally corrupt, and the political process was extremely fluid, with ministries formed and broken by means of personal relations. Elections were uniformly corrupted by administrative interference and cheating at the ballot boxes. The administrative bureaucracy should have provided leadership, continuity, honesty, and predictability under these circumstances, but it was, by and large, as corrupt as the political leadership. The old practice of bakshish was not abandoned when national independence was achieved, but continued to flourish, often with a style and innovativeness that would have astonished the Turks and others who practiced it with such skill for centuries. Throughout the entire period, corruption flourished in all areas and all levels of administrative activity. It became a way of life to offer bribes to officials to ensure action on a petition or secure a favorable outcome. It was just as customary for officials to expect and accept such bribes or favors. There is a substantial popular literature on the Balkans that treats the political systems there like "banana republics," and current serious literature increasingly verifies this image.[39]

Rejection of central authority was well anchored in the collective psyche of the Romanian peasantry; corruption, nepotism, and poor performance became just as commonplace among the politicos and the bureaucrats. The urban masses, seeing the venality of elite behavior on a much more frequent basis than their rural counterparts did, also became alienated, negatively apathetic, and, occasionally, overtly hostile. Thus, the two major political characteristics discussed thus far combined to widen the chasm between the government and the people.

A third major characteristic of the Romanian political system was the discrepancy between words and acts. Upon the establishment of independence, the Romanian leaders promulgated a constitution that emphasized democracy, honesty, thrift, and responsibility. Flowery rhetoric stressed the same values every year in parliamentary speeches, celebrations on festive days, and in official documents from the ministries of the capital. *Reality* was uniformly different. Administrative decrees that spelled out procedures in excruciating detail were habitually ignored or modified by personal fiat. The flaunting of democratic principles was constantly visible, particularly during elections. And the ceaseless rhetoric about sharing rights, duties, hardships, and successes had a definitely hollow ring to those who were not in leadership positions and thus not "on the take."[40]

The discrepancy between rhetoric and reality reinforced the popular mindset that politics is an illusion. Any political situation or circumstance has a hidden meaning; there is always the question "What's the catch?" Procedural rules, voluminous as they were, had no meaning and precious little influence on the average Romanian's behavior. The notion that something should be done because it was procedurally right or because it was one's duty had little validity. Only under circumstances in which *higher* duty (to God or to the nation) was called on could one expect the masses to perform unquestionably, without asking "What's the catch?" Under normal circumstances, popular attitudes reflected only negative apathy and cynicism. Much of this continues in contemporary Romania.[41]

Nonetheless, the Romanian masses in town and countryside had distinct political values. (These values, however, had little relationship to the behavior of elites in Bucharest or in the provincial center; in fact, they were often directly and openly opposed to the rhetoric and actions of those leaders.) There was, first of all, the sense of nationalism, which remained strong among the masses in all locations. Theirs was a rather diffuse nationalism, based on the belief that God supported the Romanian cause and emphasizing the glory of traditional leaders who had known how to forge a strong link with the people. In fact, Romanian nationalism stressed that organic link between elite and mass, especially the great leader himself, in a value set featuring important aspects of populism and the quest for the strong leader—the man on horseback who would bring law and order, predictability and reality to politics, all of which were missing in the contemporary order.

Romanian nationalism was also somewhat egalitarian, and it stressed the need for redistribution of wealth, land reform, and a return to the simple life of the village. The Christian values of love, loyalty, and sacrifice permeated much of this form of nationalism. Again, such qualities were noticeably lacking in the leaders of the country or the province.[42]

It can be argued that parochialism and apathy in themselves were expressions of political values. The *real* values of ethics, morality, and nationalism could only be expressed by ignoring the official political order and, in fact, withdrawing from it. Thus, a countervalue system developed among the masses in both town and countryside, juxtaposed to the hollow proclamations of the leadership and their bureaucratic henchmen. Life in the villages continued along its age-old paths, and the discrepancy between rural behavior and the actions of the central leaders was striking. Furthermore, the honest and loyal villager would think nothing of cheating on his duties vis-à-vis the state or central authorities. After all, *they* would cheat whenever the occasion arose, so why should he not respond in kind when dealing with *them?* The wide gap that opened between private (and local) morality, on the one hand, and public morality, on the other, is perhaps the most dangerous of chasms, because it fosters the belief that officials and leaders are, ipso facto, inferior to the masses and thus can be expected to do little good for anybody but themselves. It is extraordinarily difficult to bridge this gap; such a feat requires responsible leadership, in power for a very long period of time. Certainly, Romania has not experienced such leadership during the communist era.[43]

The political leaders of the country managed to tap into mass values and nationalism only on a few occasions. For example, the masses could be mobilized when the nation was threatened, as during the Balkan Wars and World War I. National euphoria over the acquisition of Transylvania and the establishment of historical Romania, "Romania Mare," in 1918 was another occasion. At such times, the political and religious leaders could stand together to receive the adulation of the masses—a rare show of organic unity between the political elite and the people. But, again, these were extraordinary circumstances. The daily practice of politics, Bucharest style, did not permit such unity.[44]

Some elements of the mass political culture did support specific aspects of the leaders' behavior, up to a point. For example, the *authoritarianism* of the central leadership was not inconsistent with mass values; its lack of *direction*, however, was. When the King instituted a personal dictatorship in 1938, his proclamations had strains of the populism and strong-man tendencies so often found in popular mythology about the great historical figures of Romania. Furthermore, the religious, populist, and intolerant elements of the mass movements (such as the League of the Archangel Michael and, eventually, the Iron Guard) reflected elite values as well. The point here is that both mass and elite were authoritarian, lacking in the values and traditions of civil democracy and society, and intolerant of "deviants." Thus, they lacked any notions of "unity in diversity" that are so crucial to liberal democracy in Western and Northern Europe. The chasm between elite and mass developed *inside* authoritarian value systems. As such, Romania developed entirely in the tradition of Southeastern Europe.[45]

By contrast, there was little support for the kind of organized radicalism represented by Marxism and other forms of leftist challenges so common elsewhere in Europe. The Romanian working class was small, albeit growing at a rapid pace. Most of the workers were first-generation proletarians who maintained strong ties with the village and were still steeped in traditionalism and authoritarianism; many of them remained profoundly religious. These were not the right recruits for Marxism (even though, under somewhat different circumstances and with vastly more inspiring leadership, similar proletarians in Russia could be captured for the cause). Furthermore, the Marxists in Romania tended to come from the ethnic minorities, particularly the Jews and the Bulgarians—a fact that did not endear them to the masses, whether urban or rural.[46] Despite concerted efforts by the communist leaders, and particularly the Ceausescu clan, to rewrite history, this fact cannot be erased from the *real* record. The communists had no future in Romania. They could only hope to obtain power through extraordinary circumstances, and, by the same token, maintain themselves in power by means of force or by redefining Marxism in their own image, tradition, and culture. This they did.

Notes

1. The Ceausescu regime constantly refers to this heritage as a legitimizing device; see, for example, the General Secretary's speech during Mikhail Gorbachev's visit, discussed by Anneli Ute Gabanyi, *Radio Free Europe Research*, Romanian SR/4, 29 May 1987.

2. See, for example, Nicolae Copoiu in *Flacara*, February 10, 1984, on the origins of the Romanian state.

3. The Romanian party leadership utilizes historiography for many of its claims to historical ties, e.g. in *Scinteia*, in a series of articles on Mircea the Old (a prince who ruled Wallachia in the fourteenth century), July 6 and 26, 1986.

4. R. W. Seton-Watson, *A History of the Roumanians* (Cambridge, England: Cambridge University Press, 1934), ch. I (pp. 1–17).

5. This nationalism has indeed become chauvinism. See, for example, the homage paid to the Ceausescus on the occasion of their birthdays, in *Septamina*, No. 4, January 24, 1986 (Nicolae) and *Contemporanul*, No. 2, January 14, 1984 (Elena).

6. Andrei Otetea (ed.), *Istoria Poporului Roman*, (Bucharest: Editura Stiintifica, 1970), esp. pp. 77–127.

7. Dinu Giurescu, *Illustrated History of the Romanian People* (Bucharest: Editura Sport-Turism, 1981), pp. 30–109, esp. 76–109.

8. The claim to Dacian superiority was taken to extremes with Nicolae Copoiu, a researcher at the Institute for Historical and Socio-Political Studies of the RCP Central Committee. See, for example, one of his articles in *Luceafarul*, October 16, 1982.

9. E.g. Stephen Fischer-Galati, "Romanian Nationalism," in Peter F. Sugar and Ivo J. Lederer (eds.), *Nationalism in Eastern Europe* (Seattle, WA: University of Washington Press, 1969), pp. 373–396.

10. *Ibid.*

11. Constantin C. Giurescu (ed.), *Chronological History of Romania* (Bucharest: Editura Enciclopedica Romana), pp. 27–29, accepts the notion of the integration of Romans and Geto-Dacians. Giurescu also discusses the Geto-Dacian withdrawal into the forests and mountains, on pp. 38–42.

12. Dinu Giurescu, *Illustrated History of the Romanian People*, esp. pp. 56–76.

13. *Ibid.*

14. Official glorification of this continuity is clearly exaggerated. For an analysis, see Dan Ionescu, *Radio Free Europe Research*, Romanian SR/10, 11 September 1986.

15. For a recent discussion of the issue, see Michael Shafir, "The Dispute with Hungary over Transylvania," *Radio Free Europe Research*, Romanian SR/2, 28 January 1988.

16. Fischer-Galati, "Romanian Nationalism."

17. For a superior discussion of the development of such group cohesion see John A. Armstrong, *Nations Before Nationalism* (Chapel Hill, NC: The University of North Carolina Press, 1982), esp. ch. 1 (pp. 3–14).

18. Seton-Watson, *A History of the Roumanians*, ch. I (pp. 1–17).

19. For a discussion of the confluence of nationalism and religion, see my chapter "Religion and Nationalism in Romania," in Pedro Ramet (ed.), *Religion and Nationalism in Soviet and East European Politics* (Durham, NC: Duke University Press, 1984), ch. 10 (pp. 170–187).

20. Armstrong, *Nations Before Nationalism*, ch. 3 (pp. 54–93).

21. Others have also examined this development in the Romanian case, e.g. Seton-Watson, *A History of the Roumanians*, esp. ch. VIII (pp. 192–220).

22. The importance of religious counterelites cannot be overstated. See, for example, Keith Hitchins, *Orthodoxy and Nationality: Andreiu Saguna and the Romanians of Transylvania, 1846–1873* (Cambridge, MA: Harvard University Press, 1977), esp. ch. 7.

23. E.g. Stefan Pascu, "Perioada Tendentilor de Centralizare a Tarilor Romane," in Miron Constantinescu, et al., *Istoria Romaniei* (Bucharest: Editura Didactica si Pedagogica, 1969), esp. pp. 190–204.

24. Otetea, *Istoria Poporului Roman,* esp. pp. 167–209, and 237–262.

25. On the subjugation suffered under Ottoman and Phanariot rule, see Seton-Watson, *A History of the Roumanians,* esp. ch. III (pp. 50–101) and ch. V (pp. 126–144).

26. There is a great deal of material on Transylvania. See, for example, Stefan Metes, *Emigrari Romanesti din Transilvania in Secolele XIII–XX,* (2nd ed.) (Bucharest: Editura Stiintifica si Enciclopedica, 1977), esp. ch. I (pp. 11–22) and ch. VI (pp. 71–148). See also Otetea, *Istoria Poporului Roman,* esp. pp. 460–487.

27. See my "Religion and Nationalism in Romania," in Ramet, *Religion and Nationalism in Soviet and East European Politics,* ch. 10 (pp. 170–187).

28. Dinu Giurescu, *Illustrated History of the Romanian People,* esp. pp. 331–383.

29. Seton-Watson, *A History of the Roumanians,* ch. VIII (pp. 192–220) and ch. IX (pp. 220–269).

30. Some scholars of the communist era have attempted to discuss the formation of mass attitudes and values in a systematic manner; see, for example, Stefan Pascu, *Marea Adunare Nationala de la Alba Iulia* (Universitatea "Babes-Bolyai" din Cluj, Romania, 1968), esp. ch. 1 (pp. 9–46).

31. On the establishment of the national state, see Traian Lungu, "Orinduirea Capitalista" in Miron Constantinescu (ed.), *Istoria Romaniei* (Bucharest: Editura Didactica si Pedagogica, 1970), esp. pp. 342–386.

32. Seton-Watson, *A History of the Roumanians,* esp. ch. XI (pp. 301–346), XII (pp. 346–390), and XIII (pp. 390–432).

33. On the peasant revolt, see Andrei Otetea, et al., *Marea Rascoala a Taranilor din 1907* (Bucharest: Editura Academiei Republicii Socialiste Romania, 1967), esp. ch. II (pp. 31–109) and ch. IX (pp. 787–841).

34. I have discussed the basic features of the Romanian political culture in "The Communist Parties of Romania," in Stephen Fischer-Galati (ed.), *The Communist Party of Eastern Europe* (New York, NY: Columbia University Press, 1979), ch. 71 (pp. 281–327), esp. pp. 281–290.

35. For a superb discussion of the dichotomy between city and countryside in peasant societies, see Armstrong, *Nations Before Nationalism,* ch. 4 (pp. 93–129).

36. Many of these concepts were elaborated upon in Gabriel Almond and Sidney Verba, *The Civic Culture* (Princeton, NJ: Princeton University Press, 1963), esp. ch. 1 (pp. 3–43) and ch. 14 (pp. 402–473).

37. For a discussion of party politics in independent Romania, see my "Romania" in Vincent E. McHale (ed.), *Political Parties of Europe* (Westport, CT: Greenwood Press, 1983), Vol. II (pp. 774–810).

38. Thus, the traditions of the Phanariot Greeks have been upheld to this time in Romanian politics. For a discussion of the Pharoriote period, see Seton-Watson, *A History of the Roumanians,* ch. V (pp. 126–144).

39. A good overview of Romanian politics in this period is found in Ghita Ionescu, *Communism in Romania 1944-1962* (London: Oxford University Press, 1964), ch. 1 (pp. 1-71).

40. For an analysis of this rhetoric, see, for example, Stefan Pascu, *Marea Adunare Nationala de la Alba Iulia,* esp. ch. VIII (pp. 361-381).

41. At times, the cynicism so frequently found in Romania boils over into open protest; see, for example, *Le Monde,* December 31, 1986, on a strike in Cluj in the fall of that year.

42. Many of these values have been discussed in literature even in the socialist period. See, for example, Titus Popovici, *The Stranger* (Bucharest: Meridians, 1972). On the persistence of such values in contemporary Romania, see my "Political Socialization in Romania," in Daniel N. Nelson (ed.), *Romania in the 1980s* (Boulder, CO: Westview Press, 1981), ch. 5 (pp. 142-174).

43. In fact, the performance (or lack thereof) of the Ceausescus is widening the gap every day. In addition, specific regime policies further alienate large segments of the population; see, for example, the restrictive rules on the elderly and their residencies, discussed in *Flacara,* March 21, 1986. On the chasm between the masses and the leaders in the "bourgeois" era, see Andrei Otetea, et al., *Marea Rascoala a Taranilor din 1907,* esp. ch. II (pp. 31-109).

44. One such occasion was the assembly at Alba Iulia in December 1918, proclaiming the unification of Transylvania and the rest of Romania. See Pascu, *Marea Adunare Nationala de la Alba Iulia,* ch. VII (pp. 317-361) and ch. VIII (pp. 361-395).

45. On native authoritarianism and fascism in Romania, see Peter F. Sugar, *Native Fascism in the Successor States, 1918-1945* (Santa Barbara, CA: ABC-CLIO, 1971), ch. VI (part A, pp. 101-112 by Emanuel Turczynski and part B, pp. 112-123 by Stephen Fischer-Galati).

46. R. V. Burks, *The Dynamics of Communism in Eastern Europe* (Princeton, N.J.: Princeton University Press, 1961), pp. 165-168.

3

Radicalism and
Marxism in Romania

The Roots of Romanian Radicalism

Many observers have pointed out that the radical ideas of Karl Marx
and Friedrich Engels had little effect on Romanian politics, and it is
certainly true that these ideas never produced a mass movement in that
agrarian country. In fact, in August 1944, when a coup d'etat toppled
the Fascist regime and established a coalition government with communist
participation, the Romanian Communist Party (RCP) reportedly had only
a thousand registered members. This record stands in sharp contrast to
neighboring Bulgaria, where leftist radicalism of various kinds played
a major role in the political life of the country in the interwar period,
or Yugoslavia, where Josip Broz Tito forged a powerful coalition of leftist
elements that eventually propelled him to power in that country. These
analysts, having pointed out these *massive* differences between neighboring countries in the Balkans, often puzzled over the discrepancy and
offered a number of explanations that revolved around political culture
and the allegedly submissive nature of the Romanians ("mamaliga does
not explode").[1]

The notion that radicalism was of minimal importance in Romania
needs to be examined more carefully. History shows a number of cases
in which the peasantry rose up in powerful jacqueries against oppressors
of all kinds. The most famous of these was the uprising led by Horia
and Closcan in the eighteenth century, but there was also the case of
Tudor Vladimirescu in the following century, and then, in the first decade
of the twentieth, the largest and bloodiest peasant rebellion in recent
European history. Between these periodic outbursts there were long
periods of quietude and submission, to be sure, but even these periods
harbored the seeds of the eventual explosion. Thus, mamaliga *does*
explode, provided the circumstances and the pressures are germane to

such activities. Instead of relegating Romanian radicalism to the back burner, we must try to explain its nature and its specific manifestations.[2]

While there are a number of manifestations of peasant radicalism, there is less evidence of urban revolutionary thought and behavior. In this area, Romania does stand in clear contrast to Bulgaria, which produced an active urban revolutionary movement with important tendencies towards violence, as evidenced by the bombing of the Sofia Cathedral in 1923. Furthermore, Bulgarians became important operatives for the spectacular activities of The Communist International (Comintern) including terrorist acts and actual assassinations. In Romania, on the other hand, the Marxist left was always weak (despite the efforts of recent historiography to prove the opposite). In the decades prior to independence, the leftist radicals of the city focused much of their activity on the question of national independence. And after 1876, there was a notable lack of mass support for the few radical thinkers who struggled to maintain a meaningful Marxist movement in such difficult circumstances. The nature of this difference between neighboring countries must be explored, for therein lies one of the keys to understanding the contemporary political order in Romania.[3]

Romanian Marxism Before World War I

A number of factors account for the lack of Marxist activity in Romania up to World War I. First of all, those who were acquainted with the thoughts of Karl Marx and Friedrich Engels were, by and large, urban intellectuals in a traditionally rural society. The rurality of Romania went far beyond the fact that the overwhelming majority of the population lived in the countryside. It was a psychological state of mind, as discussed in the previous chapter. In this mindset, the peasant distrusted ideas that emanated from the city because he basically distrusted the city itself, as the center of foreign or alien activities, and as the residence of foreigners, especially Jews, Hungarians, Germans, Armenians and Greeks. The heart and soul of Romania was seen to be located in the countryside, where the values of the village and the extended family prevailed. It did not help matters much that many of the intellectuals who did espouse Marxism were, in fact, non-Romanians, particularly Bulgarians and Jews, both ethnic groups that were distrusted and even despised by the Romanian masses.[4]

The urban intellectuals, for their part, were psychologically removed from the life of the village and the people who lived there. They were citified individuals in a thoroughly rural society, and they had very little in common with the "great unwashed masses" of the fields and the forests. In fact, they tended to look down on these representatives of

Romanian backwardness and longed for the day when economic development would propel Romania to the ranks of industrialized society where *real* proletarians (and hence the possibilities of *real* revolution) could be found. Finally, those intellectual revolutionaries who were non-Romanians had serious doubts about the masses of the peasantry who belonged to an ethnic group which they often despised and occasionally lumped together with the lowest of all categories, the Gypsies.[5]

Thus, many of those who professed to be Marxist revolutionaries in Bucharest, Iasi, and a few other cities were eminently Salonfähig as revolutionaries but woefully unprepared to go out and get their hands dirty in the messy business of leading masses to storm the bastions of power. It was chic to talk revolution and class society over an aperitif in one of the sidewalk cafes of the "Paris of East," but there was no question that this intellectually stimulating talk would be followed by real action outside of the pleasant, treelined boulevards of Bucharest. There was indeed a great deal of intellectual arrogance among these citified purveyors of revolution as they longed for civilization in Rome or Paris, far away from backward Romania.[6]

The enormous gap between city and countryside and the mutual alienation between those who wrote about Marxism and those who lived on the margins of survival in the countryside precluded the development of a mass movement on the left on this ideological basis prior to industrialization. But even after that process got underway in a sustained fashion conditions remained unfavorable. The emerging industrial proletariat was really made up of peasant-workers, individuals who may have left the villages in a physical sense, but with the peasant mentality retained intact. Furthermore, most of these individuals were crammed into hastily erected shanty houses and workers' hostels, where they lived together as a compact mass, isolated from other individuals and other socio-economic classes, thus impervious to influences from the urban society around them. Basically, this residential pattern simply moved the village into areas of the city, but the "peasantness" of the individuals who had made this physical move remained intact. Besides, many of the peasant-workers retained close ties with the village and went back to it with great regularity, particularly at sowing and harvesting time. In fact, there were many new "proletarians" who commuted to the city for work but retained their primary residence in the countryside.[7]

The new proletariat of peasant-workers constituted an uprooted class that had lost its traditional surroundings, but not its psychology. Still, the atomized nature of its existence made it available for mobilization by various movements, many of them radical, and many of them attuned to the mentality of these transplanted peasants. In the confusing welter of competing radicalisms, the Marxists, with their ingrained city habits and outlooks, came in way behind a number of others, some of which set the stage for elements of contemporary Marxism in the garb of "Ceausescuism." More about that later.

One of the elements of leftist radicalism in Romania during the decades between independence and World War II was populism. Populism, Romanian style, emphasized the need for political and socio-economic change to benefit "the people." It stressed the need for egalitarianism and denigrated political elites, and the emerging structure of modern society, in which there were increasing distances between the well-to-do and the masses of the population. Furthermore, this kind of populism accepted direct rule by an individual strongman; in fact, it encouraged such a system, because this form of political rule eliminated the "middlemen" of bureaucrats and representatives who were considered (and rightly so) corrupt and untrustworthy. Romanian populism also incorporated important values such as the attachment to the land and to localism, and it had an important element of religious fundamentalism as well. It was egalitarian, concerned with fundamental values of life and religion, and anti-intellectual. "Progress" was not considered worthwhile if it meant experiencing the dislocations that Western Europe and the United States had gone through, particularly secularization, the loss of traditional values of family and village, and the uprooting of traditional structures that industrialization and urbanization inevitably produced. In fact, this populism emphasized agrarian values and saw the village as the good society, with its life and its enduring values.[8]

Populism was a form of rural radicalism, but it also had an urban counterpart in Romania, which emphasized much the same set of values. Some of the urban populism saw the egalitarian society discussed above as applicable and appropriate for the city and thus a possible model for a modernized Romania, while others felt that such conditions could only be found in the pastoral setting of the village. In both cases, the model advocated differed considerably from the Marxist notions of a class society that would produce a revolution and then a classless society based upon rule by the urban, industrial proletariat.[9]

Throughout the late nineteenth and early twentieth centuries there also developed a set of political beliefs that contained elements of future Fascist thought. These elements, like Fascism, emphasized race, ethnicity, the importance of the soil and man's relationship with it. There was a great deal of romanticism involved in these ideas, based upon the notion of the "pure" individual tilling the gardens and the fields, and the corresponding adulteration of life that was associated with the city and all of its alien elements. Anti-Semitism was an important element of this package of thought, reflecting long-standing values among broad segments of the Romanian masses in the cities as well as the countryside.

The mysticism of the soil and the village was coupled with religious fundamentalism. Later on, as it became fashionable to espouse the theories of Fascism, the Romanian version took firmer organizational forms in the League of the Archangel Michael and, eventually, the Iron Guard and the other Fascist organizations.[10]

In the countryside, there were also other groups that advocated the violent overthrow of the existing order and its substitution by a new system, which would ensure greater equality and a better life for all. Some of these ideas were rather similar to the ideological foundations of the Socialist Revolutionaries in Tsarist Russia—a fact that should not be surprising, given the similarities in organization, level of development, and political traditions of the two peasant societies.[11]

All of the groups and organizations above were authoritarian in a certain sense of the word, in that they wished to substitute one form of a directed society for another. There was no willingness to accept "unity in diversity," which characterizes a civil society and a pluralistic political order. The radical movements discussed above rejected and mistrusted all or most of the elements of social and political pluralism, such as social diversification and functional specialization, respect for the rights of others, and tolerance for competing ideologies and political programs. Anti-democratic, anti-pluralistic, and anti-intellectual values and norms dominated; the emphasis was on fundamentalism in politics and religion, the notion of strong, individualized leadership, and the return to the "good old days." This had little to do with classical Marxism, with its emphasis on progress, defined as industrialization, urbanization, and secularization, nor did it bear much resemblance to those elements of the "early Marx" that stressed the need for *individual* liberation from the shackles of alienation and economic exploitation.[12]

One area in which the radical movements of Romania and Marxism did coincide was in the field of collectivism. The rural radicals emphasized the organic ties between the individual and the collectivity and could not envision a society in which the rights of the individual would be more important than the needs of the society. The same can be said for Marxism, at least the "mature" version that emerged as the dominant element as Karl Marx became more concerned with the need for a class based revolution and less interested in human alienation and its alleviation. Under these circumstances, the relevance of Marxism in Romania was distinctly limited. But there was definitely radicalism among the masses, as discussed. It bore the manifestations of its Eastern origins, emanating from the cultural traditions of Byzantium, the Sublime Porte, and Muscovy. In contrast, Marxism was a product of Western culture, the Judeo-Christian heritage, and the Enlightenment. The "cognitive dissonance" that was produced by this discrepancy put Marxism at an enduring disadvantage in Romania. It still suffers from this disadvantage, regardless of the chorus of sycophants who praise the current Leader as the "most scientific" and "progressive" of all leaders, of all times, at any place.[13]

Another distinct handicap for Marxism in Romania was the fact that the overriding political issue in that country until 1876 was national independence, and, until 1918, the reestablishment of Historic Romania, "Romania Mare," incorporating Moldavia, Wallachia, and the "lost" province of Transylvania. This nationalistic quest could be incorporated into the rural radicalism discussed above; in fact, it was an integral part thereof. But in Marxism, the emphasis was on internationalism and models of socio-economic development that were foreign (or at least not indigenous) to the Romanian experience. Marxism as such could only begin to develop as a meaningful political alternative after 1918. At that time, other debilitating elements appeared, as we shall see below.[14]

The Interwar Period

The "national question" continued to dominate the Romanian political scene even after the incorporation of Transylvania in 1918. The new state, Romania Mare, or Greater Romania, contained a large number of ethnic minorities, chief of which were the Magyars, the Germans, and the Jews. These three groups were clearly more advanced than the now dominant Romanians, and this fact caused considerable friction and resentment. The openly nationalistic policy of the Romanian government was a necessity if popular support were to be established and maintained among the masses of the ethnic majority, but it was clearly detrimental to relations between the Romanians and the minority groups. This is a political dilemma that continues to this day and indeed appears to be aggravated as a result of the policies of the Ceausescu regime.

Ethnic animosities produced political tension among the various nationality groups in Romania. They also precluded any solidarity across such boundaries, thus eliminating or severely reducing the possibilities of a political movement based primarily on socio-economic class and a common occupation. Thus, the fledgling RCP, which was formed in 1921, could not create a mass movement of workers from different ethnic backgrounds. The RCP remained small, with its mass membership primarily among the ethnic minorities and its leadership drawn from the Jewish group or even Bulgarians. Recent Romanian historiography has attempted to deny this fact, but the historical record shows that interethnic relations were so negative that precious little solidarity across the dividing lines developed in the interwar period.[15]

The early policies of the RCP also contributed to the party's isolation and its eventual illegality. During the early period of the Communist International (Comintern) the RCP associated itself with the international organization's position on the national question. And the Comintern maintained, in true internationalist fashion, that national sovereignty and state borders were anachronisms, soon to be swept away by the rising tide of revolution and international solidarity. The RCP even went so far as to associate itself with the Comintern's view that Bessarabia should be returned to the Soviet Union. This position was seen in Romania as direct betrayal of a cause espoused by the entire nation, regardless of class, and the communists found themselves in a ghetto, despised by their fellow countrymen, many of whom were workers.[16]

By 1923, the Communist Party of the Soviet Union (CPSU) had taken full control over the Comintern and its Executive Committee (ECCI). This led to the so-called "Bolshevization" of the Comintern, in which Soviet foreign policy goals became predominant, and the needs of the member parties were forcefully subordinated to the interests of Moscow. In the Romanian case, this meant slavish acceptance of the Soviet line on Bessarabia and the espousal of policy goals which had little relevance in the domestic context. This story is familiar to students of the Comintern in the 1920s and 1930s. In Romania, it ensured the continued irrelevance of the RCP and its consignment to the political fringe and eventually illegality.[17]

During the interwar period there also arose a rather powerful Fascist movement in Romania that removed any mass appeal that the communists may have hoped for. This native Fascism was well tailored to the Romanian political culture. It emphasized values that were commonly held in wide segments of the population, regardless of socio-economic class. It espoused authoritarianism and one-man leadership, concepts held in high regard by many in Romania; it proffered solutions to the economic crisis that seemed more feasible than most other plans, including the communist slogans of class struggle. Above all, Romanian Fascism was much better suited to the political conditions in an agrarian society with strong religiosity. In the 1930s the Fascist movement, together with other movements on the political right, completely overshadowed its own purposes.[18]

Communist historiography has maintained that the RCP remained important throughout this entire period and that it had a major role in various political activities during the years between the two world wars. For example, much has been made of the Grivita railroad strike of 1933 and the communist leadership that was manifested in it. During the last two decades, there has also been a flood of writing on the leadership role of Nicolae Ceausescu and Elena Petrescu in the youth movement of the party during this period. In actual fact, the RCP and its subsidiaries and front organizations remained on the fringes of Romanian politics and could do little to affect events.[19]

On the eve of World War II, then, the RCP was a minor force in Romanian politics with little prospect for an early remedy of the fringe status to which it had been consigned. The lack of success in mass recruitment, coupled with the severe repression meted out by various cabinets and especially the royal dictatorship after 1933, led to internal bickering, factionalism, and the incarceration of several party leaders. A number of others went into exile in the Soviet Union or elsewhere. The party was in the doldrums. The war changed its fortunes in drastic ways in a process that was repeated elsewhere in Southeastern and Central Europe.

The War and Changed Fortunes

The story of the Romanian involvement in World War II is well known and needs no further elaboration here. It should merely be emphasized that the fortunes of war enabled the RCP to come to power, not because of its strength in mass appeal or the relevance of its political programs, but because the geopolitical and other conditions were fundamentally altered as a result of the destruction of Germany and the rise of the Soviet Union to political and military preeminence in Southeastern and Central Europe. Added to this was the fact that the leaders of the Western alliance expressed their view that Romania was not crucial to their interests—a clear incentive for the Kremlin to attempt to manipulate matters in that country to its own advantage. The very presence of Soviet troops and the active part played by the Soviets in the Military Control Commission altered the political context in which the various groups, movements, and political parties of that country operated. The other parties must now consider the RCP a viable player and include it in their calculations. The RCP, in turn, utilized these political conditions to maximize the influence that had come its way as a result of these altered circumstances. The combination of these factors propelled the erstwhile band of hounded revolutionaries to the fore of Romanian politics in a way that would have been inconceivable even a few short weeks earlier.

The pragmatism and apathy prevailing in the Romanian political culture now worked to the distinct advantage of the RCP in terms of mass recruitment. Most individuals with any political savvy realized that the communists would play a major part in Romanian politics from that time forward, and they acted accordingly. There was mass enrollment in the RCP and its various front organizations during the fall of 1944, and the next year as the so-called "progressive coalition" was established and widened, with increasing communist influence at every juncture. Large numbers of individuals left existing parties to join the RCP; many others, who had never been politically active, now acquired party cards and other accoutrements of participation for the left. Even some of the members of Fascist organizations made this switch with remarkable facility, whereupon the more adventurous of the latter proceeded to establish themselves in positions of some authority in some of the coercive organizations controlled by the RCP. Clearly, the "fellow-travelling" tendencies of important elements in the Romanian public stemmed, in considerable measure, from the lack of real political commitment that characterized the masses in the first place.[20]

By the time that World War II was officially over, the RCP had strengthened its position in the Romanian political system to such an extent that it could no longer be dislodged. From that time onward, the erstwhile band of true believers readied themselves for the task of ruling and governing. And in that capacity, the RCP leaders also had to come to grips with the tension between nationalism and internationalism, or loyalty to Bucharest versus devotion to Moscow.

National Communism in Romania

A great deal of research has been produced on the issue of ruling communism in Romania during the period 1947 (when the RCP took power by forcing the King to abdicate) until 1965, when Nicolae Ceausescu came to power and began to develop a theoretical and practical version of Marxism-Leninism that is both national and idiosyncratic. There is no doubt that "Ceausescuism" is a form of national (and personal) communism. There *is* a certain debate about the extent to which the theories and policies of Ana Pauker and Gheorghe Gheorhiu-Dej also were nationalistic, or, the *extent* to which they displayed some such characteristics. Rather important arguments can be made both ways on this issue. For example, it is undeniable that a number of specific policies carried out by these two Romanian leaders coincided with Soviet statements, interests, and policies to such an extent that a careful observer might be convinced that coordination, imitation, and subordination most clearly characterized the relationship between Moscow and Bucharest. First of all, the Pauker leadership openly acknowledged the leadership of the CPSU in relations among communist parties, and the Romanians also readily accepted the notion that the USSR must be the leader of the socialist states. This was manifested during the ideological struggle that ended with Yugoslavia's ouster from the Cominform, and the acceptance of the Soviet definition of "Titoism" and the resulting purges which hit Romania hard, albeit less severely than a few of the other states inside the Soviet Bloc. Furthermore, the Romanians followed the Soviet lead in the rapid escalation of East-West tension, dramatically manifested in the Korean War, and Bucharest loyally accepted the Soviet version of events in East Germany during the summer of 1953, when the first open and serious challenge to Soviet supremacy and Stalinism (even after Stalin) erupted and was duly suppressed. During the period 1953–1956 Romania appeared as one of the bastions of political, ideological, and socio-economic orthodoxy just as challengers materialized and toppled the regimes of Poland and Hungary and almost produced systemic change in the latter country. Gheorghiu-Dej loyally handed over Imre Nagy and his entourage after they had sought refuge in Romania during the second Soviet invasion of Hungary in November 1956, and the Romanian leader took measures to ensure that the large and relatively compact Magyar minority in Transylvania would represent no serious threat to the stability of the Romanian regime and would remain untainted by the dramatic developments north of the border, in Hungary proper.[21]

In the socio-economic development of Romania, a "Stalinist" model was clearly followed, both under Pauker and Gheorghiu-Dej. There was massive, rapid, extensive industrialization, forced collectivization of agriculture, and a forceful campaign of mass education. All of this was coupled with energetic measures, occasionally physical, against actual or potential competitors such as the remnants of the old political parties, the various churches (particularly the Uniates, who were outlawed already in 1948), and the political purges, which removed large numbers of "Titoists," "cosmopolitanists," "Zionists," and, above all, individual fellow-travellers with inadequate or nonexistent ideological bases for membership in a ruling party of the communist type. The result of these policies were familiar for any student of the Soviet experience: The destruction of entire socio-economic classes, such as the entrepreneurial middle class, the private peasantry, and the absentee landlords; and the creation of new classes (or "strata") such as a socialist urban proletariat, an intelligentsia produced by communist-controlled educational institutions, and a collective and state peasantry, with an overlay of communist bureaucracy and security organs so familiar to any student of the communist political order. Romania, in this respect, represented strict adherence to the "model" that emanated from Moscow.[22]

Thus, the actual policies of the RCP under Ana Pauker and Gheorghe Gheorghiu-Dej followed the Soviet model closely. In theory, too, Romanian communism hewed close to the "classical" Marxist-Leninist interpretation emanating from Moscow in almost all areas. There was nevertheless a gradual shift towards a more national stance, not so much because of direct assertions on the part of the RCP leadership, but rather because of those elements of political discourse that were left out of official speeches and documents. This was clearly the case in the so-called "national question," where Gheorghiu-Dej refrained from the slavish copying of the Soviet line so common during the Stalin era elsewhere in Eastern Europe. Even after the death of Stalin there was a tendency among the East European leaders to accept the Soviet version of matters pertaining to nationalism, national boundaries, and disputed territories. Here again, the Romanians were less likely to follow suit than their "fraternal colleagues" in other capitals of the region. Towards the end of the era of Gheorghiu-Dej, there were even open statements about the importance of national sovereignty and rather strong hints that certain historical events pertaining to boundaries had represented a questionable precedence in decades past (a clear reference to the Soviet incorporation of Bessarabia in the summer of 1940).[23]

The greatest Romanian deviation from the Soviet model came in the area of economic thought, particularly as it pertained to integration and the specialization of production. In April 1963 an RCP Central Committee statement set forth on elaborate doctrine of national economic development that refuted many of the preferred Soviet axioms of modernization, specialization, and integration, directly or indirectly. The so-called "declaration of independence" of 1963 has become a landmark in Romania's quest for autonomy and subsequently economic autarky.[24]

Ceausescuism

After the death of Gheorghe Gheorghiu-Dej in 1965, the ascent to power of Nicolae Ceausescu represented a quantum leap in the development of Romanian nationalism and national communism. Nicolae Ceausescu has produced a hybrid form of Marxism-Leninism that is "sui generis" in the communist world and represents a blend of traditional values, elements of Marxist classics, and the particular (and peculiar) personal aspects that Ceausescu has brought to the development of theory. These are the basic aspects of "Ceausescuism."

Populist Emphasis

"Ceausescuism," as it has developed over time, has always been characterized by a strong element of populism, i.e. emphasis on the idea that the "people" contain within itself the fundamental values that must become the basic political guidelines for action and implementation. This belief in the "goodness" of the masses is exemplified by the General Secretary's insistence that art, literature, cinema, and other cultural expressions must be directed towards the preferences of the masses and must, indeed, derive their inspirations from those masses. During the celebrations of the centennial of Romanian independence, for example, song festivals were arranged throughout the entire country, and workers and peasants were encouraged to sing, dance, and compose music to the glory of Ceausescu and Romania (most of the time in that specific order of preference). The artistic intelligentsia was told to listen to "the people" for its profound and deep values and to derive inspiration from that source, leaving the elitism of the intellectual behind. By the same token, workers and peasants were installed on the advisory boards of theaters and journals to ensure that the values of "the people" would be adequately represented and expressed. This was an excellent control mechanism that ensured both Ceausescu's power over the intellectuals and the cultural elite and at the same time spread the word about the "folksiness" of the Leader, who liked to hobnob with the representatives of "the people" and discuss their ideas about art and literature with them.[25]

The emphasis on the masses in Ceausescuism does not lead to any real attempt by the leader to communicate with the masses in a meaningful manner. Ceausescu isolates himself from the masses and only ventures out to meet them under carefully controlled and orchestrated conditions, in which the groundwork has been laid for "spontaneous" displays of mass enthusiasm for the leader. The General Secretary apparently feels that the basic values of "the people" must be discovered by the leader himself, as he provides guidance and inspiration for all Romanians. There is clearly an element of arrogance and distrust of the masses in such an attitude, contrary to all proclamations and slogans. The "great unwashed" cannot produce the results that are inherent in them without the inspiration (at times pictured as divine) of the leader. Like Rousseau, Ceausescu proclaims a "general will"; unlike the French philosopher, he does not accept the notion that this will is available in society as such. It must be discovered, molded, honed, perfected, by the Leader himself.[26]

The Man on Horseback

The notion that the masses can only be "activated" by a strong leader is an integral part of Ceausescuism. The General Secretary distrusts elites that interpose themselves between him and "the people," and he insists on utilizing the latter to control the former. Results can only be obtained if the layers of bureaucracy are pulled away and the Leader can communicate from the top *directly* down to the masses. "The people" is to be inspired by great speeches, parades, and slogans; it is not to be trusted. The notion of limited rule is entirely alien to Ceausescu, because he rejects the idea that there can be "unity in diversity." Instead, he stresses organic government in which the leader and the people live in a harmonious and fundamentally necessary relationship; one in which the leader is indispensable, but the masses are not. This is clearly a vision of direct rule *over* the masses, not in conjunction with them, or their representatives. There are important elements of traditional Balkan leadership styles here, but also essential aspects of Leninism, as we shall see below.[27]

Traditional Romanian Nationalism and Chauvinism

As has been pointed out repeatedly,[28] Ceausescu has incorporated elements of traditional Romanian nationalism, indeed chauvinism, in his ideology and has, in fact, made them into key elements of that "package of thought." This is evident from his constant reference to the great heroes of Romanian history, such as Stephen the Great and Michael the Brave. It is to this end that Romanian historiography has been utilized— to describe and analyze the heroes of the past—thus providing the ground for a clear and unequivocal comparison with the present, tying the two sets of historical periods together into an unbroken string of Romanian greatness. Ceausescu has even elevated Vlad Tepes to an honored position in the pantheon of historical legends, primarily because Vlad is depicted as a leader who kept control over his subjects and engaged in successful defense of the fatherland against the machinations and onslaughts of foreign rulers, notably the Turks.[29] The historical record on Vlad Tepes as known in the West is rather different. He is seen as a bloodthirsty tyrant who ran his lands and his subjects with an iron hand, perpetrating vicious and cruel crimes against those subjects and others when it was seen as necessary for the maintenance of security. The domestic image that Ceausescu is promoting of Vlad is similar to the version that the General Secretary has of himself; the nature of Vlad's reign is occasionally compared with the use of force and terror currently present in Romania. In any case, the historical parallels drawn by the Romanian propaganda apparatus and the academic establishment are clear and designed to enhance the stature of the regime and its leader in the eyes of the intensely nationalistic Romanian populations.[30]

Under Ceausescu, Romanian nationalism has turned to chauvinism. The Romanians are no longer just extolling the virtues of their own history. They are doing so at the expense of others. This is clearly the case in the regime's nationality policies at home. Specifically, the major ethnic minorities, the Magyars and the Germans, have experienced policies that are designed to reduce their ethnic homogeneity in residential areas by dispersion and the immigration of large numbers of Romanians into formerly compact areas of minority residence. Furthermore, there are educational policies that have an impact on the expression of native languages in literature, the arts, and in primary and secondary educational institutions. Finally, the tone of discourse in the press, in the arts and literature, and in speeches and rallies is clearly chauvinist in its emphasis on Romanian themes, thus indirectly denigrating the importance of ethnic groups, while raising the achievements of the ethnic majority to unrealistic heights. And towering above it all is Ceausescu, claiming (directly or indirectly, through his court poets) to represent all that is noble and inspiring in the tradition of Romans and Geto-Dacians. During the last six or seven years, the chauvinism exhibited by the regime has taken an overt anti-Semitic coloration, as evidenced by a number of articles, books, and even paintings by individual writers and artists known to be close to Ceausescu and his entourage. This disturbing trend, pointed out by a number of Western observers and analysts, has not been abated by criticism from abroad, but has rather intensified, as Ceausescu defiantly pursues his goals and delusions with single-minded dedication.[31]

Isolationism, Autarky, and "Fortress Romania"

The emphasis on nationalism and the Romanian national heritage has produced side effects of considerable importance in the current political order. The most important of these is a form of isolationism, in which Ceausescu denigrates external influences, particularly Western thoughts and ideas, as detrimental to the national and revolutionary spirit of Romania and the Romanian masses. This attitude has resulted in strict censorship of all matters Western, particularly serious discussions about social and economic development and any serious scholarly examination of the problems of socialism, whether they emanate in the West or domestically. Furthermore, Ceausescu repeatedly, and with increasing vehemence, has attacked the moral depravity and ethical shortcomings of the West, emphasizing instead the "true values" of socialism and the superiority of moral and ethical education and socialization in systems under communist rule, especially Romania. This emphasis is closely tied in with the notion that Romania represents the apex of historical achievement in the ancient period and that the current regime is in the process of resurrecting this glorious tradition.[32]

The emphasis on national values and self-sufficiency in ideological and cultural matters is repeated in the economic field, where Ceausescu seems to have become obsessed with the notion that Romania must pay off all its debts and thus become truly independent. To this end, the population is being deprived of essential goods and services, which are funneled into export. Furthermore, the regime has cut back severely on technology imports from abroad, both to save hard currency and in order to further domestic research and development. Entire lines of industry have been developed to produce goods that could clearly have been bought more cheaply elsewhere. Production is being fostered, regardless of scale, in order to enhance the notion of autarky and reduce dependence upon other countries. Again, this costly line of development, which makes little sense in pure economic terms, is undertaken to produce economic conditions for which there is no basis.[33]

The Personality Cult and Megalomania

During the early years of Ceausescu's rule, there was an attempt to promote an image of frugality and sobriety among the top leadership. Ceausescu personally criticized Gheorghiu-Dej for the latter's opulent lifestyle and demanded that top bureaucrats shed their squandering ways in order to save money and set a "socialist example" for the rest of the population. This theme occasionally crops up in the General Secretary's speeches even today but we must assume that the credibility of such statements has been severely reduced after the increasing evidence of excessive consumption among the Ceausescu clan itself. In any case, there can be little doubt that the early emphasis on "socialist lifestyles" has given way to a way of life that resembles that of the pashas of old. The only difference is that the parties and the access to goods and services not available elsewhere exist behind closed gates and not ostentatiously displayed, as was the case during the rule of the Ottomans and the Phanariot Greeks. But enough evidence seeps out from the closed doors to reach a population which is increasingly pauperized, sinking deeper and deeper into the despair and hopelessness that engulfs people for whom there is no prospect of better times. The perception of a life of the leader far removed from the masses spreads, leading to further loss of credibility among the average citizen. By now, this disenchantment has clearly reached considerable segments of the artistic and scientific intelligentsia as well.[34]

The conspicuous consumption of the ruling clan is coupled with a personality cult of the General Secretary, his wife and his son which exceeds all other cases of the East European experience, surpassing even the Soviet Union during the height of the Stalin era, and matched only by the display of personalized leadership found in North Korea. It is probably no accident that Ceausescu and Kim-il-sung are close both ideologically and personally; they both run systems which have been dubbed "socialism in one family."[35]

The Ceausescu personality cult has reached heights that are ridiculed outside the borders of Romania. The General Secretary is variously described as the greatest thinker, philosopher, statesman, and scientist the world have ever seen. Some of the sycophantic prose and poetry written for him and about him describes this "oak of Scornicesti" as a living god, the sun that provides others with warmth and inspiration, and the inspirer for all mankind.[36] Personal appearances by Ceausescu are carefully orchestrated events in which the masses "spontaneously" surge forward, rhythmically chanting "Ceausescu and the people," "Ceausescu-peace," or simply "Ceausescu, Ceausescu." Children demonstrate with flags, pretty young girls in national costumes provide him with flowers, and the eyes of the workers, it is said, glow with admiration and love for this "truly remarkable man," the true son of Romania, the greatest leader the country (and at times, even the world) has ever seen. At meetings and rallies, the General Secretary obviously enjoys this adulation, but also exults in cutting off applause with the sweep of the hand, as if to demonstrate his great power even over those who praise him so effusively.[37]

Elena Ceausescu, the General Secretary's wife, is also the object of a massive personality cult, and she, too, apparently approves of it and enjoys it. The same can be said of other members of the clan, notably the first couple's son Nicu, who is now head of the RCP youth organization. Nicu's reputation as a playboy and a debaucherer has not endeared the "first family" (perhaps, under the circumstances, the "only" family) to the population.[38]

The personality cult has recently produced acts and thoughts that can only be described as megalomania. The General Secretary has demolished a substantial part of the central city of Bucharest for the purpose of constructing an entire new city to the glory of the achievements of socialism and the "epoch of Ceausescu." Old monasteries, churches, and other architectural monuments have been razed or moved, (a process which has damaged them substantially). Entire sectors of dwellings have been razed, and the population moved to housing in the suburbs, reportedly of lower quality than that which they vacated. The new, enormous boulevards are flanked by gigantic buildings which represent Ceausescu's monument to himself. This monument is likely to remain long after his demise and that of his clan.[39]

The razing of historical monuments is a curious activity for a leader who, until recently, claimed direct lineage in political terms from the great figures of the Romanian past. Such activities can only indicate that the General Secretary now considers himself above these historical figures and is determined to leave his own impact on history, while diminishing that of his predecessors. Hence the personality cult, hence the destruction of the old, hence the erection of the new and the ostentatious. And hence also Ceausescu's indulgence of those who sing his praises in a sycophantic chorus, and his punishment of those who dare hint at opposition or refuse to join the chorus of obviously exaggerated praise.[40]

Marxist Elements in Ceausescuism

While many of the aspects of Ceausescuism discussed above are idiosyncratic or culture specific, there are also a number of elements that can be clearly identified as Marxist in origin. First of all, Ceausescu believes in centralized power, controlled by a hierarchial party organization, operating under the auspices of democratic centralism. The structure of political power in Romania is very similar to that found elsewhere in the socialist world, indicating the organizational origins in the CPSU and the Soviet experience.[41]

Secondly, Ceausescu's notion of the party's role in society is similar to that of Lenin and his successors in the Soviet Union. Ceausescu, like Lenin, distrusts the masses and believes that they cannot be entrusted with power, because they are incapable of meaningful political action and must instead by led by a forceful hand. This is clear from Ceausescu's behavior, despite his flowery rhetoric about "the people" and the "organic unity" between himself and the masses.[42]

Thirdly, Ceausescu is committed to the notion of forceful change from the top down in the political and socio-economic order—another fundamental element of Leninism. This approach is manifested in the forceful transformation of Romania from an agrarian to an industrial society at breakneck speed, regardless of costs. This "revolution from above" in the political and socio-economic realms is only possible through a voluntaristic approach to political leadership and the acceptance of "the great man" theory of history. These elements are also vintage Leninism.

Fourthly, Ceausescu, like Lenin, adheres to the notion of a frontal attack upon problems of all kinds, and often simultaneously. This "storming" approach is costly, but it presumably gets the job done, and quickly; it is, in other words, effective, but not efficient. There is no reason here for incrementalism.[43]

Finally, Ceausescu adheres to all of the basic tenets of Marxist-Leninist economics and social policy, notably public ownership of the means of production, rapid and forced industrialization, collectivization of agriculture, and the relegation of service industries to a tertiary position in the economy. His approach to the implementation of these goals is so orthodox that there can be no real reform under Ceausescu—hence the overt defiance emanating from Bucharest as Mikhail Gorbachev engages in glasnost and perestroika in the Soviet Union and demands reform in Eastern Europe as well.[44]

Ceausescu differs sharply from Marx, and also to some extent from Lenin, in his clear disregard for the opinion of others, such as his colleagues in the party leadership and the various technical and managerial experts who are needed to run the increasingly complex society that is Romania. His style of leadership and his encouragement of the personality cult surrounding him are very different from Lenin or Marx and represent an aberration of some very fundamental tenets of Marxist and Leninist ethical principles. But most importantly, he differs from the principles of leadership recruitment and cooptation, which in all other East European systems increasingly revolve around the need to get the best and most skillful individuals into leadership positions for better, more rational, and more meaningful decision-making and implementation. In Ceausescu's Romania, leadership selection is haphazard, based upon whim and personal preference, loyalty and submission. It produces a leadership that is easily controlled, because it has no skills other than allegiance to the leader and his family and hence no possible base for privilege and power outside the clan. It is a system uniquely suited to personal power and uniquely ill-equipped for the needs of a modern society.[45]

Ceausescuism and Political Legitimacy

It is clear from the discussion above that Ceausescuism is a theory, a style of operation, and a set of parameters for acceptable behavior by subelites. As a theory, it is a hybrid of nationalism, chauvinism, Marxism-Leninism, and idiosyncratic elements of Nicolae Ceausescu's own thought. It contains a core of basic tenets that are constantly violated in practice, thus producing a sense of unreality, friction, and a Kafkaesque atmosphere of insecurity, anxiety, and erratic behavior. As a style of operation it is characterized by extreme centralization of power, irrationality, and bombastic symbolism with little to show in terms of practical results. As a set of parameters for subelite behavior Ceausescuism is fluid and unpredictable, because personal whim and dramatic changes in favors and disfavors characterize Ceausescu's leadership style, thus rendering predictable parameters and standards of performance invalid and dependent upon the attitudes of the movement in the inner circles of the Ceausescu-Petrescu clan.[46]

Ceausescuism is the politics of rhetoric which has little or no reference to actual behavior. It is the politics of irrationality as well as terrible realism as the country sinks further and further into poverty and despair as a direct result of regime policy. The enormous (and growing) discrepancy between the expanding personality cult and the totally unsubstantiated claims to achievement, on the one hand, and the reality of decline and pauperization, on the other, has removed any vestige of political legitimacy that the regime may have had in earlier periods, such as the summer of 1968, when Ceausescu's angry defiance of the Warsaw Pact during the invasion of Czechoslovakia rallied the masses around him. This was clearly the high point of the regime. Since then, legitimacy has slowly dwindled. Today, the masses are exhausted, dispirited, cynical. The characterization of Robert Tucker of the Brezhnev era as "swollen state, spent society" is even more apt for Romania. The vitality of the Latin culture has been sapped; the arts and literature are reduced to sycophancy; economic activity is geared to export or to gigantomania in construction, an investment program that has become very counterproductive, now draining badly needed resources, and basic disregard for the needs of the population. Ceausescuism as theory is idiosyncratic and inconsistent. As a leadership style, it is sui generis and thus interesting and tragic at the same time. As a political and socio-economic program, it is a failure. But as a mechanism for the establishment, maintenance, and expansion of personal and clan power, it is extraordinarily successful. It is not national communism, but personal communism, communist nepotism. As such, it represents a new form, worthy of serious study and commentary.

Notes

1. Robert R. King, *History of the Romanian Communist Party* (Stanford, CA: Hoover Institution Press, 1980), esp. ch. 1 (pp. 9–39).

2. On the Horia and Closcan uprisings, see Seton-Watson, *A History of the Roumanians*, esp. pp. 186–187. The most detailed study of the 1907 peasant uprising is Andrei Otetea (ed.), *Marea Rascoala a Taranilor din 1907.*

3. Recent Romanian historiography overemphasizes the level of revolutionary activity in the country during the period between the two world wars. See, for example, Andrei Otetea, *Istoria Poporului Roman*, esp. pp. 519–545.

4. Ghita Ionescu, *Communism in Rumania 1944–1962*, esp. ch. 1 (pp. 1–59).

5. Fischer-Galati, "Romanian Nationalism," esp. pp. 373–380. See also Nicolae Iorga, *Istoria Literaturii Romanesti* (Bucharest: 1925–26), esp. vol. II.

6. The dichotomy between city and countryside has been brilliantly discussed by John A. Armstrong, *Nations Before Nationalism*, esp. ch. 4 (pp. 93–129). Much of the literature of the period between the two world wars also reflect this dichotomy; see Iorga, *Istoria Literaturii Romanesti*, vol. II.

7. The concept of peasant-workers is discussed in considerable detail by Ivan Volgyes in his *The Peasantry of Eastern Europe* (New York, NY: Pergamon Press,

1979), 2 vols. See also my "Rural Transformation in Romania," in *ibid.*, vol. II, ch. 6 (pp. 77–123).

8. At times this populism became authoritarian, even fascist. For an analysis of this phenomenon, see Henry L. Roberts, *Rumania: Political Problems of an Agrarian State* (New Haven, CT: Yale University Press, 1951), esp. pp. 130–186. Romanian fascism has been discussed in great detail by Eugen Weber, "Romania," in Hans Rogger and Eugen Weber (eds.), *The European Right* (Berkeley, CA: University of California Press, 1966), pp. 501–574.

9. *Ibid.*

10. The philosophy of Corneliu Zelea Codreanu, the inspirer of organized fascism in Romania, is found in his *Pentru Legionari* (Bucharest: Editura Miscarii Legionari, 1937).

11. Roberts, *Rumania: Political Problems of an Agrarian State*, pp. 130–186. See also David M. Mitrany, *The Land and the Peasant in Romania* (London: Oxford University Press, 1930).

12. Marxist thought in Romania was, in fact, rather rudimentary in this period. Recent Romanian historiography overemphasizes the performance in this field. An interesting account of radicalism and authoritarianism in interwar Romania is Lucretiu Petrascanu, *Sub Trei Dictaturi* (Bucharest: Editura Forum, 1946).

13. Marx frequently spoke of the "idiocy of rural life," and the ethos of Marxism is urban. Romanian collectivism, on the other hand, was rural in thought and action. See Roberts, *Rumania: Political Problems of an Agrarian State*, pp. 130–186.

14. The importance of the quest for reunification of Transylvania with Moldavia and Wallachia is discussed in Stefan Pascu, *Marea Adunare Nationala de la Alba Iulia*, esp. ch. V (pp. 125–160).

15. The *official* view, however, is that the various nationalities struggled together under the leadership of the communist party. See, for example, L. Banyai, *Pe Fagasul Traditiilor Fratesti* (Bucharest: Bibliotica de Istorie, 1971), esp. pp. 163–202.

16. King, *History of the Romanian Communist Party*, ch. 1 (pp. 9–39).

17. The increasing centralization of the Comintern has been documented in Bela Kun, *Kommunisticheskii Internatsional v Dokomentakh* (Moscow: Partiinoe Izdatel'stvo, 1933), esp. pp. 397–415.

18. For a good discussion of fascism in East-Central Europe, see Peter F. Sugar, "Conclusion," in Sugar, *Native Fascism in the Successor States*, ch. VIII (pp. 145–156). More specifically on Romania, see N. M. Nagy-Talavera, *Green Shirts and Others: A History of Fascism in Hungary and Romania* (Stanford, CA: The Hoover Institution, 1970).

19. Typical of the glorification of the RCP in the interwar period is Ion Oprea, "Perioada dintre cele doua razboiale mondiale," in Miron Constantinescu, et al., *Istoria Romaniei*, esp. pp. 451–500. Nicolae Ceausescu has continued in the same vein; see, for example, his speech to the thirteenth RCP congress, November 1984, in *Scinteia*, November 19 and 20, 1984.

20. The early years of coalition politics in postwar Romania have been discussed by Ghita Ionescu, *Communism in Rumania 1944–1962*, ch. 4 (pp. 94–107) and ch. 5 (pp. 107–126).

21. E.g. Stephen Fischer-Galati, *Twentieth Century Rumania* (New York, NY: Columbia University Press, 1970), esp. pp. 109–128.

22. Zbigniew K. Brzezinski still has the most detailed work on this period in his *The Soviet Bloc* (New York, NY: Frederick A. Praeger, 1963), pp. 90–100. See also my *Modernization in Romania since World War II*, ch. 5 (pp. 141–171).

23. For a detailed discussion of this problem, see Robert R. King, *Minorities Under Communism: Nationalities as a Source of Tension among Balkan States* (Cambridge, MA: Harvard University Press, 1973), esp. pp. 220–241.

24. One of the most celebrated of these discussions was printed in *Scinteia*, March 9, 1963.

25. Much of what I have to say about Ceausescuism is derived from the voluminous writings of the RCP leader and his many speeches. For one example of such a speech, summarizing much of his thinking, see *ibid.*, November 19, 1984 (speech to the thirteenth congress of the RCP). As for the ideas of mass culture, see *Saptamina*, December 3, 1976, on the "popular" festival "Hymn to Romania," which emphasized mass participation in defining and executing cultural policy.

26. A recent insightful analysis is Vladimir Tismaneanu, "Ceausescu's Socialism," *Problems of Communism*, January-February, 1985, esp. pp. 60–66.

27. For a recent elaboration of the Ceausescu philosophy, see his opening speech to the RCP national conference in December 1987, printed in *Scinteia*, December 15, 1987.

28. See, for example, Tismaneanu, "Ceausescu's Socialism." I have also discussed this in "Romania's Growing Difficulties," *Current History*, November 1984, pp. 375–398.

29. George Cioranescu, "Vlad the Impaler—Current Parallels with a Medieval Romanian Prince," *Radio Free Europe*, RAD Background Report/23 (Romania), 31 January 1977.

30. *Ibid.* See also Ceausescu's claim to the national heritage in his speech to the thirteenth RCP congress in *Scinteia*, November 19, 1984.

31. The latest round in this chauvinism can be seen in the current polemic with Hungary over the treatment of Magyars in Transylvania, e.g. *Era Socialista*, April 10, 1988.

32. An example of this emphasis on autarky can be found in Ceausescu's denunciation of most favored notion status in trade relations with the U.S., after the Senate voted to suspend such status for Romania temporarily, due to civil rights violations. For the official Romanian position, see *Scinteia*, June 28, 1987.

33. Nicolae Ceausescu has, in fact, appointed himself as the chief planner of Romania in order to ensure the continuation of this policy. This was done in January, 1988, when Ceausescu signed a decree implementing the 1988 plan without the formal approval of the RCP Central Committee (which had been required by precedent) or the Grand National Assembly, (whose approval is required by law). The General Secretary's decree was published in *Romania Libera*, January 14, 1988. For an analysis of this episode, see Paul Gafton, "Ceausescu Becomes Romania's Chief Planner," *Radio Free Europe Research*, Romanian SR/5, 29 March 1988.

34. On the disillusionment of intellectuals, see Mihai Sturdza in *ibid.*, Romanian SR/6, 29 April 1988. On the personality cult, see Eugen Barbu's piece on the occasion of Nicolae Ceausescu's sixty-eighth birthday in *Scinteia*, January 26, 1986; Elena Ceausescu was glorified in *Luceafarul*, January 4, 1986, by Ilie Purcaru.

35. The clan nature of Romanian politics was further strengthened by recent changes in the party leadership, which brought trusted associates to the top and concentrated power based on acquaintance rather than performance. At the national RCP conference in December 1987, several alternate and one full member were appointed to the Central Committee; these were mostly Ceausescu loyalists. For details on the conference, see *Scinteia*, December 17, 18, and 19, 1987.

36. See, for example, laudatory articles on Nicolae Ceausescu in *Saptamina*, January 24, 1986, and *Flacara* of the same date; *Scinteia*, January 26, 1986, and *Romania Libera* of the same date.

37. I have personally witnessed this on many occasions. For a typical discussion of the "Leader" meeting with the people, see *Scinteia Tineretului*, June 30, 1986.

38. Examples of the glorification of Elena can be found in *Luceafarul*, January 4, 1986, *Saptamina*, of the same date, and *Scinteia Tineretului*, January 5, 1986.

39. Even Mikhail Gorbachev voiced his concern over the destruction of historic buildings during his visit to Romania; see TASS, May 25, 1987.

40. Examples of such courageous dissenters are Karoly Kiraly, formerly a member of the Central Committee and a county RCP first secretary, and Mihai Botez, a well-known intellectual (who was subsequently allowed to leave for the U.S.). Botez expressed his concern in *L'Express*, May 28, 1987. On Kiraly's stand, see *Radio Free Europe Research*, Hungarian SR/6, June 30, 1987.

41. Ceausescu's established views on this subject can be found in his speech to the tenth RCP congress, in *Congresul al X-lea al Partidului Comunist Roman* (Bucharest: Editura Politica, 1969), esp. pp. 64–69.

42. On this alleged organic unity, see his speech to the recent RCP national conference in *Scinteia*, December 17, 1987.

43. This approach continues unabated, but results are still lacking. The General Secretary has occasionally admitted failures, but continues to blame others. See, for example, his speech to the plenum of the Central Committee on October 5, 1987, published in *ibid.*, October 6, 1987.

44. Ceausescu has specifically rejected the notion that policies elsewhere in Eastern Europe may be appropriate for Romania; e.g. *ibid.*, February 25, 1987.

45. An example of this tendency is the decision that the Permanent Bureau of the Supreme Council of Economic and Social Development will be the "supreme command" (Ceausescu's words) of the Romanian economy. Nicolae Ceausescu heads this bureau. Several positions in the leadership are now ex-officio, which means that Ceausescu loyalists further invade other positions in the hierarchy. Ceausescu's speech can be found in *ibid.*, June 23, 1987; for a good analysis of this process, see Paul Gafton, *Radio Free Europe Research*, Romanian SR/6, 3 July 1987.

46. The realities of power stand in sharp contrast to the rhetoric of the "Leader." See, for example, Ceausescu's speech at the recent party conference, in *Scinteia*, December 15, 1987.

4

Romania as a
Modernizing Society

The peculiar blend of nationalism, chauvinism, and Marxism-Leninism that constitutes Ceausescuism as a doctrine carries within it important elements of a modernizing program which is designed to lift this erstwhile backward country into the ranks of the industrial societies of the world and then to proceed to post-industrialism and the technological stage. This modernizing doctrine is also a blend of classical Marxism, Soviet-style, Leninist concepts, and the personalistic views of Nicolae Ceausescu and his entourage. Taken together, all these elements form the Romanian modernization program as conceived by Ceausescu's predecessors and implemented in a personalistic way by the present leader of Romania.

The Marxist-Leninist Aspects

Marxism-Leninism emphasizes industrialization, urbanization, collectivism, top-down rule, and frontal assaults and "storming."

Marx was a product of the industrial revolution and, as such, he emphasized the need for industrial development as a lodestar of all development. Consequently, industrialization has been a key feature of all communist development plans ever since the Russian Revolution; it was also an article of deep faith prior to the establishment of communist power anywhere. All contemporary Marxists in Europe are dedicated to industrialization, and this is true for most leaders who profess Marxism in the Third World as well. Ceausescu is a mainstream Marxist in this respect, as we shall see later.

Urbanization

It may be argued that industrialization ipso facto carries with it the process of urbanization. In fact, the two processes are inextricably intertwined. The modernizer basically has two choices in the way he or she approaches the nexus between industrialization and urbanization: Factories may be located in already existing cities, because the infrastructure of buildings, transportation, communications, and labor is in place, or they may be built in the countryside, thereby immediately starting the process of urbanization required to provide these necessary elements of the production process. Either way, urbanization and industrialization are in a symbiotic relationship, so that one is inconceivable without the other.[1]

Marx, of course, recognized this relationship, and he advocated urbanization partly because of this realization. But there is much more to his enthusiastic emphasis on the process of developing cities. He was a committed urbanite, convinced that only in an urban setting could human progress be expected and facilitated. He spoke disparagingly about "the idiocy of rural life" and emphasized the cumulative effect of industrial activity, education, and cultural ferment that can only be achieved in an urban setting. In this respect Marx drew his inspiration from the centuries of urbanity that had developed, first in the Mediterranean basin, the Greek city-states, and Rome, and subsequently in the cities and towns of Central and Northwestern Europe. This element of Marx clearly establishes him as a Westerner, psychologically far removed from the present societies and cultures of Eastern and Southeastern Europe, where urbanity declined and almost disappeared with the dismantling of the Roman and Byzantine empires.[2]

Collectivism

The "early" Marx focuses on the individual, in the sense that he is concerned about human alienation and the need to alleviate or remove it. The more "mature" Marx focuses on collectivism, the condition of the individual as a member of a collectivity, primarily a socio-economic class. The individual's life is determined by the conditions of his or her socio-economic class. This is a prominent feature of Leninism and even more a core aspect of Ceausescuism.[3]

The notion of collectivism is crucial both as a philosophical screen of perception and as a mechanism for organizing the economy. It is so firmly held even by contemporary "Marxists" that they refuse to draw obvious conclusions from economic malfunctioning and lagging popular commitment in the economic sector, which now constitutes the primary problem of all communist systems in existence.

Top-down Rule

Marx believed in the revolutionary capabilities of the industrial proletariat, but he was also convinced that there was a definite need for strong, even elitist, leadership of that proletariat (the "vanguard" theory). Leadership was conceived as a top-down process. Historical necessity demanded that a vanguard would lead others, if need be, with coercive methods. This aspect of Marxism was later enhanced by considerable measure by Lenin, who defined the vanguard party in terms much more elitist than Marx or Engels. Leninism was further enhanced in practice on this score by Stalin and all other practicing communist leaders in Europe and elsewhere. Nicolae Ceausescu is clearly a product of the Leninist school of thought on leadership.[4]

Frontal Assaults and "Storming"

Since Marx believed in the notion that history moved in predetermined ways and in an established direction of progress, it followed logically that each stage of historical development would reach its full fruition in all areas before it was ready for the dialectic leap to the next stage. Consequently, the changes that would be brought about as a result of this leap would be multivariate; the whole gamut of problems associated with underdevelopment could be attacked at once, and not incrementally.

Ceausescuism and Development

Nicolae Ceausescu is a committed Marxist, insofar as he firmly believes in the main aspects of Marxist developmental doctrine. He is also a Leninist, because he is firmly committed to those aspects of leadership and development that are most strongly associated with Leninist norms of behavior and organization. Other aspects, however, are clearly national in character or even derivable from the idiosyncratic notions of Ceausescu as an individual. Taken together, these elements produce a highly original "package" of modernization and development which is, in fact, in the process of implementation. It behooves us to take a very close look at this doctrine and the ramifications of it, and then to proceed to examine the results of its implementation.

The Ceausescu Notion of Industrial Development

Since ascending to the apex of the Romanian political system in 1965, Nicolae Ceausescu has been firmly committed to the rapid and thorough industrialization of this country. This notion has been in the mainstream of Marxism and the Marxist-Leninist experience, and he has, in fact, emulated the Soviet model on this score to a larger extent than anyone else in contemporary Eastern Europe. Specifically, this acceptance of the Soviet model has resulted in a firm commitment to rapid, extensive industrialization with an emphasis on the heavy and extractive industries, the fuels sector, transportation, and construction. The Ceausescu goal is to make Romania one of the major producers of steel, iron, heavy machinery, rolling stock, and other elements of heavy industry. This commitment, which is now more than two decades old and actually constitutes a continuation of policies and programs established as early as 1945, reflects the obsession of all Romanian leaders after World War II with the backwardness of the country they inherited after the destruction of the "bourgeois landowner" system. It also reflects the acceptance and enthusiastic furtherance of those aspects of developmental policy that represented Stalin's version in the Soviet experience after the initiation of the five-year plans. Romania, like the other states of Eastern Europe, enthusiastically implemented Stalinist industrialization doctrines in the period 1947/48–1953; Romania alone has continued on the same path in the 1970s and 1980s and has, in fact, accelerated the pace of this implementation.[5]

Another aspect of Ceausescu's doctrine is the notion of gigantomania. The RCP leader is firmly committed to huge factories, grandiose construction projects, and ongoing tasks so large that they defy technical capabilities and economic resources, let alone the manpower of the nation. Examples include the petrochemical combine at Pitesti, the Iron Gates project on the Danube River, the Danube-Black Sea Canal, and the razing and reconstruction of much of downtown Bucharest. From an economic point of view, these are, in part, irrational projects and their continued implementation can only be explained by doctrinal stubbornness and commitment on the part of the RCP leadership, particularly the General Secretary himself as well as his close family associates in the clan.[6]

Nicolae Ceausescu is also determined to spread industrial development throughout the entire territory of Romania, regardless of cost. This has resulted in the location of industrial projects in areas which have little or no infrastructure such as roads, housing, water and sewer systems, or schools and other necessary corollaries to development. Much of Romania looks unfinished, as a gigantic construction site, and much of it actually remains unfinished, because the completion rate of Romanian industrial projects is dismal, resulting in huge losses of equipment, labor, and machinery that never goes into production. This is indeed doctrinal commitment to extensive industrialization.[7]

Up to the mid-1970s, the Ceausescu industrialization program could proceed at a relatively high speed, because the necessary ingredients for such extensive development were at hand. For example, there was a surplus of labor which could be drawn from the pool of rural residents, thus providing the expanding but inefficient industrial plants with a crucial ingredient. There was a surplus of raw materials, because Romania is more richly endowed from nature than most of its neighbors. Fuels, particularly oil, were available domestically or through barter trade with certain partners such as Iran. But the energy crises of the 1970s changed these conditions drastically. Fuels became much more expensive, and after the demise of the Shah in 1979, Iran no longer accepted payment for oil in inferior Romanian goods. Domestic oil wells ran dry, the forests were depleted, and decades of irrational farming took their toll on the fertility of the soil. Urbanization depleted the labor pool to such an extent that extensive industrialization ran up against shortages of this indispensable ingredient. The Ceausescu program was now confronted with the need for *intensive* development in this crucial area.[8]

The Revamped Industrialization Program: Production Through Symbolic Rewards

Faced with the need to react to drastically altered conditions, Nicolae Ceausescu changed his industrialization program, now focusing on the need for intensive development through greater productivity. Such productivity was to come from three basic sources, namely, improved technology and a harder work climate, a faster pace, and greater commitment by the individual worker. As a result of this doctrinal adjustment, Romania began an aggressive program of importing technology and industrial and technological espionage, and attempted to encourage various forms of Western participation in Romanian industrial production. Romania soon became a large debtor in the international monetary market. There were massive efforts to expand exports in the West, primarily of finished industrial goods, but also of agricultural commodities. There was also a flurry of Western activity in various cooperative enterprises on Romanian soil. After a few years, however, this effort floundered, because Romania had little to offer in terms of quality goods, and because the rapidity of the bureaucratic system reduced or eliminated the possibilities of Western firms doing serious business on a large scale in Romania. Bucharest was left with a large foreign debt, technology that could not be efficiently absorbed in the industrial plant, underutilization of costly imported machinery, and a great deal of waste.[9]

The reaction of the Ceausescu regime to this self-made predicament was characteristic. The General Secretary proclaimed an austerity program, reduced energy consumption by administrative fiat, increased production quotas, speeded up his investment program, allocated increasingly scarce resources to production rather than consumption, and forced greater exports of saleable commodities such as foodstuffs, thus further lowering the standard of living. The leadership became obsessed with autarky; it drastically reduced imports of all kinds, including technology, instead forcing the development of homemade technology, which, in most cases, was significantly inferior to available resources elsewhere, particularly in the West. Exhortation and propaganda took the place of goods and services. Coercion (or the threat thereof) became an essential element in the extraction of output, since there were few material incentives for the individual worker to produce. Bombastic declarations about the achievements of Romania attempted to belie the reality of decline and pauperization. The discrepancy between rhetoric and performance increased. Nicolae Ceausescu responded by even more fervent declarations of commitment and achievement, and with an expanded program of autarky designed to reproduce the elements of extensive industrialization which had existed twenty years earlier. This program, while focusing on political indoctrination and a higher level of regime interference in individuals' lives, is nevertheless an integral part of the Ceausescu industrialization plan and should be discussed in this vein here.[10]

Recreating the Past:
Romania's Population and Indoctrination Program

As the labor supply dwindled through urbanization and a liberal abortion program that became the chief method of birth control in Romania, the regime watched in dismay. During the last decade, the Ceausescus and Petrescus decided to do something about it. Abortions have become outlawed except for a few categories of medical emergency. The mass media keep a steady drumbeat about the need for each couple to have multiple children, at least three, as a patriotic duty. Women are periodically subjected to gynecological examinations to determine that they are not using birth control or that they have not had abortions. Various incentive programs have been established to ensure greater "people production." Vigilante squads in factories, offices, and other places of employment continuously carry the message about the need for more children and threaten dire repercussions if prevention of pregnancy is sought by anyone, married or not. All in all, this program exceeds anything undertaken elsewhere in Eastern Europe, and it even goes beyond the attempts undertaken during the 1930s in the Soviet Union to control the behavior of groups and individuals. The only comparable program is China's efforts at birth *control* through the use of the local community organizations to ensure the low birth rate of women in that overpopulated country.[11]

The Ceausescu population program, if successful, would recreate the pool of plentiful labor, thus ensuring one of the crucial ingredients for extensive industrialization. It would make it possible for the current (or future) regime to ignore the real issues of economic developments, namely, legitimacy and material incentives. As such, it is a quixotic attempt to refute the basic laws of economic development now recognized all over the region and particularly in the central leadership of the CPSU.

While the successful implementation of the population program would solve some of Romania's problems in the future, the babies produced today will not enter the active industrial pool for fifteen to twenty years. In the meantime, measures must be taken to ensure greater production by these currently in the labor force or about to enter it. Elsewhere in Eastern Europe, this goal is pursued through material incentives and an effort to improve the service sector. In Romania, the solution is seen in more exhortation, more propaganda and indoctrination, more control. The politicization of Romanian life from top to bottom in the sense of *mobilization* of the masses for work is palpable, frantic, at times hysterical in appearance. The cynicism and detachment of the masses are equally evident as a dispirited people shuffles from empty stores to markets devoid of produce. The Ceausescu industrialization program is sui generis. As such, it is criticized and rejected even by Romania's allies, particularly the Soviet Union itself. These facts notwithstanding, the "revised" Ceausescu plan remains and even intensifies as the country heads toward the last decade of this century.[12]

Urbanization

Nicolae Ceausescu is committed to the process of urbanization because it is a necessary corollary of industrialization. Still, he is not an urbanite by conviction, which was the case with Karl Marx and Friedrich Engels. Nor does he come from an urbanized culture in which life in the city was held in high regard as the epitome of civilization—a condition found in Mediterranean societies, particularly as a result of the splendor of the Greek city states. The cultures of Western and Northern Europe, which experienced urbanization later, nevertheless became city oriented *before* the onset of the industrial revolution, thus producing a mindset that considers the city and citification as worthwhile places and processes in their own right, and not as a necessary product of industrial development. Romanian culture was oriented towards the peasant and the village, as discussed in Chapter 1. Nicolae Ceausescu is a product of this culture and a son of the village of Scornicesti. He is not an urbanite, but a transplanted peasant living in the capital. This has a great deal to do with his programs of urbanization and the results of these programs.[13]

Extensive industrialization tends to perceive urbanization as a dependent variable. The factories are constructed first, and the urban infrastructure of housing, schools, hospitals, roads, water and sewage systems, and other elements of the necessities of life subsequently or simultaneously develop. This produces cities and towns that resemble the jerry-built agglomerations of early industrialization everywhere. Since everything is unfinished, there is no time or opportunity for the new community to "settle down" and acquire its own culture. Instead, the workers are really "peasant-workers" whose attitudes and values resemble that of the village, and not the city. Plants and cities develop without an urbanized culture. Expanding islands in the sea of rurality, these places are in a hybrid existence, neither village nor real city.[14]

Ceausescu, as a product of rural traditions, tends to distrust city dwellers, and particularly those elements of city life that require physical proximity to cultural institutions, processes, and artistic life, the intellectual. The General Secretary has made his views clear on a number of occasions, stressing the need for artists, writers, and intellectuals to stay close to the masses, to listen to the "voice of the people" and to be guided by it, and to draw their inspiration from this rich source. This outlook has become policy. During the 1970s, for example, there were numerous "festivals" of popular culture in which the workers were encouraged to sing and dance, to compose songs to the glory of Romania, and to supervise the intellectuals and the artists, in order to limit their elitist tendencies. Ceausescu is the primary representative of the proletcult notion in Eastern Europe today, reflecting his faith in the workers (who, nevertheless, must be guided). The Leader has built cities as physical manifestations, but he has not accepted the notion of the city as a concentration of culture and urbanity. In this sense Ceausescu is not a Marxist.[15]

Collectivism

The early Marx wrote eloquently about the need to reduce or eliminate human alienation and exploitation, thus focusing on the individual inside the social and economic context. At the same time, even the early Marx was a collectivist in the sense that he identified the driving force of history as socio-economic classes and the conflict that develops between them. The later, revolutionary Marx was clearly and unequivocally a collectivist who examined the ways and means whereby one class, the industrial proletariat, would reach power and exercise it in the name of socialism and of history. It is *this* Marx who became the inspirer for those who used his ideology to capture, hold, and exercise power.

Nicolae Ceausescu is a collectivist who not only distrusts individualism in political terms, but also produces and executes policies designed to eliminate individualism in the social setting, in economic relationships, in the arts and literature, and in education. Individual men and women can only find self-fulfillment inside the collective, inside society as a whole. Individual rights are granted, not given at birth; they are granted if and when the collective finds it opportune and necessary to do so. Political and organizational collectivism permeates all of society and sets the stage for the processes that lead to political decisions and, consequently, the nature and quality of individuals' lives on a daily basis. Collectivism is taught in the schools, in the workplace, in the controlled media, in political and social discourse of all kinds. There is less room for individual initiative in *any* area of societal activity in Romania than any other system in Eastern Europe, including the Soviet Union. The regime seeks total control and fails to achieve it only because of a lack of skills, not because of a scarcity of will. In many ways, this aspect of the contemporary Romanian political system is the greatest deviation from the norms of the rest of Eastern Europe in the 1980s.[16]

While Ceausescu emphasizes collectivism for the rest of Romanian society, he is also convinced that he, and only he, can determine the needs of "the people," the direction in which the collectivity that is Romania should be going. Only he can determine the specific social, economic, cultural, and political policies of the system. Nicolae Ceausescu has gathered in his hands the greatest amount and concentration of power in the communist world today, with the possible exception of Kim-il-sung in North Korea. Ceausescu's policies are intensely personalistic, in that they represent his interpretation of Marxism and Marxism-Leninism, mixed with his notions of Romanian history and Romanian greatness, his loves and prejudices, and his commitment to "socialism" as he see its, coupled with his hatred of "capitalism," which, by all accounts, is tangible and almost palpable. This kind of personalistic rule is distinctly un-Marxist and also deviates from Leninism as practiced by Lenin, but it resembles the leadership style of Stalin. In any case, Nicolae Ceausescu is only a partial Marxist on the dimension of collectivism. As in other fields, the Romanian leader is sui generis.[17]

While the Ceausescu regime deviates from Leninism in leadership style, particularly in the lavish and opulent personal lives led by the Ceausescu-Petrescu clan (as compared to the austere, almost ascetic Lenin), there are other aspects of Leninism that can be found in Ceausescu and his entourage. For example, the Romanian leader shares with Lenin a certain skepticism about the capabilities of the masses and a corresponding conviction that the essential qualities of the masses can only be brought out by elites. In Lenin's case, that elite was the communist party; in the case of Ceausescu, it is the Leader himself. The organic relationship between leader and masses is necessary for the fulfillment of the capabilities residing in the masses; without it, there can be no such realization. Under these circumstances there can be no delegation of authority, no sharing of power, no real possibility for other individuals or groups to really participate in the process of policy-making and implementation. Other political leaders are adjuncts of the Leader himself, primarily executive organs tasked with the successful, speedy, and efficient implementation of the Leader's will. The Leader must surround himself with a "clan" of close associates who have been trained and have acquired his outlooks, goals, and values. At the same time, very few individuals, if any, can be trusted to fully acquire these values and capabilities, hence the rapid turnover of political figures at the top of the Romanian hierarchy (the rotation of cadres also helps reduce the possibility that others may build power bases for the purpose of challenging the Leader himself). This attitude corresponds with Lenin's conviction that the masses only possess "trade union consciousness," and that the party itself must provide the leadership necessary for the revolution and the subsequent exercise of power. Elitism inside a collective entity such as a political party is different from elitism centering around an individual, however, and in this respect, Ceausescu has carried Leninist notions of political leadership beyond anything envisioned by the "father of communism."[18]

Top-down Rule

As pointed out by many analysts, Marx believed that revolution would only occur when the socio-economic base was ready for it, i.e. when each historical style had reached its fullest fruition. The revolution would then be the political fulfillment of processes which had run their full course, and the new political order would correspond perfectly to the conditions of the socio-economic base after a relatively short period of transition, known as the dictatorship of the proletariat. When the time comes for this theoretical postulate to be put to the test in a society which was not "ready" for the socialist revolution, communist power was established in the political system and superimposed upon a socio-feudal, semi-capitalist base. The only way to bring the political super-structure and the socio-economic base into correspondence was through the radical transformation of the base through top-down rule. The five year plans in the Soviet Union were the first attempt at such a policy; it was later copied by all of the East European systems during their period of Stalinism (1947/48-1953). Top-down rule was a natural consequence of the actual conditions in Russia and also of Leninism as a theoretical construct. Nicolae Ceausescu is the quintessential Leninist in this respect. Romania remains the most heavily centralized and controlled political and socio-economic system in all of Eastern Europe. Lip service to reform and decentralization has never been followed up by serious political change, and, in the meantime, the centralization of power in the hands of a few individuals, particularly Nicolae and Elena Ceausescu, effectively precludes any notion of reform or change. Decisions of all kinds in Romania are made at the top, implemented by decree, and often changed at the will by the Leader and his consort while in the process of implementation. This is indeed the epitome of top-down planning, execution, and control.[19]

The results of this kind of policy are manifold and often contradictory. There is extreme direction at the top, but all others are reduced to mere executors of the clan's decisions. Consequently, no one dares show initiative, and no one wants to be held responsible for mistakes or even achieved results, because those results may be deemed inadequate by fiat at the very top. "Drift" ensues; unless a decree from the Leader materializes, no implementing decisions will be made, and nothing happens. The dismal performance of the Romanian economy during the 1980s is in large measure attributable to this leadership drift just below the apex of power (and at all lower levels). This lack of performance infuriates Ceausescu and his wife Elena, who then habitually choose to interfere at all levels of management, even at the grass roots, by personal visits to factories and farms. While they castigate officials, perhaps even fire them, they also receive the "accolades" of the workers and peasants, who have been gathered for "spontaneous" demonstrations of love and adoration.[20]

This kind of leadership approach creates extreme insecurity in leadership cadre at all levels. Demoralization sets in; corruption flourishes as each bureaucrat and manager attempts to reap the maximum benefits of his or her privileged position in the shortest time possible, before a transfer or demotion takes place. The system "ratchets down" on the scale of performance, and the spiral continues downward. Mere personnel changes cannot deal with this problem; only fundamental changes in attitude can do this, and, as known, attitudes change very slowly. Thus, Romania will suffer the result of the Ceausescus' managerial style long after the demise of the two principals, and perhaps even their successors in the clan.[21]

Top-down leadership depends heavily upon the decisions of the top leadership, particularly in a system as centralized as Romania. Nicolae and Elena Ceausescu are extraordinarily fickle leaders. They frequently change the criteria for performance in mid-stream, as it were, thus invalidating all criteria of plan fulfillment and success. Furthermore, they have frequently granted privileges and then removed them, and promised concessions to key groups in society, only to take these away after a period of time. The result of this is enduring skepticism and cynicism among the masses and key societal elites, with attendant problems of performance. All of this contributes to the continued downward slide in performance. In this respect, Ceausescuism is Leninism but with the opposite effect of Leninist top-down leadership. Instead of increasing production and performance, it hampers and severely reduces it.[22]

Storming and Overcommitment of Resources

Marx, convinced that society would be ready for the *political* revolution that ushered in socialism, did not confront the problems of underdevelopment and lack of "synchronization" between society and polity. Lenin, as a practicing political leader, was obliged to deal with this discrepancy. The frantic efforts which he launched to develop Russia economically and socially, were enhanced in a most dramatic fashion by Stalin, whose policies represented a full-blown effort to bring polity and society into correspondence with each other through rapid, forced, and multifaceted development of the latter. Stalin perceived the need to attack all problems of underdevelopment at once, to "storm" the bastion of underdevelopment, and to conquer it in the shortest possible time. This approach to development required massive doses of resources and manpower, the epitome of extensive development. Overcommitment of resources and corresponding waste, some of it horrifying in nature, ensued. This feature of Leninist and Stalinist development policy is not Marxist, but has become a standard feature of communist modernization policies. In this respect, Nicolae Ceausescu is in the mainstream of communist approaches to the question of development.

Socio-economic "storming" has remained a prominent feature of the Romanian experience up to the present time just as most of the other East European political leaders began to examine the notion of extensive industrialization and the need for reform, decentralization, and an emphasis on individual labor productivity. During the forty years of communist modernization in Romania, the emphasis has always been on massive infusions of men, materials, and investment funds. Huge industrial complexes have sprouted all over the country, as exemplified by the Pitesti petrochemical complex, the Slatina steel mills, and the refineries on the Black Sea coast. Gigantic construction projects have been started, and some are actually finished; examples include the Iron Gates and the Danube-Black Sea Canal, as mentioned above. Other projects, which defy reason in an economic sense, are underway. The most conspicuous of these is the "reconstruction" of much of downtown Bucharest as discussed in Chapter 3.

This approach is amplified by attempts to make Romania into one of the major industrial powers of the world in the shortest possible period of time. A frantic investment program has been pursued for several decades, draining the spending power of the population and relegating consumer goods and food production to a secondary or tertiary position on the ladder of economic and political priorities. Educational deficiencies were "attacked" through massive programs that initially produced considerable results in that they eradicated illiteracy and began the process of developing a socialist intelligentsia of high quality. During the 1980s, however, education has been pauperized in a variety of ways, from reduced funding and a shift towards vocational training to excessive political control and disruption of the educational process because of shortages of all kinds, such as heat, electricity, and essential supplies. (In recent years, Romanian schools have been closed during the winter months because of lack of heat).[23]

The "storming" approach is also reflected in the mentality of the leadership, particularly the Ceausescu clan. No project is seen as too large, no plan target, however inflated, is perceived as unrealistic, no demand on time and effort is conceivably excessive. Nicolae Ceausescu persists in establishing plan targets that are clearly unrealistic in terms of the socio-economic capabilities of the country. Furthermore, he routinely revises the plans upwards in the middle of the planning cycle, apparently without much consultation with experts, planners, or workers. When these plans are routinely underfulfilled (as can be expected) the General Secretary launches another round of personnel reshuffling and firings, then proceeds on the same path as before. This cycle of events has repeated itself throughout the last two decades a number of times, always with predictable results. Storming does not work, particularly in a society which is now exhausted, dispirited, and devoid of reserves, human, machinery, or resource wise.[24]

The developmental "style" discussed above is inherently wasteful. It is, perhaps, effective under certain circumstances, because it gets the job done in those areas that have the highest priority, but it is most assuredly not efficient, because resources are expended at a very high rate of consumption. Overcommitment of resources presupposes the existence of a resource pool from which reserves can be drawn. This pool is now virtually empty all over Eastern Europe. Nowhere is this more true than in Romania. Nowhere is it more tragic, because this country had a much greater pool to start with. For example, Romania was once one of the major oil producers of Europe, but must now import most of the crude used by inefficient factories and other economic enterprises. The large refinery capacity that was constructed during the last twenty years is underutilized because Romanian resources are inadequate to purchase the necessary quantities of crude. By the same token, forest resources have been severely depleted, and reforestation programs are insufficient for reproductive needs. The soil is also worn out in many areas, due to excessive utilization of the one-crop system and corresponding insufficient rotation of crops or fallow harvesting. Other examples could clearly be added, but it is not necessary. Overcommitment of material resources is no longer possible, because there are no longer such resources to be utilized and expended in this way.[25]

Mobilizing Human Resources:
Ceausescu and Political Socialization

An important part of the regimes that are known as communist is the utilization of human resources for the fulfillment of political and socio-economic goals. These are, literally, *mobilization* regimes, where the political leaders organize, orchestrate, and utilize individuals and groups for the achievement of goals that are ideologically or doctrinally determined by the leaders themselves, mostly without regard to the views of the mobilized mass. People do not participate in decision-making; they merely perform tasks that are assigned to them by the leaders who, in turn, claim to speak for the interests of the nation, of the internationalist cause, of peace and progress. Any analysis of communist development programs must take into account this crucial resource, and must recognize that an essential part of extensive development is precisely the overcommitment of *human* resources for goal fulfillment.

Such overcommitment is risky and costly in two major ways. First of all, at some point the modernizing regime will run out of easily accessible manpower, because everyone will be employed, more and more people will live in the cities, and the rural pool of underutilized, available people will dwindle and then disappear altogether. This is a development which has caught up with all of the East European systems, including Romania, which had greater reserves since it was less developed to start with. Thus entered the era of communist power with a greater rural labor pool than the other East European states. Despite this relative advantage in the field of human resources, even Bucharest is now feeling the pinch in labor reserves. Most of the productive elements have been moved from the countryside to the cities and towns. The human resources left in the villages are older, or less enterprising, or in some other way less than would be expected, and even their numbers are dwindling. There simply is less to draw from. In the next decade, even this marginal pool will be drained. Only two solutions remain: Increase the birthrate (see above), and increase the productivity of each worker, each peasant, each functionary. Nicolae Ceausescu is devoting his considerable energies to both of these solutions in his typical fashion of top-down leadership, storming, and exhortations.

The second problem with extensive use of human resources is the likelihood that this asset, like all others, will wear down and will need repair. Humans need incentives, material or spiritual, for the self-sustenance and the renewal that must accompany each day at the office, in the factories or fields. Such rejuvenation comes not only from material incentives and the satisfaction of material needs, but also from emotional satisfaction, entertainment, hope, goals and dreams for the future, particularly the future of one's children. These elements are all essential "spare parts" for the human engine, as demonstrated repeatedly and conclusively by social and industrial psychology.

Ceausescu's Romania is singularly lacking in these resources. Even the regime admits that the population is lacking in the spirit, the drive necessary to achieve existing goals and setting new ones. Social science research conducted in Romania shows a dispirited population which is concerned with survival, not progress. People who replaced hope for the future with cynicism about the present. Individuals seek relief from a reality that is, at best, dreary, through alcoholism and retreat from society. The steady growth of various forms of social pathology and disruptions such as hooliganism, increase in the divorce rate, and crime, (some of it violent), illustrate the pathologies of the current societal order. The regime-controlled press reports a great deal of slovenliness at the workplace, corruption among officials, and theft and pilferage among the work force. Furthermore, the regime is open about the generally low labor productivity throughout all branches of the economy as well as the lack of enthusiasm exhibited for the fulfillment of the socio-economic goals established by the leadership. Thus, there are massive problems in the system, even by official admission. One can imagine, then, that real conditions are much worse, bordering on a real crisis of considerable scope and duration.[26]

Nicolae Ceausescu and his close associates are well aware of these problems and have taken decisive, even drastic, measures to deal with them. These measures are consistent with the emphasis on top-down leadership, storming and overcommitment of resources, and the notions of ideological achievements found in "Ceausescuism" and discussed in some detail above. The Ceausescu program of mobilizing human resources is complex, of long standing, and represents a throwback to an era of social mobilization which ended after Stalinism in most of the rest of Eastern Europe.

The following elements can be said to represent the basic aspects of the Ceausescu "human mobilization plan":

First, there is a continued emphasis on political socialization and indoctrination and an apparent conviction that these mechanisms will, in fact, induce people to work harder. Many analysts trace this emphasis on indoctrination to the summer of 1971, when Ceausescu visited China and apparently became deeply impressed with the ideological achievements of the Great Proletarian Cultural Revolution. For other analysts, 1971 merely represents the year in which Ceausescu felt secure enough at the top of the political pyramid to implement his long-standing views and convictions. It is not necessary to determine the exact starting point of the campaign for our purposes here; suffice it to say that at least since 1971, Nicolae Ceausescu has implemented a program of mass indoctrination designed to extract even greater amounts of socio-economic performance from the population while offering little in the way of material incentives. All branches of the RCP have been mobilized to spread the message of ideological fervor, the danger of deviationism, the false allure of "Western" thought and ideas, and the need to perform more and better for the cause of socialism and peace. The party congresses have become little more than an orchestrated show of enthusiasm for the leader, and there are numerous other meetings between the congresses themselves in which various functional groups, such as the Council of Socio-Economic Development, meet to discuss the latest successes and ways to improve further. The General Secretary and his wife also make frequent visits to economic enterprises, in which they receive the orchestrated adulation of the masses, exhort them to greater performance, criticize officials, and, in general, reaffirm the need for continued ideological vigilance and economic performance for the glory of greater Romania.[27]

The ideological messages blasted at the Romanian citizenry from all angles and in all conceivable situations are, presumably, designed to produce the "new socialist man and woman." These are individuals with a higher level of commitment to socialist society and to their duties in that society, superior ethics and morality, and a deeper understanding of their individual lives as components of the collective. The new socialist individual will, in turn, help establish socialist culture and the socialist nation—entities that are qualitatively superior to the selfishness, greed, and individualism of capitalist society, the West in general, and, by implication, other systems run by communists less committed or less skilled in the quest for the new individual.[28]

The notion of establishing a new society is not unique to Ceausescu and his clan, but most of the rest of the communist world has abandoned this quest in favor of greater pragmatism and a simple concern for staying in power. Nicolae Ceausescu's program is a throwback to an earlier period of communist rule, when idealism was an important part of the political program of all parties in this category. It is thus curiously out of touch with contemporary reality even in the communist world. It is even more incongruous because of the obvious discrepancy between slogans and reality, and the widening gap between the elite and its opulent lifestyle, on the one hand, and the pauperized and dispirited masses, on the other hand. Furthermore, many in the essential stratum of the socialist intelligentsia, those crucial experts needed to run a modernized society, have lost faith in the exhortations of the top leadership, because their efforts have not resulted in improvements in their lives, but rather greater demands, more rhetoric, and more exhortations. Thus, it is literally true that Ceausescu and some of his close associates believe in the idea of the new socialist individual, but nobody else does. The chasm that thereby develops between the small elite and the rest of the population is wide and probably unbridgeable.[29]

The RCP General Secretary is also concerned with the need to improve the vocational skills of the population so that the technical tasks of modern society can be fulfilled. Thus, the political messages emanating from the top leadership stress greater efficiency, reliability, punctuality, skills, and honesty among the work force, and the corresponding need to do away with "old" attitudes, values, and behavior concerning work. This vocational emphasis does carry elements of commonality with similar campaigns elsewhere in communist-ruled Eastern Europe, where the onset of the technological revolution and the communications changes brought about by the computer as a tool of mass interaction both fascinate and scare the old apparatchiki in the top political leadership. What is missing in Romania is the realization that the ideological indoctrination program and the vocational skills emphasis of political socialization must be matched by a third component, more material incentives and better services. Without this third component, the other two will fail. This is understood by growing numbers of Romanian intellectuals and even some party leaders below the top of the political pinnacle, but not by the clan.

A second mainstay of the Ceausescu mobilization plan is the personality cult and the emphasis on personalistic rule discussed above. Nicolae Ceausescu is apparently convinced that he, and only he, can inspire the population to the performance level required, through ideology and not through material payoffs. On this basis, the General Secretary constantly interferes in economic management and technical processes, thereby upsetting any notion of orderly procedures. He frequently recycles personnel, thereby assigning blame for failures and removing any chance of "empire building" among his subordinates, but this precedence clearly reduces performance, because the top leadership in the economic sector is unable to act with any consistency before many are removed, recycled, or demoted. This is a waste of talent and human resources, because it underutilizes a great many capable individuals whose skills are sorely needed in the economic sector and elsewhere in a system where performance is at rock bottom. It only makes sense from the vantage point of a political leader who is convinced about his own skills as the *only* inspirer of the masses. Furthermore, it reflects Nicolae Ceausescu's deep-seated mistrust of bureaucrats, technocrats, and the process of delegation of authority. The General Secretary has determined in his own mind that he is the *only* individual who can lead the workers, peasants, and intellectuals to the achievements of the new socialist (and ultimately communist) order. The palpable failures in performance, then, are due to the inadequacy of lower cadre and actually tend to reinforce his convictions.[30]

Given these tendencies and trends, there is little reason to believe that the centralization of power and the emphasis on top-down management now in evidence will be reduced or changed in any major way while the current leadership remains in power. Instead, one should expect further escalation of the trend towards personalistic leadership, cult of the personality, and top-down management. Furthermore, as economic results remain unsatisfactory and actually decline over time, the RCP leader will emphasize the need for a "campaign" style of management and "storming" in the fulfillment of plans. This is likely to involve even more actual mobilization, by military means, of the human resources that are still available in Romania. Given the results that this approach has provided in the past, it is likely that the actual performance of the system will continue to decline under present management. This inevitably brings up the question of how much more can be tolerated in the Romanian political culture. More about this later.

The final major element of the Ceausescu plan to mobilize the human resources at hand is represented by autarky and nationalism. The RCP leader is clearly determined to achieve his version of a socialist society by means of domestic resources only, without major reliance upon the outside world, be it other communist-ruled systems or the West. This is partly driven by Ceausescu's determination to eliminate the foreign debt that was accumulated during the 1970s; in part, it is caused by his conviction that the Romanian people, if properly led, has within it the kind of genius that will make outside influences unimportant. By the same token, he is also convinced that as the inspired leader of this potentially gifted nation he can (and will) realize this genius single-handedly, in an organic relationship with the masses, thus propelling Romania to a position of leadership for the rest of the world and, by implication, a model for emulation by others. Up to the present time, Ceausescu has been rather cautious in billing *his* Romania as a model for others, with an obvious realization that such open advocacy is likely to produce reactions among others, and most importantly the Soviets.

At the same time the implications of his statements and programs should be clearly understood.[31]

Autarky is clearly an outmoded notion in the autumn of the twentieth century, and it has been abandoned by virtually everybody else (with the possible exception of the Albanians, and even post-Hoxha Tirana has begun to break out of its self-imposed isolation). In Ceausescu's case, autarky is coupled with nationalism, and perhaps even ethno-chauvinism, which postulates the superiority of the Romanian nation in ethical and cultural terms. Given this notion of superiority, autarky may make a certain sense, because a superior collectivity does not need other, less developed, entities for inspiration. Ceausescu wants to relate to the rest of the world from a position of strength, not weakness. There is clearly an element of messianism in this approach. The trouble is that few seem to believe the message anymore.

Notes

1. There is a great deal of literature on the concept of "modernization," and also on "urbanization." See, for example, S. N. Eisenstadt, "Varieties of Political Development: The Theoretical Challenge" in S. N. Eisenstadt and Stein Rokkan (eds.), *Building States and Nations* (Beverly Hills, CA: Sage Publications), 1973), pp. 41–73; and Stein Rokkan, "Cities, States, and Nations: A Dimensional Model for the Study of Contrasts in Development," in *ibid.*, pp. 73–99. The argument on the relationship between modernization and urbanization has been made by Karl W. Deutsch, "Social Mobilization and Political Development," *The American Political Science Review*, September 1961, pp. 493–575. A superb discussion of urbanization and urbanism is John A. Armstrong, *Nations Before Nationalism*, esp. ch. 4 (pp. 93–129). For a discussion of the roots or urbanism, see, for example, Ernst Kirsten, *Die griechische Polis als historisch-geographisches Problem des Mittelmerraumes* (Bonn: Dümurler Verlag, 1956).

2. For a discussion of the process of deurbanization in the Balkans, see Robert Lee Wolff, *The Balkans in Our Time*, ch. 4 (pp. 50–69).

3. Nicolae Ceausescu makes this point every time he speaks. One of the most comprehensive statements on this subject was his speech to the thirteenth RCP congress in November 1984, printed in *Scinteia*, November 19, 1984.

4. The emphasis on Stalinist planning and management is restated with great regularity. For a recent statement, see Ceausescu's speech to the plenum of the RCP Central Committee on March 28 and 29, 1988. The statement was printed in *Agerpres*, March 29, 1988.

5. This commitment is reflected in the state budget for 1988, printed in *Scinteia*, December 25, 1987. See also Ceausescu's speech to the party conference in December, 1987, printed in *ibid.*, December 17, 1987.

6. The RCP General Secretary has continued his plans for "rebuilding Bucharest" despite severe criticism from abroad as well as at home. One of his

favorite recent projects is a gigantic television tower (450 meters high) in the city. This project was discussed by *Scinteia Tineretului* on May 21, 1987.

7. This commitment is constantly restated. One example will suffice, namely Nicolae Ceausescu's speech to the plenum of the Council of Working People and the Supreme Council of Economic and Social Development, on June 25 and 26, 1986, printed in *ibid.*, June 26, 1986.

8. The depth of the economic crisis produced by such policies is sometimes reflected in discussions by party officials themselves, e.g. *Scinteia*, December 17, 1982. In October, 1987, the General Secretary himself admitted failures but attempted to blame others for them (Ceausescu statement to the RCP Central Committee, *ibid.*, October 6, 1987).

9. By the mid-1980s, Ceausescu had become obsessed with the need to reduce domestic consumption by virtually eliminating imports and accelerating exports. This policy has resulted in food rationing in Romania. For an analysis, see Dan Ionescu, "Food Rationing in Brasov," *Radio Free Europe Research*, Romanian SR/ 4, 4 March 1988.

10. This pattern is revealed in countless speeches and interviews. One of the most characteristic was his speech to the October RCP Central Committee plenum, published in *Scinteia*, October 6, 1987.

11. The Romanian anti-abortion laws are among the toughest in the world. See Sophia Miskiewicz, "Demographic Policies and Abortion in Eastern Europe," *Radio Free Europe Research*, RAD Background Report/179, Eastern Europe, December 8, 1986. The Romanian media occasionally reveal that illegal abortions take place, e.g. *Femeia*, February 1986; *Muncitor Sanitar*, December 23, 1986; *Scinteia Tineretului*, June 23, 1986.

12. Ceausescu has made his position clear in the face of direct and indirect pressures for Romanian reform by the Soviet Union and other Comecon countries. See, for example, his speech in *Scinteia*, January 27, 1987.

13. For a superb discussion of the importance of urbanism, see John A. Armstrong, *Nations Before Nationalism*, esp. ch. 4 (pp. 93–129).

14. I have discussed this in considerable detail in my *Modernization in Romania since World War II*, esp. ch. 5 (pp. 141–171).

15. The festivals during the 1970s were prime examples of this attitude. For a discussion of this program, see *Saptamina*, December 3, 1976. See also Ceausescu's speech on this subject in *Scinteia*, October 23, 1976.

16. The Romanian authorities are becoming more and more repressive against dissenting elements of the population because such elements are outside the collectivity so treasured by the leadership. For a detailed discussion of this, see Vladimir Socor, "Repressive Measures Against Protesters," *Radio Free Europe Research*, Romanian SR/1, 13 January 1988.

17. A great deal of literature has been summarized here. For a recent major statement of his philosophy on this and related subjects, see the General Secretary's speech to thirteenth RCP congress, in *Scinteia*, November 19, 1984.

18. I have discussed this phenomenon in my "Romania's Growing Difficulties," *Current History*, November 1984, pp. 375–389.

19. See *ibid.* See also recent changes in the RCP leadership structures that further strengthen the clan's hand, (at the national RCP conference in December 1987, the proceedings of which were published in *Scinteia,* December 17, 1987).

20. See my paper "Leadership Drift in Romania," presented at the annual convention of the American Association for the Advancement of Slavic Studies, Boston, MA, November 1987 (to be published by *Comparative Communism* in 1989).

21. See *ibid.* See also Ceausescu's scathing attack on the performance of the nomenklatura in *Scinteia,* February 21, 1987.

22. Thus, there is a schizophrenic element in Ceausescu's speeches; on the one hand, he talks about the glorious achievements of Romania, but on the other, he castigates subordinates. Extolling his own leadership, he also spends much time blaming subordinates for failures. See, for example, his speech to the RCP Central Committee in October 1987, published in *ibid.,* October 6, 1987.

23. One of the most recent outbursts of student unrest as a result of cutbacks of all kinds in education occurred in Iasi in May 1987. The demonstrations were reported by *Le Monde,* May 27, 1987. Nicolae Ceausescu has reportedly stressed the need to respond to such "provocations" with more austerity and tighter controls. On the latter, see his speech, reported in *Scinteia Tineretului* on January 27, 1987 (before the latest demonstrations).

24. Romania is the last of the East European countries to put more emphasis on personal loyalty and ideological "purity" than on expertise. In fact, the emphasis on indoctrination and ideology has increased in recent years. At this time, the proportion of apparatchiki in the top leadership is higher than it was at the beginning of the Ceausescu era, and the proportion of real exports lower. For an analysis, see "'Reds' Squeeze Out the 'Experts'," *Radio Free Europe Research,* Romanian SR/11, 2 October 1986 (article by M.S. and VVK).

25. Even CMEA statistics reveal the depth of the socio-economic crisis in Romania. For an analysis, see Vladimir Socor, "Social Hardships Reflected in CMEA Statistics," *ibid.,* Romanian SR/1, 6 February 1987.

26. Sometimes this cynicism turns to satire and anti-regime humor. A current favorite in Bucharest is the saying that "Ceausescu is spreading darkness with the speed of light." See Crisula Stefanescu, *ibid.,* Romanian SR/7, 26 May 1988. For an overview, see my "Social Deviance in Romania," in Ivan Volgyes (ed.), *Social Deviance in Eastern Europe* (Boulder, CO: Westview Press, 1978), ch. 6 (pp. 113–159).

27. This is a summary of clan behavior for a number of years. Nicolae Ceausescu has restated his position on this topic many times, e.g. at the RCP national conference in December 1987, as published in *Scinteia,* December 17, 1987.

28. For a discussion of political socialization under Ceausescu, see, for example, my chapter "Political Socialization in Romania: Prospects and Performance," in Daniel N. Nelson (ed.), *Romania in the 1980s* (Boulder, CO: Westview Press, 1981), ch. 5 (pp. 142–174).

29. One example of intellectuals rejecting Ceausescu's policies is Mihai Botez, who now resides in the West. His interviews with the Western press while he

still resided in Romania earned him a number of repressive measures by the authorities, including banishment to the provincial city of Tulcea. His interviews were published in *L'Express*, May 29, 1987; *La Stampa*, March 16, 1987; *Le Figaro*, February 27, 1987; *The Christian Science Monitor*, March 3, 1987.

30. The personality cult is especially outrageous every January, when both Nicolae and Elena celebrate their birthdays. For the latest round of this, see *Scinteia*, January 26, 1988 (Ceausescu's speech to the "Solemn Homage Meeting" at the Socialist Republic Palace). See also statements by Nicolae Giosan, Chairman of the Grand National Assembly, who glorified Ceausescu in *Saptamina*, January 25, 1980. The cult of Elena Ceausescu approaches that of her husband; see *Femeia*, January 1988.

31. The General Secretary did reject the notion that Soviet-style glasnost and perestroika would be applicable to Romania. See, for example, his speech on this subject, published in *Scinteia*, January 27, 1987.

5

Implementing Ceausescuism:
The Vehicle of the Party

The doctrinal blend that is Ceausescuism would be nothing more than a curious theoretical construct except for the fact that it has become the official policy of Romania for the last two decades. Such official policy, in order to be implemented, must have a number of executive vehicles. In Romania, as in other communist-ruled systems, this vehicle is the communist party, the RCP (Romanian Communist Party) and its auxiliaries and front organizations of various kinds.

The Mechanism of Policy Implementation:
The RCP Structure

On November 23, 1984, *Scinteia* announced the elections to the top RCP bodies at the conclusion of the thirteenth congress. This established the power structure of the party for the period up to the next congress, to be held in 1989. The main bodies of the party are the Political Executive Committee (PEC), the Secretariat, and the Central Committee. There is also a Central Revision Commission, which tends to be a body for dignitaries who are accorded some recognition but minimal influence.

The membership of the PEC after the thirteenth congress was as follows:

Nicolae Ceausescu, General Secretary

Iosif Banc	Alexandrina Gainuse
Emil Bobu	Manea Manescu
Virgil Cazacu	Paul Niculescu
Elena Ceausescu	Constantin Olteanu
Lina Ciobanu	Gheorghe Oprea
Ion Coman	Gheorghe Pana

Nicolae Constantin
Constantin Dascalescu
Ion Dinca
Miu Dobrescu
Ludovic Fazekas

Ion Patan
Dumitru Popescu
Gheorghe Radulescu
Ilie Verdet
Stafan Voitec (Voitec died in 1985)

A rather large number of individuals were elected as candidate members to this top executive body. They were:

Stefan Andrei
Stefan Birlea
Nicu Ceausescu
Leonard Constantin
Gheorghe David
Marin Enache
Petru Enache
Mihai Gere
Maria Ghitulica
Nicolae Giosan
Suzana Gadea
Nicolae Mihalache

Ioachim Moga
Ana Muresan
Elena Nae
Marin Nedelcu
Cornel Pacoste
Tudor Postelnicu
Ion Radu
Ion Stoian
Gheorghe Stoica
Iosif Szasz
Ioan Totu
Ion Ursu
Richard Winter

The Secretariat had the following composition:

Nicolae Ceausescu, General Secretary

Iosif Banc
Emil Bobu
Ion Coman
Petru Enache

Constantin Radu
Ion Radu
Ion Stoian
Ilie Verdet

The Central Committee had 265 full members and 181 candidate members. On the Central Revision Commission there were 75 members.[1]

As is customary in communist parties, certain individuals served in two or more capacities at the top of the party hierarchy, thus enhancing their power and stature. Iosif Banc, Emil Bobu, Ion Coman, and Ilie Verdet (and, of course, Nicolae Ceausescu) were full members of the PEC and also members of the Secretariat. Petru Enache, Ion Radu, and Ion Stoian were candidate members of the PEC and full members of the Secretariat. All of the members in these two top bodies were also full members of the Central Committee.

The congress produced relatively few changes in the top leadership bodies as compared to 1979, the time of the twelfth congress. Only Miu Dobrescu was added as a full member of the PEC. Dobrescu, whose career was primarily in various county party bodies, is clearly a close associate of the Ceausescus, especially Elena Ceausescu. His appointment further strengthened the power of the clan.

Among the candidate members to the PEC, there were some changes. Dobrescu was promoted to full membership. Stefan Mocuta, who was elected a candidate member in 1979, retired after the 1984 congress. There were also new faces in this body, namely Nicolae Giosan (an agricultural expert); Tudor Postelnicu, whose career has been in the security apparat (he became head of the Department of State Security in March 1978); Ioachim Moga (primarily an RCP county apparatchik); Gheorghe David, an agricultural expert and, since January 1984, Minister of Agriculture and the Food Industry; Marin Nedelcu, county party leader in Brasov since 1983; Nicolae Mihalache, another agricultural expert, at the time of his appointment first secretary of the Constanta County RCP body; Maria Ghitulica, since 1982 first secretary of the Vrancea County RCP; finally, Gheorghe Stoica, who became first secretary of Dolj County. Stoica, an old RCP leader, was moved from the Secretariat to the PEC at the 1984 congress, because his new position is incompatible with membership in the Secretariat. (The same happened to Lina Ciobanu, a former member of the Secretariat, who became the head of the General Council of Trade Unions earlier in 1984). Finally, the General Secretary promoted his favorite son Nicu to candidate membership in the PEC. Nicu was earlier made head of the UCY (Union of Communist Youth) and thus also Minister of Youth.[2]

On December 8, a few weeks after the thirteenth congress, the PEC appointed a Permanent Bureau from among its membership. The Permanent Bureau is the inner circle of power in Romania and deserves our attention. The new Bureau in 1984 was made up of Nicolae Ceausescu, Emil Bobu, Elena Ceausescu, Gheorghe Radulescu, and Ilie Verdet (all of whom were on the Bureau in 1979 as well); the only "newcomer" was Manea Manescu, who was a member of the Bureau in the period 1974–1979.[3]

The appointment to the top bodies of the RCP at the thirteenth congress came from two rather different categories of people. First of all, there were a number of old party apparatchiki, particularly from the most important county party bodies, or individuals who may have started elsewhere but had recently been appointed to county positions. The second category was made up of younger economic and managerial experts, particularly in agriculture; two of these individuals (David and Nedelcu) had been personal counselors to the General Secretary. In the case of Manescu, a former economist with extensive experience in bodies such as the Supreme Council for Economic and Social Development and, in the period 1974–1979, Prime Minister of Romania, a major comeback took place. Manescu may have been called back to help manage the deepening economic crisis, or he may have used his close family connection with the Ceausescus for readmission to the inner circle; in any case, Manescu's appointment strengthened the clan's position further at the top of the RCP.[4]

Almost as interesting is the list of individuals who were dropped from the Bureau or the PEC altogether. This applies to Iosif Banc, who was both a member of the PEC and the Secretariat after the 1979 congress; Cornel Burtica (who was ousted from the Central Committee); Virgil Cazacu, Nicolae Constantin, Paul Niculescu, Dumitru Popescu, Petru Enache, Ion Patan, and Stefan Andrei. Banc, Cazacu, Constantin, Niculescu, Popescu, and Patan all retained their membership on the PEC, but removal from the Bureau was still a demotion. Petru Enache and Stefan Andrei experienced an even steeper decline, since they only became candidate members of the PEC at the thirteenth congress.[5]

Most of those who were removed from the inner circle in 1984 were somewhat younger than the core group that remained after November 1984. It appeared that Nicolae Ceausescu, in his distrust of *all* officials, had decided to surround himself only with family members and his oldest cronies, thus further isolating himself from the rest of the RCP and the governmental structure as well.

As discussed in general terms above, the RCP hierarchy was shaken by a number of personnel changes after the thirteenth congress. In November 1985, Stefan Andrei was appointed a secretary of the Central Committee in charge of economic matters. Andrei thereby gave up his post as Foreign Minister. Andrei was joined in the Secretariat by Cornel Pacoste, an engineer by training but with considerable experience in the youth movement, in foreign affairs, and in county party administration. Another addition was Maria Ghitulica, whose career was primarily in the Grand National Assembly and in county party administration.

Ilie Verdet and Ion Radu were released from the Secretariat to make room for the newcomers. Verdet became Minister of Mining, and Radu first secretary of the Brasov County RCP body. Both of these positions were incompatible with further service on the Secretariat, according to both the old and the new RCP statutes.

The November 1985 changes were apparently followed by a reshuffling of responsibility with the Secretariat. Petru Enache was switched to the area of international relations inside the Secretariat, while Stoian took Enache's place as chief ideologist.[6]

Between November 1984 and September 1986, further changes took place, particularly in the government (see below) but also in the RCP hierarchy. Two of the candidate members of the PEC were removed (Marin Enache and Nicolae Mihalache). Three new members were appointed; they included Mihai Marina, Ilie Matei, and Vasil Milea. This body then remained stable in terms of membership until August 18, 1987, when Petru Enache, who was named a candidate member at the thirteenth congress, died. In the meantime, Iosif Banc was dismissed from the ranks of full members of the PEC (March 1987). Then, in October, Stefan Andrei and Constantin Radu were dismissed from the Secretariat after they became deputy prime ministers, and were replaced by Constantin Mitra, Ion Radu, Radu Balan, and Gheorghe Tanase. Ion Radu made a further advance in his career by being appointed to the PEC as a candidate member. He was joined on that body by Neculai Ibanescu.[7]

Ceausescu also attempted to remove Gheorghe Stoica from his position as candidate member to the PEC as well as first secretary of the RCP in Dolj County, allegedly because of faulty performance. The PEC made no effort to follow these allegations with a formal expulsion, however; the result was that Stoica remained in both positions, at least for the time being, despite the denunciations by the party leader.[8] One might speculate about the ramifications of this development, including the possibility that the top apparatchiki rallied around one of the "grand old men" of the party in open defiance of the General Secretary himself.

On December 14 to 16, 1987, the RCP held a national conference in Bucharest. Such conferences are normal occurrences between the party congresses, but this latest conference was rather unusual in that it was postponed twice, probably because of growing resistance in elements of the apparat against the increasingly high-handed rule of the Ceausescu clan. At the conference, Ceausescu harshly criticized these elements and others for faulty performance and inadequate party spirit. He also denounced the handling of the Brasov demonstrations of thousands of workers in November and promised improvements in the standard of living. This sharp criticism had been preceded by decisions of the PEC on November 27 against the apparat for a variety of failures. Already on November 23 several of the leaders of the Dolj judet party committee had been dismissed, including Matei Gheorghe, the first secretary, who had occupied his position for only two months.[9]

The National Conference ended on December 16 with the appointment of twenty-one individuals to the RCP Central Committee, all of them Ceausescu loyalists. Twenty of these new full members were promoted from the ranks of alternates, and one was a newcomer to this august body. The promotions came as a surprise, because the PEC, after meeting on December 11 and 13, had failed to make any such personnel recommendations. These developments produce speculation about a power struggle in the top leadership between Ceausescu and other senior elements.[10] If this was indeed the case,the General Secretary won, because his men were appointed.

Most of the individuals promoted in December 1987 were relatively young, suggesting a relationship with Nicu Ceausescu, up to then, head of the UCY. Three of them had been appointed judet first party secretaries (Carol Dinu, Galati judet; Ion Deaconu in Teleorman judet, and Maria Stefan, Salaj judet); their promotion to full membership in the Central Committee ensured that all county RCP leaders now had such status.[11] Others promoted included Major General Stefan Gusa, Chief of Staff since 1986, and Lieutenant General Aristotel Stamatoiu, Deputy Minister of the Interior. These two promotions indicated Ceausescu's concern with the need to keep good relations with, and control over, the elements of coercive power in the country.[12]

The changes instituted at the top of the RCP hierarchy during the fall of 1987 represent the latest major shakeup. It is true that Nicu Ceausescu was removed from the position of UCY and appointed to the position of First RCP Secretary in Sibiu County in November, but this did not entail his dismissal from the status as candidate member of the RCP PEC.[13] Then, an unusual calm settled on the top RCP nomenklatura for the winter of 1987–88. One can only assume that the game of "musical chairs" at the top of the RCP will continue later in 1988 and beyond to the end of the Ceausescu era.

Reshuffles in the governmental structure have been at least as extensive during the last few years (see below). The constant changes take several forms, as follows. First of all, several individuals have been dismissed because of faulty performance. In some cases, this is clearly true, because the constant reshufflings and the cronyism of personnel selection in Romania have cast up individuals who are clearly incompetent. In other cases, however, the dismissed individuals are clearly scapegoats, made to suffer for the inadequacies of the economic processes and mechanisms currently in existence in Romania. These structural deficiencies include the irrational decisions made by the General Secretary and his close associates, which are frequently contradictory and thus impossible to implement. Ceausescu has admitted faulty economic performance, but he has consistently blamed it on others and has, in fact, used these problems as a vehicle for his own power enhancement and the corresponding reduction in the power and influence of any and all actual or potential rivals.

The second criterion for personnel changes is old age and poor health. The Romania elite is beginning to grow older, and this certainly takes its toll on executives, particularly those in important positions who live with a great deal of stress and insecurity on a daily basis. During the last few years, there have been a number of cases that fall into this category.

Party Structure and Membership Composition

At the thirteenth congress, the RCP established a Political Executive Committee with twenty-three full members and twenty-five candidates. The Secretariat had ten members, subsequently expanded to eleven. There were 265 full and 181 candidate members of the Central Committee. This represented a considerable expansion in size of some of the RCP bodies. At the tenth congress in 1969, the Permanent Presidium (the contemporary version of the PEC) had eight members; the Secretariat had seven. There was also an Executive Committee, consisting of twenty-two full and eleven candidates. By 1973, the Presidium had been expanded to nine full members, while the Executive Committee now had twenty-one full and seventeen candidates. There were nine RCP Central Committee secretaries.[14]

The eleventh RCP congress in 1974 was the scene of considerable organizational simplification. The Presidium was abolished. The Executive Committee was made up of twenty-three members and thirteen candidates. The Secretariat had seven members. The Executive Committee now became the Political Executive Committee. At the eleventh congress, a Permanent Bureau was established inside the PEC, consisting at first of five members, then expanded to nine members, including Elena Ceausescu.[15]

No basic changes in structure took place at the twelfth congress in November 1979. The PEC was expanded to fifteen members (from the original five after the eleventh congress). The Secretariat remained stable in numbers. The Central Committee had a total of 408 members, up slightly from previous congresses. The twelfth congress was remarkable mostly for what it did not do: It did not produce massive reorganizations; it did not recycle many of the top leadership; and it did not create a special position for Elena Ceausescu (rumors had assumed that the position of Deputy General Secretary would be created for her). Apparently, Nicolae Ceausescu had decided that such an overt expression of nepotism would be excessive. To this day, Elena Ceausescu is "merely" a member of the Permanent Bureau of the PEC, (but she is apparently in charge of cadre matters, the most important function in the party next to that of the General Secretary himself).[16]

At the thirteenth congress, the structure of the top party bodies again remained basically untouched, with a large Central Committee, a small

Secretariat, an expanded Political Executive Committee, and, after a few week's relapse, the election of a Permanent Bureau. But this seeming structural permanence masked significant personnel changes, as noted above. And these personnel changes were the crucial elements in the development of increased centralization of power and the cult of the personality. *That* remained the permanent and crucial aspect of RCP policy during the period 1979–1984 and indeed beyond.[17]

The RCP, through its General Secretary, prides itself on being the party of the whole people, and of the nation. To this end, it attempts to recruit to its ranks individuals from all walks of life, "representing" the people and making the RCP at the grass roots into a microcosm of Romanian society. At the same time, the Ceausescu era has witnessed growing emphasis on the party's recruitment efforts among workers, women, and young people, while the peasantry has been downgraded as a recruiting area, like the intelligentsia for parts of the period in question. The emphasis on recruitment of women bears the clear mark of Elena Ceausescu's influence, while the quest for more young members is a natural enough inclination, particularly as the Romanian party, like all East European communist parties, must worry about the tendencies towards gerontocracy and the attendant stagnation. One would also assume Nicu Ceausescu's influence here. The heavy push for more "workers from the bench," on the other hand, is less understandable except as a reflection of Nicolae Ceausescu's personal preferences and his distrust of intellectuals of all kinds. The workers, presumably, still represent the "healthy" elements of proletarian consciousness that must be fostered as a counterweight to the elitism and arrogance of the intelligentsia.

These criteria for recruitment are reflected in the membership statistics provided by the General Secretary in his reports to the party congresses in the period 1969 to 1984 (and subsequently). The percentage of total membership made up of "workers" was 43 in 1969, 48.4 in 1974, and 56 in 1984. The share of "peasants" or "collective farmers" declined in the same period from 28 percent in 1969 to 22 percent in 1974 and 16 percent in 1984. The representation of the intelligentsia has remained more stable (22.8 percent, 21 percent, and 21 percent, respectively). The percentage of women has improved rather steadily over the same period. In 1974, for example, 25 percent of the total membership was made up of women. In 1984 it stood at 32 percent. The increase in female membership and the proportion of workers was due to a conscious policy of recruitment. Thus, between the twelfth and thirteenth congresses, 80 percent of new recruits to the ranks of the party were workers. Twenty-five percent of these newcomers came from the youth organization of the RCP. Fully 46 percent of the new members were women.[18]

The RCP prides itself on the faithful reflection of the country's ethnic structure in the rank and file membership. At the eleventh congress in 1974, Romanians constituted 89 percent of the total membership, while the Hungarians had 8 percent. At the end of 1975, 87.67 percent were Romanians, 7.68 percent Hungarians, and 1.94 percent Germans. By 1984, the Romanians had more than 90 percent of all members, 7 percent "Romanians of Magyar nationality," and 0.75 percent "Romanians of German nationality." The General Secretary also proudly reported that 23 percent of the total membership in 1984 was made up of people under thirty years of age; approximately 51 percent were between thirty and fifty, and the rest of the members above fifty. The recruiting emphasis on young people had therefore borne some fruit over the years of the Ceausescu era.[19]

At the thirteenth congress, Ceausescu also provided some interesting information on the RCP structure at the grass roots. In his report to the congress, he pointed out that there were 72,517 base organizations in the party. There were 7,879 party committees in enterprises and institutions, 2,705 communal committees, 243 city and municipal committees, and 41 judet (county) organizations, including the city of Bucharest. It is clear from this that the RCP has covered all areas of the country with a dense network of party organizations that also take into account the occupational diversity of a country rapidly developing towards industrial maturity.[20]

The General Secretary went further in his description of the RCP by stating that approximately 365,000 party members are "active" in territorial base organizations. In enterprises, institutes, and agricultural units the number of activists is 142,000. Communal, municipal, and city organizations muster another 90,000 such activists, while their number in county (judet) committees was approximately 5,000. A further 550,000 members are important for their work in various fields and activities of societal life.[21]

The full-time, professional party activists in the apparat itself numbered 10,000 in 1984, according to the RCP General Secretary's report. There were also 7,000 apparatchiki in the state apparatus, and a further 4,300 in the various mass organizations of Romania (e.g., youth and women's organizations, the Front of Socialist Unity, the trade unions, and others). Thus, the "inner circle" of the Romanian political elite in 1984 constituted ten to fifteen thousand individuals (considering the fact that there is a considerable amount of overlapping membership in such leadership positions).[22]

The organizational development of the RCP continued after 1984. At the end of that year it was officially reported that there were 95,000 party organizations, of which approximately 3,000 were merged with government bodies at the county level and below, particularly in towns, cities, and municipalities. The bulk of the party is therefore organized in enterprises, agricultural units, and official bodies such as government ministries, the armed forces, and the police. The social composition of the party showed that 58 percent of the members were workers, 16 percent peasants, 21 percent engineers, technicians and other intellectuals, and 8 percent pensioners and housewives. Women now accounted for 33 percent of the total membership. The top party leadership is still committed to strengthening the worker and peasant element of the base membership (at a time when the social composition of the population as a whole is moving towards more intellectuals and other "middle class" categories).[23]

During 1985, a number of important developments took place in the personnel policies of the RCP. First of all, a purge of certain categories took place, primarily among the so-called "leading cadre" (who were defined as constituting 190,000 individuals). During the year, 9,786 individuals from this category were dismissed, mostly for poor performance and various forms of malfeasance. This still did not fully account for the fact that the RCP at the end of 1985 had 3,357,205 members, as compared to 3,465,064 at the end of the previous year; the discrepancy of 107,859 members signifies a more thorough purge at levels below that of "leading cadre." Some of the shortfall may also be caused by attrition in the older age groups. The RCP Central Committee reported, with an air of satisfaction, that those under forty now constituted approximately half of the membership of the RCP. In the "activist" ranks, 53.7 percent were under forty-five; among enterprise directors and chief engineers 40.4 percent fell below this age bracket.[24]

The importance of females among the activists also increased. In 1980, 16.9 percent of the members in this category were females, but in 1985 the figure was 26.0 percent. Female membership in the various front organizations rose from 26.8 percent to 35 percent in the same period. During these five years, women also became more important as state officials (in 1980, 5.0 percent of such officials were women, but in 1985 the percentage had risen to 9.3 percent).[25]

Scinteia shed further light on the structure of the top RCP leadership in an article in March 1987. According to this article, the official nomenklatura consists of approximately 200,000 individuals, 10,700 of which are classified as "RCP Central Committee nomenklatura." There are 194,235 individuals in the "county, municipality, and city party organizations' nomenklatura."[26] Given the nature of the Romanian system's "government by clan," one can safely say that a very small number of individuals rule *over* the twenty-three million citizens of Romania, with few avenues for anyone else to influence decision-making at the top. Again, Romania runs counter to the trends of the rest of Eastern Europe, where a broadening of the political base is currently underway.

Operational Principles: Democratic Centralism

The RCP, like all communist parties, operates on the principle of democratic centralism, but has added a special twist to this concept, due to the extreme centralization and personalization of power in the hands of the so-called "clan" of Ceausescus, Petrescus (the relatives of Elena Ceausescu) and associated other individuals. According to this principle, then, debate may take place inside a party unit until a decision has been made on any given topic, but subsequently, decisions must be loyally obeyed. In the RCP since the ascent of the clan, this centralizing principle has been taken to its logical extreme, which is the subordination of all party life, all debate, all decision-making, to the whim of the top leadership. Debate is really routinized endorsement of statements made at the top, and affirmation of party principle is little more than the slavish execution of the personality cult. "Intra-party democracy" usually manifests itself in two ways, namely the "spontaneous" and "fervently supportive" decisions of all regional and local party bodies to praise the General Secretary for initiatives he has undertaken or, alternatively, routinized initiatives undertaken to show affection for the Leader on certain occasions, such as his birthday (and that of his consort). This extreme form of democratic centralism tends to reduce the party's capabilities of rational decision-making, thus enhancing the possibilities, indeed likelihood, of mistakes, drift, and sloganeering and a corresponding lack of problem-solving capabilities.[27]

Democratic centralism also involves the upward flow of personnel, according to established bureaucratic principles, and implemented through these principles as well as cooptation of individuals and categories beyond the established procedures. Furthermore, leadership elements are frequently recruited by means of the "coattail effect," manifested by personal relationship between individual leaders. There is a substantial literature on this subject, and thus no need for a detailed description of these principles here. What is needed is a detailed examination of the RCP version of this principle of "democratic centralism."

At the thirteenth congress of the RCP in November 1984 the party adopted new statutes which regulate the operation of the apparat and thus the recruitment procedures of the party. These new statutes significantly alter the principles of "upward flow" and, correspondingly, enhance the personal power of the General Secretary and his immediate entourage. For example, the statutes set age limits on individuals serving in party bodies at all levels, with the exception of the Political Executive

Committee (PEC), the RCP version of the Politburo. Even here, these limits may be applicable, should the PEC so decide. This rule allows the central leadership to rotate out cadre of long standing who may have established significant power bases of their own.[28]

Other elements of the statutes restrict the ability of the party rank and file to influence leadership selection. Up to 1984, it was technically possible to nominate leaders from the floor of the congress, or to question names that had been put into nomination. This right resulted in a major embarrassment for Ceausescu at the twelfth congress in 1979, when the old communist Constantine Pirvilescu questioned the General Secretary's candidacy and castigated his policies from the floor in front of delegates from the entire world and also a number of Western newsmen. This possibility no longer exists. The 1984 statutes specify that nominations must be determined at the pre-congress meetings of the county party bodies. As we shall see later, Ceausescu has always maintained iron control of these regional bodies, thus eliminating the chance of disruption from this quarter.[29]

The new status also establish the principle that at least one third of the membership of the Central Committee must be rotated at each RCP congress. Skillful use of this principle would allow the top leadership to get rid of oppositional elements, factions, and individual "undesirables" while promoting others who are more pliable and reliable. In addition, the statutes limit membership in the party to individuals who have already been members of the Union of Communist Youth (UCY). If the top leadership can maintain control over the UCY, it can effectively regulate the recruitment patterns with the party itself, thus further reducing the opportunity for oppositionist or dissident elements. It should also be pointed out that, until the fall of 1987, the head of the UCY was none other than Nicu Ceausescu, favorite son of the first couple.[30]

Another element in the new statutes further streamlines the flow of personnel into the RCP leadership. According to the unanimous decision of the 1984 congress, certain bodies now have ex officio membership on the PEC as either full or alternate members, specifically the leader of the trade union federation, the head of the UCY, and the top official of the National Council of Women. The principle is clear: Appoint your people to these positions, and you automatically have their votes on the PEC. By the same token, the statutes state that the county RCP secretaries are represented on the PEC; the specific number and the individual choices are up to the Central Committee plenum.[31]

This represents a considerable increase in central control over the recruitment process, but there is more. All individuals who are appointed to posts abroad (most importantly ambassadorships) must renounce their membership in higher party bodies for the duration of the appointment (this also means that they cannot be appointed or elected to such party positions while they serve abroad).[32]

The statute changes discussed above collectively amount to a serious restriction on the lower ranks of the RCP in terms of personnel initiatives, and a correspond strengthening of the power of the General Secretary. It establishes the RCP as clearly the most centralized of all the communist parties in Eastern Europe on this crucial dimension.

Operational Ethos:
The Conscience of the Nation

The 1984 statutes represent both an innovation and expansion of the operational ethos of the RCP. In the main, philosophical, portion of the statutes, the party is defined as "the vital center of our entire nation, the guiding political force of the Socialist Republic of Romania, the organizer and catalyst of the creative energies of all the working people in our homeland, of the entire people." By contrast, there is no reference to the role of the party as "the vanguard of the working class." References to the dictatorship of the proletariat have also been removed. Instead, the RCP is depicted as the chief caretaker of the well-being of the people and the protector of the independence and sovereignty of the nation. A symbolic indication of this national emphasis is the statement that the national flag is now also the party flag.[33]

The statutes also eliminate most references to "Marxism-Leninism," instead discussing "objective, universally valid laws of economic and social development." There are also copious references to "scientific socialism" and "dialectical and historical materialism." Finally, the RCP has discontinued its use of "proletarian internationalism" and "socialist internationalism," both of which are still part of the vocabulary utilized by the Soviets to discuss relations with non-ruling communist parties and with the so-called socialist community. The RCP instead utilizes the terms "international solidarity" and "new unity." The implication is that each unit in the "commonwealth" has greater autonomy and equal status.[34]

The 1984 statutes are merely an overt expression of the long-standing emphasis on nationalism and national sovereignty that has characterized the Ceausescu era. The statutes are actually a relatively mild version of the emphatic statements about this issue that have appeared in the highly controlled Romanian press. For example, an article in the RCP monthly, *Eva Socialista* (the theoretical journal of the RCP), stressed that class interests must be coordinated with national considerations and cannot be separated from the main manifestations of those considerations, especially sovereignty and territorial integrity. These assertions of the need for sovereignty have increased in frequency and intensity as the Kremlin continues to demand reform and glasnost in the East European states as well as in the Soviet Union itself. The RCP leadership clearly wants to continue its centralistic policies without Soviet interference, under the genesis of national sovereignty.[35]

The RCP, then, sees itself as the embodiment of the needs, wishes, and aspirations of the Romanian nation, to an extent that subordinates other, more traditional roles of a communist party, such as "the vanguard of the proletariat." The RCP thus makes an exaggerated claim to be the party of the whole people in a more strident manner than any other of its sisters in Eastern Europe.

Operational Style: The Rotation of Cadre

The RCP, more than any other party in Eastern Europe, is known for its frequent rotation of cadre inside the party hierarchy and between the party and the governmental bureaucracy, which is staffed with high party officials according to the principle of "overlapping membership" and "interlocking directorates." Every year there is a dizzying set of personnel changes, frequently accompanied by reorganizations of the various bureaucratic agencies that this personnel headed. For example, in the spring of 1984, the Chairman of the State Committee for Prices, the Minister of Agriculture and the Food Industry, and the Minister of Electric Power were all replaced with other bureaucrats of roughly the same standing, thus implementing the principle of "rotation of cadre." During the month of March that year, five new members of the RCP Central Committee Secretariat were elected, while one of the incumbents was moved to the Central Collegium, a body with little power. In June, there were important changes in the Ministry of Foreign Affairs. The Ministry of Internal Trade also suffered considerably during the spring and summer of 1984, as several deputy ministers were dismissed, probably as scapegoats for the dismal situation in retail trade.[36]

The RCP pre-congress changes in Romania did not stop there, however. Much of the propaganda apparat was purged, and the heads of *Scinteia*, radio and television, and Agerpres were removed. The editor-in-chief of *Scinteia* then became the head of the Department of Religious Affairs, thus producing other changes in this body. Finally, this round of purges also saw the dismissal of Ion Iliescu from the National Council of Water Resources. Iliescu had once been one of the "best and brightest" among Ceausescu's young lieutenants, so this dismissal represented yet another step in the downward fortunes of this man. The Director of the Central Statistical Board was also removed.[37]

The spring and summer purges picked up again in the fall of 1984, prior to the thirteenth congress. In October, the head of the Central Council of the General Confederation of Trade Unions was removed but also made a Deputy Prime Minister, thus suffering rotation rather than a serious demotion. The replacement was a woman (Lina Ciobanu) who had been appointed to the Central Committee Secretariat in the spring, thus serving in that position for only a few months. She became the sixth chairperson of the trade unions in five years.

Later in October, the Deputy Minister for Mines was replaced, as was the Minister of Oil. The Minister of Tourism and Sports was also dismissed. These changes in the course of a few months were not atypical; in fact, they represented the continuation (and perhaps acceleration) of a trend underway for several years. As stated by Anneli Maier:

> Another, and perhaps the main, reason for the frequent changes in high-level personnel is Ceausescu's lack of confidence in the members of the nomenklatura. By shifting them repeatedly from one position to another, he reduces or excludes the possibility of their building a power base for themselves from which to threaten his own autocratic rule. These changes, suggesting an increasing sense of insecurity on Ceausescu's behalf, are in sharp contrast to the steady rise and consolidation of the positions of the members of the Ceausescu clan.[38]

The pace of personnel change, which had been frantic during the congress year of 1984, slowed in 1985, but did not fully abate. In December 1985 the Minister of Foreign Affairs (Stefan Andrei) was moved to the Central Committee Secretariat and replaced by a relative newcomer to high office, Ilia Vaduva. Two other secretaries were also appointed, while two were removed. Since the dismissed individuals were primarily responsible for economic matters, it was clear that they had been made scapegoats for the failures of the economy, (which are really systemic and not attributable to any one individual).[39]

During December the Minister of National Defense, Constantine Olteanu, was also removed, shortly after he had made an official visit to the Soviet Union, thus prompting speculation about disagreements between Ceausescu and the armed forces. The replacement, Vasil Milea, is clearly a Ceausescu loyalist.[40]

The year 1986 witnessed a number of major changes in the RCP hierarchy. The following positions changed hands: two deputy premierships, the Foreign Minister, the Foreign Trade Minister, and the Chairman of the Committee for People's Councils. All of these changes took place among Ceausescu loyalists, so political performance was clearly not the reason for the dismissals or the reappointments. Again, the principle of rotation and the sensitivity of many of the tasks performed may have been the main reasons.[41]

During 1987 further changes took place. The Supreme Council for Socio-Economic Development, which has great powers of strategic economic planning, was given new powers, and concurrently, its membership was expanded to include two additional first vice-chairmen. At the same time, several new members were added ex officio. All of this strengthened the position of Nicolae Ceausescu and weakened that of Constantin Dascalescu, the Prime Minister, who is First Vice-Chairman of the Council (Ceausescu is ex officio Chairman as State President).[42]

In February 1987, the Minister of Light Industry, Alexandrina Gainuse, was removed, but then, surprisingly, moved to the position of judet party first secretary, which is certainly a promotion. Here, then, the reshuffling must have had motivations other than punishment. In September, the Minister for the Heavy Equipment Industry and the Minister for the Wood Industry and Building Materials were both replaced. At the same time, several ministries were merged (Ministry of the Chemical Industry and the Ministry of the Petrochemical Industry), while the Ministry of Mines, Oil and Geology was divided into three. Two days later, new ministers were appointed for these new posts. Later in September, three deputy prime ministers were dismissed, as was the Chairman of the State Committee for Prices. There were also some personnel changes at the Ministry of Foreign Trade and International Economic Cooperation. Finally for the hectic month of September 1987 another deputy prime minister and the Minister for the Electrical Power Industry were dismissed, and replacements were named shortly thereafter.[43]

This was only the beginning of a major purge. On October 3, 1987, the PEC dismissed the Minister of Technical-Material Supply and Control of Fixed Assets, the Minister of Internal Affairs, the Minister of Electrical Engineering, the Minister of Justice, and one deputy prime minister. On October 5 four new Central Committee secretaries were named after two incumbents had been named deputy prime ministers. Two new alternate members of the PEC were also elected.[44]

During the following week, the General Secretary's son, Nicu Ceausescu, was released from his position as head of the UCY. He was later named first secretary of the Sibiu County Committee of the RCP—a promotion which strengthens his potential claim to his father's mantle. Gheorghe Stoica, one of the grand old men of the RCP, was dismissed by Ceausescu from his position of First Secretary of the Dolj judet RCP committee, but later indications are that he continues to serve in that capacity as well as his position as an alternate PEC member. This may be an example of a Ceausescu "rotation" that was successfully resisted by the rest of the top RCP hierarchy.[45]

The virtually continuous reshufflings, purges, and reorganizations of the RCP and various governmental bodies during the last few years cannot fail to have a detrimental effect upon the performance of these bodies. There is no time to settle into a position and learn its intricacies before another transfer is effected. Furthermore, the constant changes clearly produce extreme insecurity among cadre, thus reducing their productivity further. Such constant reductions also reduce output, which, in turn, results in more dismissals, more reorganizations. Nicolae Ceausescu and his close entourage refuse to deal with the real causes of the country's problems, namely their own gravely flawed policies. In the meantime, the principle of rotation has reached ludicrous proportions. They reduce the apparat to a mere executive organ of the clan's predilections and irrationalities and cannot provide the crucial input on political, socio-economic, and cultural matters that is so desperately needed for a country in deep crisis. In fact, the subordinate role of the RCP and state apparats is directly responsible for much of this crisis. At the same time, such personnel policies enables the Ceausescu clan to garner even greater amounts of power in their hands. The somewhat cynical analyst may say that the failure of the system itself is directly proportional to the success of the clan in its quest for personal power. This is indeed a Balkan approach to politics.

The Routinization of Rank and File Participation

The rapid turnover of party leaders at all levels of the RCP hierarchy reflects a certain leadership style that we may label "organizational Ceausescuism." This approach to organizational questions is repeated in the General Secretary's dealings with the rank and file of the party. Verbally committed to democracy in the RCP, Ceausescu has elevated his clan to a point where the average party member has little or no effect upon decision-making and is reduced to a static element in the mass mobilization practiced by the clan. The flow of rank and file participation is predictable in the extreme, because it has been practiced with great consistency throughout the entire Ceausescu era (twenty-three years by now), and shows no sign of abating. In fact, there has been an intensification of these patterns of behavior during the last few years, which have been dubbed "full-fledged Ceausescuism" by some observers.[46]

There are several aspects to this routinized political behavior. First of all, the party at the grass roots is engaged in endless meetings in which the RCP member is expected to participate. Such meetings may take place in the member's apartment building or other living place, or it may occur at his or her place of employment (in practice, both apply with considerable regularity). At such meetings, the local party boss routinely delivers himself of a speech which praises the Ceausescus, endorses the economic plan (including the inevitable call for overful-fillment of production quotas that have been artificially and arbitrarily increased in Bucharest a few days earlier), demands greater ideological vigilance, chastises members for lack of enthusiasm and activity on behalf of the party, and then ends with a ritualized cry of support, once again, for the "glorious leadership" of the country. The more enterprising local leaders will also venture into matters that must be rather strange and thus unknown to them, such as foreign policy. The local leader will pay homage to the image of Romania abroad, which has been enhanced to unknown levels of respect through the wise leadership of Nicolae and Elena Ceausescu. After such speeches, the necessary decisions are made and endorsed, and the renewal of pledges of increased production and enhanced vigilance are transmitted to the next higher party body, there to become part of a report which extols the new heights of performance reached at *that* level. The tide of political sloganeering and ritualistic claims of success thus rolls from the bottom to the top of the hierarchy, creating entirely false notions of achievement. As for the local party members, they tend to yawn and go home after such a meeting, fully cognizant of the unreal aspects of their behavior but equally convinced that such behavior is necessary and realistic in terms of their political survival and fortune. There is realism inside the unreal in this set of behavior patterns, and it creates a powerful sense of schizophrenia and irrationality that seems to permeate all of society, only accentuated in the party itself.[47]

The boredom of the average party meeting is repeated at workplaces all over the country as the RCP activists fan out to inform workers, peasants, and intellectuals about the latest decisions at the center and the great wisdom that they represent. The activist invades the precious free time of the worker to read the latest proclamations, and he frequently interrupts the flow of work in the fields to make announcements and discuss matters pertaining to the five year plan. Throughout, the activist attempts to generate the kind of artificial enthusiasm that can only sound and seem hollow in the face of the continued worsening of the standard and quality of life for the average individual in Ceausescu's Romania. Again, there is an artificiality and unreality about the life of the average party member that strikes every observer of the local scene. This artificiality is also a powerful and unremitting force in the life of those who must endure it.[48]

The routine of local party life is occasionally broken by the arrival of a "higher up," a dignitary from the regional or county party organization. When this happens, another form of routinized behavior is produced which we may call "synthetic enthusiasm." The script runs like this: Advance parties of apparatchiki appear days ahead of the actual visit and make sure that all elements of the program are completely worked out, especially the "spontaneous" display of popular enthusiasm among the rank and file. Flags are distributed, leaders who will conduct the chants and slogans are appointed, the handing over of flowers is rehearsed, and the enthusiastic reports of shock workers and other outstanding performers are written, learned verbatim, and delivered in practice sessions. Buildings may be spruced up, floors cleaned, and rusty machinery hidden. The stores and markets acquire stocks of goods that have not been seen in months (and will disappear for untold weeks after the visit). Banners are made and strung. Perhaps a brass band or a workers' choir will be rehearsed to produce the patriotic songs so loved by the party brass.

On the day of the visit, behavior patterns rarely vary. The rank and file line up, express their great pride and enthusiasm, pledge support and further efforts, praise the local, regional, and county bosses, and finally express their "undying" support for the "son of the people," "the oak of Scornicesti," and his consort, "the most beloved daughter of Romania." The leaders leave, the rank and file troop back to work, and the dreary reality of contemporary Romania reasserts itself with unremitting force.[49]

The scenes played out through a visit by regional or county dignitaries are repeated on a much larger scale if the Boss himself, the General Secretary, should decide to visit. If the visit is at the county level (and it frequently is), months of preparation precede the "spontaneous outbursts of joy" produced by the party membership. Again, there comes a day after the departure of the Leader, and stark reality is once again upon all, RCP card or not. Students of political socialization call this process, this gap between slogans and reality, the process of "reality testing," or living with the fictitious aspects of the political order. In Romania, this reality gap is wide and expanding, creating a yawning abyss between the rulers and the ruled. So far, the Ceausescus have managed to teeter on the brink rather than to fall into that gap.[50]

The Insecurity of the Apparat

Routinized political behavior among the rank and file is coupled with a second major characteristic of RCP life, namely the extreme insecurity of party cadre below the pinnacle of power but above the local party bodies. There is a large stratum of leaders here, as many as two hundred thousand, as discussed above. These individuals live a life of relative privilege, because they have access to goods and services not available elsewhere, but they are also beset by extreme insecurity, caused by the excessive and fickle demands from the political center, on the one hand, and the cynicism and malperformance of the masses of the people and the rank and file of the RCP, on the other hand. These individuals lack the enormous power and the protection that exists at the top of the pyramid, and they are also unable to retreat into cynicism, amoral familism, or withdrawal, which characterize the average Romanian citizen, and the average party member. The intermediate leadership cadre are measured by their performance. They are expendable. And they are insecure to an extreme. Here is a considerable political and organizational asset that is continuously shifted around, purged, harassed, and blamed for problems that are, in large measure, caused by the premier blamer, the General Secretary and his close entourage. There is no other country in contemporary Eastern Europe (Albania included) where the apparat is so beleaguered. The relationship between this kind of insecurity, low performance, and various forms of cheating, of "beating the system" (see below), is clear and unmistakable. Only a top leadership obsessed with the need to amass more and more power in a few hands could treat its own intermediate cadre in such a fashion.[51]

The insecurity of intermediate cadre, I would submit, is different from the problems often faced by the top leadership just below the pinnacle of power, even though the latter is also subjected to the frequently played game of musical chairs. But in the case of major leadership figures, they have considerable power, and they usually have some protection; if they are removed, they normally end up in other, lesser, but still worthwhile positions. (The cases of utter disgrace of such top figures are relatively few and involve special circumstances in most cases). The intermediate leaders, on the other hand, may face unemployment, jail, or menial jobs which are likely to be made even more unpalatable by workers who resent having a former "boss" on their production line. The intermediate apparatchik must perform and survive. He has the most undesirable job of all cadre in contemporary Romania. It is no wonder that he has decided, individually and collectively, to attempt to make his position on the front line personally worthwhile.

Bakshish, "Arrangements," and the Apparatchik

As the intermediate party worker examines the world, he or she is immediately struck by the discrepancy between the power that is available vis-a-vis subordinates and the general public, on the one hand, and his utter impotence in relationship with the top leaders in Bucharest, on the other hand. Coupled with this peculiar form of schizophrenia comes the realization that one day, perhaps sooner, perhaps later, he is likely to be transferred, thus losing his perks or his power, however limited, over current subordinates. This realization is clearly a powerful incentive to utilize present advantages for maximum personal benefit, while there is still time. Thus, the apparatchik at this level is likely to engage in corrupt practices aimed at acquiring goods, services, and money. This is often done through collusion with others, creating a dense network of "family groups" at the local and regional levels, in which officials help each other and protect each other against the demands of higher authority and at the expense of the general population.[52]

Behavior of this kind is also encouraged because of the frequent policy changes emanating from the center and the excessive and unrealistic demands that are made upon the nomenklatura at this level. The establishment of protection groups becomes a necessity for survival, and corruption becomes the main vehicle for producing a little "slack" in the system so that individual apparatchiki can have a chance to survive and make the system work, however imperfectly. It should be stressed that a system such as Romania, with clear pathologies of decision-making and goal setting at the top, may require ways of "beating the system," and may require the extensive use of behavior that is usually called corruption, in a pejorative sense, elsewhere. In any case, this kind of behavior, while rational for the apparatchiki involved in it, is costly for society as a whole, and it contributes significantly to the political, socio-economic, and moral malaise of Romania in the 1980s.[53]

"Drift" and Indecision

The intermediate apparatchik, while busy attempting to maximize his or her position while it lasts, is also unwilling to take initiatives or make decisions that may get him into trouble. He prefers to wait until detailed instructions arrive from Bucharest, and then to carry them out to the letter, thus minimizing his own responsibility while maintaining the opportunity to blame others for likely failures. There is no incentive to assess the local situation, to make independent decisions, to maximize opportunities, because such initiative depends upon the performance of others for its success, and that performance is not likely to be forthcoming. The result of all this is minimalist thinking, avoidance of any kind of risk taking, and lack of activity. The Romanian political system is again bifurcated; on the one hand, there is excessive centralization and interference by the top leadership, particularly Nicolae and Elena Ceausescu, but, on the other hand, there is "drift," non-action by virtually all of those who are located further down on the organizational pyramid. The results of this situation are entirely predictable: There is faulty performance and "buck passing," and nothing gets done. This, in turn, infuriates the General Secretary and leads to further purges, more pathology, increased drift. The system ratchets down and down. The crisis deepens. And the General Secretary produces yet another set of solutions. To these we must now turn.

The Ceausescu Fix:
Populism, Reorganization, Admonition

While the outside observer can clearly understand the pathologies of the current Romanian system and the interrelations of its parts, the General Secretary, who is primarily responsible for them, fails to understand. Therefore, his solutions to the problem are inadequate, and in fact, contribute to the further aggravation of the situation at hand. The situation thus worsens every time the Ceausescu "fix" is applied. Under these circumstances, there is virtually no possibility that real solutions can be found during the present regime. The only question is whether or not the thought processes and values of the intermediate nomenklatura have been changed is such a fundamental way that they will never be remedied. If the latter is the case, the "Ceausescu epoch" will acquire a distinction that is unique among communist political systems.

The specific elements of the Ceausescu "fix" are as follows: First the General Secretary affixes blame for admitted failures on others, especially the intermediate nomenklatura. An example of this is the whole set of events surrounding the massive demonstrations that took place in the city of Brasov in the fall of 1987. There, thousands of workers marched on the party building, then destroyed furniture, records, and banners, and finally extracted concessions from an intimidated local and regional apparat. Subsequently, Ceausescu blamed the local leaders, promised improvements, and then paid out production bonuses ahead of time—an unheard of phenomenon in Romania.

The second element is usually a purge, in which "responsible" officials are fired, others are brought in, and the game of musical chairs continues. The third step is a form of reorganization, in which ministries, planning agencies, or other structures at various levels of the hierarchy are merged, separated, obliterated, or recreated. Finally, the cycle of poor performance and malfeasance is repeated, and so is the Ceausescu fix, but with little results other than the sound and fury of an outraged General Secretary denouncing his subordinates and proclaiming his undying devotion to the masses and to the people.[54]

The approach to problem solving in the RCP is a factor of Ceausescu's populist tendencies, as discussed above. By now, other, personalistic aspects have also intervened, specifically unwillingness to accept responsibility, belief in the infallibility of the leadership genius, and perhaps irrationality. These severe deficiencies will continue to plague the system as long as the Ceausescu and Petrescu clan remain ensconced at the top of the RCP pyramid.

Conclusion

In comparison to the other communist parties of Eastern Europe, the RCP is more centralized and hierarchical than any other. It is also dominated by old apparatchiki to an extent unknown elsewhere. Its ideological rigidity is markedly more pronounced than the fraternal organizations across the borders; it may even exceed the orthodoxy of post-Hoxha Albania. There is little room for input into the decision-making process of the RCP by rank and file members, and even the technical and managerial elites, so crucial for the running of a modernizing society, have little impact unless they happen to be coopted into the ruling clan or otherwise become acceptable to the small clique of leaders clinging to the last bastion of fully personalized rule in contemporary communist Europe. The processes of elite recruitment and retention are idiosyncratic and fully dependent upon the whims of the top leaders, notably Nicolae and Elena Ceausescu and a few other family members and cronies. Skills and forcefulness may be a real handicap under these circumstances, while sycophantic behavior is rewarded, and the ability to divine the attentions of the clan ahead of time and then implement them is the crucial ingredient for political success. Thus, bureaucratic rigidity is alleviated by personalistic politics perpetuated by a few individuals reveling in the exercise of unrestrained power. This may be the worst of all possible scenarios: Bureaucracy operates slowly, sluggishly, and only in response to direct orders from the nation's capital, for reasons discussed above, and there is little if any room for bright individuals with independent minds. Bureaucracy places its leaden and unresponsive hand on such people and pushes them away. At the same time, the confusing but dominant ideological caveats of Ceausescuism eliminate other ways of doing business, a particularly anachronistic fact as the rest of the communist world is groping for ways to improve efficiency, performance,and alternative thought processes.

Below the summit of supreme power there is confusion, drift, stalemate, fear, greed, and cynicism, all of which contribute to the malaise and faulty performance discussed earlier. Unpredictability lessens initiative and encourages toadyism. The results are now there for all to see: A country in a deep political, economic, moral, and spiritual crisis, on the one hand, and a leadership which is more and more isolated but, at the same time, increasingly more powerful. Few if any serious observers would fail to notice such a massive failure.[55]

The Romanian paradox still haunts us, however, for it can be cogently argued that the Ceausescu era has also been a huge success; it all depends upon the units and criteria of measurement and how the observer reads the evidence. For example, any individual who sets out as a young man to capture power and ends up like Nicolae Ceausescu is a political success, at least for himself. If the objective is to enhance the power of those to whom one is close, the present leadership, exercising rule by clan, is a huge success. And if the aim is to establish unfettered power, in which procedure, constitutions, the behavior of other actors, and the alleged constraints of institutions and structures become irrelevant, the Ceausescu epoch has produced startling achievements for the clan. Finally, if the objective is to establish rule so unlimited that basic notions of logic and common sense can be ignored with impunity, Nicolae Ceausescu is ahead of all of his colleagues in the rest of Eastern Europe by a considerable margin. Furthermore, the ability to control others and prevent the formation of meaningful counterelites is a stroke of political genius. One only has to contrast the widespread notions of distrust, even hatred, of the Ceausescus with their iron control over much of the apparat and the elements of coercive power, the armed forces and the police, to understand the magnitude of this success. If he is so bad, why does he not fall? The answer is simple: On the crucial dimension of obtaining, retaining, and expanding power, Nicolae Ceausescu is very good indeed. He is so good, in fact, that he has succeeded in transforming a whole country of twenty-three million people, for better or for worse. Let us now examine the program of societal transformation which Nicolae Ceausescu sought to implement.

Notes

1. The membership of the leading bodies of the RCP was published in *Scinteia*, November 23, 1984

2. An excellent analysis of the congress was produced by Anneli Maier, *Radio Free Europe Research*, Romanian SR/18, 14 December 1984.

3. The new Permanent Bureau was announced in *Scinteia*, December 9, 1984.

4. A great deal of material has been summarized here, both from Romanian and Western sources. See also, Maier, Romanian SR/18, 14 December 1984.

5. *Ibid.*

6. See *Financial Times*, November 17, 1985. See also Anneli Maier, "Foreign Minister Replaced, Appointed Central Committee Secretary," *Radio Free Europe Research*, Romanian SR/17, 17 December 1985.

7. An indispensable summary of the many personnel changes in the RCP is Anneli Maier, *ibid.,* Romanian SR/10, 11 September 1986. See also *Agerpres,* October 3, 1987, and *Scinteia,* October 2, 3, and 4, 1987.

8. See Paul Gafton, "Changes in the Nomenklatura," *Radio Free Europe Research,* Romanian SR/11, 15 October 1987.

9. The dismissal was announced in *Scinteia,* November 28, 1987.

10. See *ibid.,* December 17, 1987.

11. Based on biographical analyses of the RCP leadership at the judet level. Much of this information has been gleaned from the Romanian press; another indispensable tool is *Radio Free Europe Research.*

12. Analysis based on sources listed in number 11. above. See also the official announcements in *Scinteia,* December 17, 1987.

13. The appointment was announced in *Buletinul Oficial,* October 21, 1987.

14. The 1984 congress was concluded with a full membership list in *Scinteia,* November 23, 1984. For details on the tenth congress, see *Congresul al X-lea al Partidului Comunist Roman,* pp. 749–758. On the leadership cadre in 1973, see my *Modernization in Romania since World War II,* Ch. 21 (pp. 33–68).

15. For an analysis of Elena Ceausescu's rise to power, see Anneli Maier, "Elena Ceausescu Marches On and Up," *Radio Free Europe Research,* Romanian SR/17, 17 December 1985.

16. *Ibid.*

17. *Scinteia,* November 23, 1984 (on the leadership cadre at the thirteenth congress).

18. Based on *Congresul al X-lea,* and *Scinteia* for the months of November, 1974, 1979, and 1984.

19. *Ibid.*

20. *Scinteia,* November 19 and 20, 1984.

21. See also Trond Gilberg and Vernon V. Aspaturian, *The Soviet and East European Party Congresses* (prepared for the U.S. Government), esp. pp. 140–168 (Gilberg).

22. *Scinteia,* November 19, 1984.

23. These figures were provided in *ibid.,* April 3, 1985.

24. These figures were provided at a plenum of the RCP Central Committee in April 1986; see *ibid.,* April 8, 9, 10, and 11, 1986.

25. *Ibid.*

26. *Ibid.,* March 29, 1987.

27. See my "Romania's Increasing Difficulties," *Current History,* November 1984, pp. 375–389.

28. The statutes were adopted on November 22, 1984. See *Scinteia,* November 22 and 23, 1984.

29. *Ibid.*

30. In late October, Nicu Ceausescu was appointed First Secretary of the judet party in Brasov Judet (see *Buletinul Oficial,* October 21, 1987).

31. *Scinteia,* November 22 and 23, 1984.

32. *Ibid.*

33. *Ibid.*

34. The statutes were also published in the RCP theoretical journal *Munca du Partid*, December 1984, pp. 2–20.

35. Ceausescu's position on this issue is parroted by his close lieutenants; see, for example, Stefan Andrei in *Scinteia Tineretului*, January 26, 1987.

36. For a detailed discussion of these changes, see Paul Gafton, "Government Reshuffle," *Radio Free Europe Research*, Romanian SR/7, 19 April 1984 (on the changes in the Ministry of Agriculture, Ministry of Electric Power, and the State Committee for Prices). The changes in the RCP Central Committee were reported in *Agerpres*, March 21, 1984. The other changes discussed here were reported in *Scinteia*, June 17, 1984 and *Buletinul Oficial*, June 6, 1984.

37. Paul Gafton, "A Reshuffle That May Be a Purge," *Radio Free Europe Research*, Romanian SR/10, 18 July 1984.

38. *Ibid.*, Romanian SR/16, 2 November 1984.

39. These changes were reported in *Financial Times*, November 19, 1985.

40. Olteanu's dismissal was made public by *Buletinul Oficial*, December 17, 1985.

41. See Patrick Moore, "Another Personnel Shuffle," *Radio Free Europe Research*, Romanian SR/10, 11 November 1986.

42. Ceausescu announced these changes in a speech to the Supreme Council. See *Scinteia*, June 24, 1987.

43. Gainu's dismissal was announced in *Agerpres*, February 4, 1987; her appointment as first secretary of a judet party body was made in *Buletinul Oficial*, February 20, 1987. The governmental changes discussed are analyzed by Paul Gafton, *Radio Free Europe Research*, Romanian SR/11, 15 October 1987.

44. Gafton, Romanian SR/11.

45. Nicu Ceausescu's appointment was announced in *Buletinul Oficial*, October 21, 1987. Stoica was criticized by Ceausescu at the Central Committee plenum, but *Buletinul Oficial* of October 6, 1987, listed Stoica as a member of the PEC *after* the criticism was made. Two terse announcements of the plenum's start and finish were made in *Scinteia*, October 5 and 6, 1987.

46. A relatively recent analysis of this is Vladimir Tismaneanu, "Ceausescu's Socialism," *Problems of Communism*, January-February 1985, pp. 50–67.

47. This process was repeated endlessly during the preparations for the thirteenth RCP congress. For an analysis, see Gilberg and Aspaturian, *The Soviet and East European Party Congresses*, pp. 140–144 (Gilberg).

48. The faulty performance of party cadre was discussed at a plenum of the RCP Central Committee on March 28 and 29, 1988. The proceedings and decisions of the plenum were discussed in *Scinteia*, March 29 and 30 and April 1, 2, and 3, 1988.

49. A typical example of such a "working visit" was the trip undertaken by Nicolae and Elena Ceausescu to Galati judet, reported in *Scinteia Tineretului*, September 24, 1987.

50. Ceausescu continues to blame the rank and file and the RCP leadership below the pinnacle for these problems. See, for example, his speech to the RCP national conference in December 1987, in *ibid.*, December 17, 1987.

51. While exaggerated in its description of clan venality and the insecurity of honest apparatchiki, the book by Ian Mihai Pacepa (former security chief,

now in emigration in the United States) entitled *Red Horizons* (New York, NY: Regnery Gateway, 1987) illustrates this insecurity in ways that have been discussed by others as well. The effects of this on intellectuals has been described by Mihai Botez; see, for example, his interview with *L'Express*, May 28, 1987. An article in *Saptamina* by a prominent film critic refers to the problems of insecurity, censorship, and arbitrary policies in this area (*Saptamina*, February 27, 1987).

52. Such malfeasance is severely criticized by Nicolae Ceausescu and other members of the clan, but they are themselves guilty of producing the conditions that create mass corruption. For a recent statement of the General. Secretary's views, see his speech to a recent Central Committee plenum, published in *Scinteia*, March 30, 1988.

53. See my "Romania's Growing Difficulties," *Current History*, November 1984.

54. Based upon a great deal of material from official Romanian sources as well as *Radio Free Europe Research*. See also Tismaneanu, "Ceausescu's Socialism."

55. The depth of the crisis was discussed by Paul Gafton, "A Deep Disruption of the Standard of Living," *Radio Free Europe Research*, Romanian SR/4, 29 May 1987. The economic conditions have continued to worsen since then.

6

Modernization, Ceausescu-style

Nicolae Ceausescu is a communist modernizer whose policies fall squarely within the parameters of modernization policy as practiced in the Soviet Union and Eastern Europe since the establishment of communist regimes there. In fact, the Romanian leader has continued the policies of Stalinist modernization beyond the Soviets themselves, and he has maintained his commitment to such policies at a time when others have abandoned them, out of necessity or conviction. Romania, therefore, once again, emerges as the maverick in Eastern Europe in the 1980s and most likely beyond our decade.

Modernization Through Industrialization

Since the inception of the five year plans in the Soviet Union in the late 1920s, communist modernizers have emphasized industrialization as the key to economic development. This was, indeed, a natural decision in a country which was severely underdeveloped in this field, and it was also good Marxism in the sense that Marx emphasized the industrial mode of production as an indispensable ingredient of the modern society, and the industrial proletariat as the primary revolutionary force. It may be argued (and a number of scholars and participants in the process have so argued) that the *specific* forms of industrialization adopted by Stalin were not necessarily the best, or even the most "Marxist."[1] Be that as it may, the fact remains that Stalinist industrialization became the norm for all of the successors in Eastern Europe (and often in other parts of the world as well). And when the communists came to power in Romania in August 1944 as part of a coalition, the stage was set for such an industrialization drive once they had consolidated their power. That consolidation was completed in 1947 with the abdication of the King and the establishment of a republic. Beginning in 1947/1948, the RCP launched a massive industrialization drive. It is still underway, remarkably unchanged for decades.

Romania was indeed well suited to Stalinist modernization through industrialization. In 1947 it was still basically an agrarian society with some pockets of industrial development in and around the major cities, and particularly in Transylvania. There was an ample supply of labor in the countryside which could be quickly mobilized. Romania had extensive resources of oil, natural gas, minerals, timber, and other raw materials necessary for industrial development. There already was an industrial base in the oil industry, which was the largest in Europe outside the Soviet Union. Land was plentiful and provided ample opportunities for the construction of factories, rail lines, and other elements of the infrastructure needed for industrial expansion. In many ways, Romania in 1947 resembled the Soviet Union in the late 1920s in terms of socio-economic and demographic characteristics.[2]

The Romanian model of industrialization closely followed the Soviet experience. Economists and development analysts call this approach "extensive industrialization." Basically, the regime chose to build new factories, man them with peasant labor, and move ahead with maximum speed, regardless of cost in human or economic terms. The results of such an industrialization process were dramatic and quick to materialize. Factories sprang up everywhere, hundreds of thousands of individuals left the village for a place to live in the burgeoning cities, while many others remained in the village but commuted to the plants, thus taxing an already strained transportation system. New construction abounded throughout the country. The factories hastily built and put into operation were often shoddily made, their production technology wasteful and polluting, and the infrastructural support of housing, roads, sanitary facilities, and schools and hospitals lagged far behind. The quality of life in these industrial cities was bleak, with hard work, lines for food and services, and the unremitting pressures of political control against the backdrop of the chimneys and smokestacks belching forth black, acrid smoke from the blast furnaces and the factories working day and night.[3]

The Romanian emphasis on extensive industrialization had another Stalinist feature which it has retained to this day: It emphasized the heavy and extractive industries of steel, machine building, mining and railroad construction, again in typical Stalinist fashion. The consumer goods industries remained far behind, and services of all kinds were classified as unproductive and therefore downgraded. The ethos of the village, so important for the survival of the Romanian nation in times of foreign occupation and assimilationist pressures, was shunted aside by a regime bent upon enforcing its own ethos, that of Marx and urbanization. The frantic pace with which the industrialization program was instituted closely resembled the "storming" of the 1930s in the

TABLE 6.1   The Development of Industrial Production in Romania, 1938-1955
(1938 = 100)

	1938	1948	1950	1955
All industry	100	85	147	299
Group A	100	92	167	363
Group B	100	79	129	240
Electrical and Thermal Energy	100	156	248	576
Coal	100	87	137	207
Oil	100	72	87	171
Mining	100	64	81	172
Machine building	---	---	100	283
Metals production	---	---	100	307
Chemical industry	100	100	168	494
Textile industry	100	91	172	299
Food industry	100	62	107	181
Steel (tons)	132,681	186,069	319,766	569,518
Iron (tons)	283,982	353,374	554,580	766,165

Source: Republica Populara Romina, Directiunea Centrala de Statistica,
Anuarul Statistic al R.P.R. 1957 (Bucharest: Editura Stintifica, 1957),
pp. 79, 83.

Soviet Union, and the costs were heavy, albeit small in comparison with the bloodbath that engulfed the first socialist state during the great purges of that crucial decade.[4]

It may be debated whether the Romanian leadership under Ana Pauker merely mimicked the Soviet approach or actually believed in the virtues of this method of fundamental societal transformation. Perhaps both factors were present; after all, Pauker was a Muscovite who had spent many years in the Soviet Union and had become steeped in Stalinist methods and outlooks. At the same time, there was general agreement in the political elite (extending beyond the communists) that Romanian underdevelopment was unacceptable and must be erased in the shortest possible time. No matter what the real motivations, the policies that were implemented were Stalinist in form, content, speed, and thoroughness. Table 6.1 illustrates the development of industrial production up to the end of the Stalin era (which, in fact, has extended to the present time in Romania in terms of economic policy). Based on official Romanian statistics, the table shows dramatic increases in the level of industrial production for the first eight years of communist industrialization. A caveat is in order when it comes to Romanian statistics; they are frequently erroneous in some manner, at times because of inaccurate computations, but often (and increasingly as we move through the Ceausescu era) containing conscious biases. Still, there can be no doubt that the gains in this period were impressive. The figures in this table

TABLE 6.2   The Development of Industrial Production in Romania, 1955–1965
             (1950 = 100)

	1950	1960	1965
Total industrial production	202	340	649
Group A	217	397	823
Group B	185	277	457
Agricultural production	162	171	193
Trade and commerce	184	260	485
Real income	125	185	226

Source: Republica Socialista Romania, Directia Centrala de Statistica,
Anuarul Statistic al Republicii Socialiste Romania 1970, (Bucharest: 1970),
p. 104.

indeed show the benefits of Stalinist modernization policies upon under-developed countries such as Romania.

The end of Stalinism in the Soviet Union did not produce similar developments in Romania, at least in the field of industrial policy. There was a change in leadership, to be sure; Pauker was purged and succeeded by Gheorghe Gheorghiu-Dej, who was a "local" and not a "Muscovite," having spent the war years and part of the 1930s in Romanian jails. But the new leader was as much a Stalinist in economic policy as Pauker had been. Therefore, the industrialization process continued unabated, and it continued to emphasize the heavy and extractive industries, while all other industrial activity and the service sector continued to fall behind the pace of development. Table 6.2 shows this conclusively for the period up to Gheorghiu-Dej's death in 1965.

The death of Gheorghe Gheorghiu-Dej set the stage for the advent to power of Nicolae Ceausescu and the implementation of the peculiar, idiosyncratic notions of development harbored by the General Secretary and discussed in some detail above. In the field of industrial policy, however, the new leader continued the trends which had been established as early as 1947, emphasizing the further (and rapid) development of the heavy and extractive industries. Gradually, as the Ceausescu era wore on, the number and range of products were enlarged, and there is indeed some truth to the claims by the Ceausescus that literally hundreds of new products were developed in Romanian industry. At the same time, the investment program continued unabated, producing more and more factories in older cities and also developing new cities in many areas of the country. Extensive industrialization remained the main focus of the Ceausescu regime. Table 6.3 shows this development quite clearly.

TABLE 6.3   The Development of Industry in Romania, 1965-1985
            (1938 = 100)

	1965	1975	1980	1984
Total industry	957	31 times	48 times	56 times
Group A	14 times	48 times	78 times	91 times
Group B	591	16 times	23 times	26 times
Coal	400	851	11 times	13 times
Oil and gasoline	333	512	616	631
Machine building, metal working	23 times	109 times	198 times	240 times
Textiles	663	20 times	33 times	36 times
Food stuffs	382	748	10 times	11 times

Source: Republica Socialista Romania, Directia Centrala de Statistica,
Anuarul Statistic al Republicii Socialiste Romania, 1985, (Bucharest: 1985),
p. 78.

The growth rates of Romanian industry were indeed impressive, even if some of the figures produced may have been inflated. This was so even after the industrialization program had produced a sizeable base, thus belying the notion that extremely high growth rates are only possible if one starts from a low level of development. In the Romanian case, the growth rates were maintained through very high levels of investment and a correspondingly low level of growth in consumption. In fact, there were times during the Ceausescu era when consumption actually declined; this has especially been the case during the 1980s, when the accumulated problems of three decades of extensive industrialization finally caught up with the economy. Table 6.4 shows the level of investment throughout the socialist period, while Table 6.5 examines the rate of increase of the national income as claimed by official Romanian statistics.

The driving force of the industrialization program carried everything before it during the Ceausescu era, forcing all other economic activity to conform to the needs of industry. In contradistinction to the other systems of Eastern Europe, Romania continued to push for further heavy industrialization beyond the limits that could reasonably be expected and beyond the area of meaningful return. Today, the massive industrialization program has produced an infrastructure that produces goods no longer needed, particularly in the West. Despite such evidence, the program continues, as if it had taken on a life of its own. Perhaps it has in the mind of Nicolae Ceausescu and the other members of the clan.[5]

A prolonged program of extensive industrialization depends for its success upon the continued availability of plentiful fuels, raw materials, and manpower. These ingredients are unfortunately no longer available

TABLE 6.4 Investment in Romania under Communist Rule

(a) 1950-1956 (in millions of lei at 1955 prices)

	1950	1951	1952	1953	1954	1955	1956
Total investments	5649.7	7952.1	10,586.2	13,463.4	11,874.6	13,178.1	14,784.3
Thereof: Productive capacity	4870.7	6910.8	9266.5	11,566.2	10,054.8	11,157.2	12,118.4
(Total and % of total)	86.2%	86.9%	87.5%	85.9%	84.7%	84.0%	82.0%

In the sum of 5649.7 million lei in 1950, 50.5% went for construction, 36.0% machinery and instruments, 8.6% drilling; by 1956 these figures were 54.4%, 30.2%, and 7.1% respectively.
(Source: Anuarul Statistic al R.P.R. 1957, p. 147).

(b) 1956-1965 (in millions of lei at 1959 prices)

	1955	1960	1965
Total investments	14,585	27,665	47,177

(Source: Republica Socialista Romania, Directia Centrala de Statistica, Anuarul Statistic al Republicii Socialiste Romania 1981 (Bucharest, 1981), p. 386).

In 1955, 85.5% of investments went into material production; in 1960 it was 83.5%, and in 1965, 86.2%. In 1955, 52.3% of all investments went for construction, 32.0% for machinery and equipment, 9.2% for geological exploration, and 7.2% for drilling. In 1960, the figures were 48.1%, 36.2%, 5.8%, and 4.7% respectively, and in 1965 the figures were 45.5%, 39.4%, 4.6%, and 3.9%.
(Source: Republica Socialista Romania, Directia Centrala de Statistica, _Anuarul Statistic al Republicii Socialiste Romania, 1970_ (Bucharest, 1970), p. 452).

(c) 1965-1975 (in millions of lei at 1963 prices)

	1965	1975
Total investments	47,014	137,731

(Source: _Anuarul Statistic 1985_, p. 198).

Of the total of 47,014 million lei invested in 1965, 49.8% went to construction, 34.9% to equipment, and 5.5% to drilling and exploration. In 1975, the proportion of these categories were 41.9%, 47.9%, and 2.5%
(Source: _Anuarul Statistic 1985_, p. 199).

(d) 1975-1980 (in millions of lei at 1977 prices)

	1975	1980
Total investments	139,674	210,451

(Source: _Anuarul Statistic 1985_, p. 198).

In 1975, 47.1% went to construction, 42.9% to equipment, and 2.4% to geological exploration. In 1980, the figures were 41.0%, 49.3%, and 2.0%.
(Source: _Anuarul Statistic 1985_, p. 199).

(continues)

TABLE 6.4 (continued)

(e) 1980-1981 (in millions of lei at 1981 prices)

	1980	1981
Total investments	223,877	207,954

(Source: Anuarul Statistic 1985, p. 198).

In 1981, 43.1% of all investments went for construction, 45.7% for equipment, and 2.7% for geological exploration.
(Source: Anuarul Statistic 1985, p. 199).

(f) 1982-1984 (in millions of lei at "current prices")

	1982	1983	1984
Total investments	216,354	230,743	244,714

(Source: Anuarul Statistic 1985, p. 198).

In 1982, 45.2% went for construction, 43.2% for equipment, and 3.2% for geological exploration. Corresponding figures for 1983 were 47.2%, 42.0%, and 2.6%; for 1984 it was 46.3%, 42.8%, and 2.9%.
(Source: Anuarul Statistic 1985, p. 199).

TABLE 6.5 Officially Claimed National Income per Capita, 1950-1985 (1900 = 100)

	1955	1960	1965	1970	1975	1980	1984
National income per capita	181	238	354	482	784	11 times	12 times

(Percent increase per year during the period 1951-1984 = 7.6)

Source: Anuarul Statistic 1985, p. 42.

in the same amounts and at the same price; the oil crisis of the 1970s demonstrated this with great clarity to everybody, including the Romanians, but the latter seem not to have learned the lessons, at least not adequately. By the end of the decade, however, Bucharest was forced to take drastic measures to deal with severe shortages of fuels and raw materials. As usual, the draconian measures that were undertaken were at the expense of the average citizen. Thus, it was he or she who must suffer the blackouts and the reduction of electrical power, while industry received its quota and wasted it, as usual. It was also the average car owner who suffered gasoline lines and gas free days; industry and official vehicles, on the other hand, had enough fuels to waste in their customary manner.[6] Throughout the entire period, little was done to improve the service industry, even though it was quite clear that future economic expansion would come from intensive development (i.e. each worker produces more) and that this would require goods, services, and other incentives for the average worker. As shown by Table 6.6, the service industries, particularly retail trade, remained woefully inadequate.

Towards the end of the 1980s, then, Romania finds itself saddled with a large but decaying industrial plant which is inefficient and noncompetitive, producing low quality goods that cannot be sold on the open market except by means of dumping or special trade arrangements. The work force cannot produce more intensively because of old-fashioned machinery and because of the lack of incentives. At the same time, economic performance *must* improve, or the system will clearly stagnate and deteriorate even further. This is a problem of major magnitude for all of the communist systems of Eastern Europe and the Soviet Union, and Romania may be the worst case, because its service industries are among the most inadequate in the region, and the capabilities of the consumer goods industries are primarily oriented towards export. The economic crisis besetting this unfortunate country, therefore, is not temporary, but permanent, not accidental, but systemic. Only systemic change can solve it.[7]

TABLE 6.6 Retail Trade and Service Establishments, 1955-1984

	1955	1960	1965	1975	1980	1984
Stores (all kinds)	33,393	36,609	38,920	45,936	49,526	52,014
Food stores:	7,812	10,361	12,562	16,240	17,588	17,630
Thereof:						
meat and fish	1,028	1,508	1,421	1,423	1,499	1,419
bread	1,980	2,076	2,621	2,636	2,679	2,488
fruits and vegetables	875	1,161	1,709	3,118	2,998	3,161
Other stores:	11,770	14,224	14,091	18,225	20,897	23,463
Thereof:						
textiles and shoes	1,849	2,716	3,278	5,859	6,957	8,071
metals, chemicals	1,059	1,273	1,557	2,822	3,417	4,313
toys and children's						
equipment	3,812	3,437	2,834	2,575	2,497	2,433
furniture	193	262	350	548	682	844
cosmetics	76	141	182	210	288	398
books and papers	1,326	988	1,238	1,789	2,014	2,153
petroleum products	653	731	883	831	811	773
gasoline stations	425	408	382	522	513	469
construction materials	276	385	406	482	684	649
department stores	604	758	1,224	2,475	2,550	2,248
mixed stores	13,207	11,266	11,043	8,996	8,491	8,673
restaurants	1,190	816	950	2,673	3,410	3,793
buffets, bars	6,070	7,017	7,774	8,506	9,326	10,094
cafeterias	674	785	1,195	3,071	3,558	3,930

Sources: For 1960-1984, Anuarul Statistic 1985, p. 249; Anuarul Statistic 1970, p. 534 (for 1955).

Technological Innovation

Communist rulers are emphatic about the need to acquire and utilize the newest technological innovations, and Ceausescu and his predecessors are no exception. Throughout the entire history of communist-ruled Romania the leadership has conducted a policy of enhancing the domestic capacity in this area and also acquiring foreign technology through barter, transfer, or espionage. The emphasis on the individual ingredients of this policy changed over time, but the mix was always there.

During the Stalin era and into the late 1950s, Romania relied heavily on Soviet technology and various forms of assistance provided by Moscow. Much of the early industrial plant of Romania was provided by the Soviets, who also skimmed off profits and production through the mechanism of the joint companies, the sovroms. Towards the end of the decade, greater Romanian autonomy was made possible by the removal of Soviet troops, and gradually, Bucharest's reliance on the eastern neighbor subsided. Economic (and thus also technological) nationalism began to appear in a number of decisions about plant locations, product mix, and the machinery to be utilized in the production process. There was more emphasis on autarky, and the beginnings of a focus on more economic and technological cooperation with the West. The process of removing Soviet tutelage came to a climax in April 1963, when the Romanians rejected Khrushchev's ideas about a division of labor inside the Comecon that would have left Romania with primarily agricultural responsibilities. The so-called "declaration of independence" of April 1963 set the stage for a period of economic orientation towards the West, in which Romania would export various goods and services to the capitalists in return for advanced technology.[8]

The emphasis on economic autonomy took Romanian foreign trade in the direction of Western Europe, the United States, and Canada, where markets were established for Romanian foodstuffs, textiles, and raw materials, while technology was imported on a massive scale. Furthermore, there was considerable emphasis on various forms of joint ventures which would provide Western capital and technology, matched with Romanian facilities and manpower, occasionally also marketing of the finished product in areas of the world not easily available to Western firms, especially in Africa and Asia. This phase lasted until the middle of the 1970s.[9]

At some point in the middle years of the previous decade, decisions were made in Bucharest to reduce the dependence on the West that had developed during a decade of active trading and technology importation. At the same time, it was becoming more and more clear to Western firms and banks that ventures in Romania were not overly profitable because of the low level of worker productivity and the inefficiency (sometimes venality) of the bureaucracy. This mutual cooling off of Romania's economic relations with the West resulted in drastic reductions of technology import, inadequate servicing of machinery already acquired, and a considerable slowing down of the diffusion of such technology throughout the Romanian economic system. The regime became obsessed with the drastic and rapid reduction of the foreign debt and a corresponding increase in the development of domestic technology. The regime cut off much of the academic exchange that had existed with the West and launched a number of projects at home that were designed to produce computers, advanced electronic machinery, robots, and various other devices that could sustain the drive from the industrial to the technological era. Simultaneously, Romanian espionage abroad was stepped up, and Bucharest became an active partner in the sharing of intelligence inside the Soviet alliance system.[10]

The result of these developments was a further reduction in the capabilities of the Romanian economy and thus a step backwards in the quest for intensive development. As Ceausescu's megalomania became further established, he became excessively sensitive to criticism from the outside world and further tightened the control over information, thus practically eliminating Romania's participation in the international exchange of ideas so vital to the enhancement of technology. The General Secretary began to extol the virtues of manual labor rather than machinery, and even discussed the advantages of horses over tractors in the agricultural sector.[11] By the time of this writing, the RCP leadership has voluntarily renounced "most favored nation" status in the United States because of Washington's criticism of its human rights record. This means both significant losses in export revenue and a further reduction of technology transfer. Autarky has reached its final, irrational, peak.[12]

The turning inward that occurred in Romania during the second half of the 1970s continued with accelerated tempo during this decade in all areas of activity, with the question of technological autarky representing the most visible element. At the present time there is no sign that the Ceausescu clan will reverse this trend; on the other hand, there are plenty of indications that it will be further accelerated before it has run its course. These developments are profoundly disturbing to the scientific and technological intelligentsia in Romania, whose members feel a kinship with the rest of the world in this field. During the last few years, several of them have come forward with criticism of regime policies, suggesting that the RCP is following a policy that will lead to the utter isolation of Romania from the world community. One such individual, Mihai Botez, has been particularly outspoken, and he has paid for this by experiencing various forms of discrimination (such as removal of all computer facilities from his jurisdiction). Botez was recently transferred from Bucharest to Tulcea in the Danube Delta—hardly a place for a futurologist and technical expert. Botez is merely the best known example of a tendency found throughout the entire country during the zenith of the Ceausescu epoch.[13]

Even some elements of the nomenklatura have begun to express concern over the deepening isolation of Romania from the world scientific community. One of the former bright stars of the regime, Ion Iliescu, recently spoke out in a remarkably candid piece in an established journal. Iliescu expresses the same concerns as Botez, but expands on them to include the rest of society, not merely the technical and scientific intelligentsia. According to Iliescu, present tendencies in decision-making remove a massive number of talented individuals from the pool of contributors to the well-being of society, thus reducing or eliminating the chances that may still exist for renewal and better performance. Iliescu's piece, which is a thinly disguised attack on rule by the clan, suggests more widespread concern among elements of the apparat itself; the publication of the piece in a journal of considerable stature indicates an element of "protection" for Iliescu in high places. It is interesting in this context to mention rumors that now make the rounds in Bucharest that Iliescu is Gorbachev's favorite candidate for Romanian perestroika and glasnost. If such is the case, Iliescu's survival, even in the reduced state in which he has found himself since the late 1970s, will depend upon the extent of his protection.[14]

Agricultural Policy

The development of heavy industry represented only one of the main elements of communist modernization in Romania as well as in the rest of the communist world. An indispensable companion policy was collectivization of agriculture, which was carried to varying degrees of completion throughout the entire region. In Romania, the regime proudly proclaimed in 1962 that the country was fully collectivized, with the exception of a few areas in the mountains, where topography and settlement patterns made such a policy unenforceable.[15] The achievement of full collectivization may be considered a watershed for a number of reasons, especially in terms of political and social results, but it did not in itself represent a clear change in *policy*. In fact, the completion of collectivization was a logical result of policies underway since 1947, and these policies continued unabated after the 1962 announcement as well.

The main aspects of this policy are underinvestment, low priority for the training of agricultural personnel and the provision of machinery and equipment, the conscious creation of a political and societal ethos that emphasizes urbanization and industrialization, thereby denigrating the agricultural sector and rural life to a secondary and less important position in the collective psyche of the new order, and, finally, the utilization of the rural manpower pool as a provider of labor for the high priority areas of economic development, such as industrialization. Tables 6.7, 6.8, 6.9, and 6.10 illustrate these aspects of conscious policy and also their intended and unintended consequences, especially the poor record of agricultural production that has beset this erstwhile "breadbasket of Europe" for four decades.

These tables show a pattern that is familiar throughout the entire region of Eastern Europe and is only remarkable in Romania because of the great agricultural resources possessed by that country. Underinvestment in agriculture has been dramatic, with the predictable result of lowering production, or at least experiencing production increases that are totally inadequate for the population increase and the consumption patterns which have developed in Romania during the last two decades. Throughout this period of time the modernization process has changed the way in which people structure their diet, with a significant higher intake of meats and vegetables. The regime itself has assiduously promoted the notion that the economic plans of the system have been successful,

TABLE 6.7 Investments in Agriculture, 1950–1985 (industrial investment in
           parenthesis next to agricultural figures)

(a) 1951–1965 (in 1959 prices) (millions of lei)

1951–1955	1956–1960	1961–1965
6,436 (33,292)	19,430 (44,992	37,462 (92,811)

(b) 1966–1975 (in 1963 prices) (millions of lei)

1966–1970	1971–1975
51,555 (165,388)	76,966 (277,243)

(c) 1976–1980 (in 1977 prices) (millions of lei)

1976–1980
124,899 (458,566)

(d) 1981–1984 ("current" prices) (millions of lei)

1981	1982	1983	1984
32,090 (105,490)	32,818 (101,545)	36,627 (111,684)	40,039 (124,094)

Source: Anuarul Statistic 1985, pp. 204–205.

TABLE 6.8   Urbanization in Romania, 1930–1985

Date	Total population	Cities and towns	Suburbs	Rural Communes
12/29/1930	100.0%	20.1%	1.3%	78.6%
01/25/1948	100.0%	22.0%	1.4%	76.6%
02/21/1956	100.0%	27.1%	4.2%	68.7%
07/01/1960	100.0%	27.8%	4.3%	67.9%
07/01/1965	100.0%	29.8%	3.9%	66.3%
03/15/1966	100.0%	32.6%	5.7%	61.7%
07/01/1970	100.0%	36.9%	3.9%	57.2%
07/01/1975	100.0%	39.2%	4.0%	56.8%
01/05/1977	100.0%	43.6%	3.9%	52.5%
07/01/1980	100.0%	45.8%	3.8%	50.4%
07/01/1981	100.0%	46.9%	3.2%	49.9%
07/01/1982	100.0%	48.4%	3.1%	48.5%
07/01/1983	100.0%	49.0%	3.1%	47.9%
07/01/1984	100.0%	47.2%	3.1%	47.7%

(1930, 1948, 1956, 1966, and 1977 were official census years)

Source: Anuarul Statistic 1985, p. 12.

TABLE 6.9 Rural Occupation Structure and Income, 1900–1985

	1900	1965	1975	1980	1984
1. Work force in agriculture (percent of total)	74.1%	56.5%	37.8%	29.4%	28.9%
2. Women in agriculture (percent of total)				16.1%	19.9%
3. Income per worker:					
(a) agriculture (lei/month)	243	939	1,531	2,160	2,663
(b) industry (lei/month)	341	1,066	1,602	2,307	2,812
(c) construction	383	1,081	1,838	2,494	3,135
4. Agriculture specialists (total)		24,148	37,502	47,322	58,564

(1975: total agriculture 390,800; women 58,800)
(1965: total agriculture 329,800; women 35,800)

Sources: Anuarul Statistic 1985, pp. 60–68, 194; Anuarul Statistic 1981, p. 131; Anuarul Statistic 1976, p. 75; Anuarul Statistic 1966, p. 126.

and thus the population would have a more "scientific" diet. It is only during the last five years or so that Nicolae Ceausescu has taken it upon himself to proclaim a "new" scientific "diet" that includes a significantly reduced consumption of all kinds of foodstuffs which are in short supply in contemporary Romania. This new diet has reduced meat consumption to 8.5 kilograms per year per person (based on information from Brasov). Actually, there was no meat in Brasov in January, March, and July of 1987. The "scientific" diet is, of course, nothing but a fig leaf for the dismal failures of the Romanian agricultural sector, and this failure is directly attributable to faulty policies on the part of the clan itself.[16]

Table 6.11 illustrates the change in the diet of the Romanian population during the period 1960–1975. Table 6.11 shows the changes in that consumption pattern for the 1960s and 1970s, and it also compares this diet to other East European countries. Table 6.12 is the "scientific" diet as established by Ceausescu in November 1985. The statistical evidence produced above shows an economic sector in severe crisis, but the picture is considerably worse. The recorded production increases are usually based on grain in the fields, fruit on the trees, meat on the hoof, an so on; nothing is said about the actual harvest in the grain elevators, the fruits and vegetables available in the stores and the markets, and the meat available to the consumer. In actual fact, much is lost through slow or inadequate harvesting, spoilage, slow transportation to markets, and siphoning off of foodstuffs by middlemen. The statistics

TABLE 6.10 Agricultural Production, 1950-1985 (1938 = 100)

	1950	1955	1960	1965	1970	1975	1980	1984
(A) Total production	74	120	126	143	157	214	258	307
1. Thereof:								
vegetable	65	119	118	133	136	181	209	271
animal	94	123	145	163	201	287	365	385
2. State farms	.							
(a) Number of workers	161,800	155,200	224,000	301,300	292,300	251,700	199,800	337,400
(b) Cattle	60,500	84,700	236,300	515,300	631,000	807,100	905,300	957,300
(c) Cereals (thousand tons)	205.9	549.1	1,526.1	3,009.6	2,455.2	3,381.5	4,207.0	4,755.0
(d) Meat (thousand tons)			127	227	364	561	731	756

	1962	1965	1970	1975	1980	1984
(B) Collective farms						
1. Number of farmers	5,398,000	4,680,000	4,626,000	4,419,000	4,011,000	3,745,000
2. Cattle	1,577,200	1,955,800	2,147,800	2,582,400	2,973,100	3,099,800
3. Cereals (thousand tons)	6,721.0	8,387.7	6,746.3	9,835.9	12,947.4	14,226.5
4. Meat (thousand tons)	177	257	313	515	645	525

Source: Anuarul Statistic 1985, pp. 142-145; Anuarul Statistic 1964, pp. 238-239.

TABLE 6.11 Consumption Patterns of the East European Countries, 1960-1975
(per capita consumption)

	1961-1963	1972-1974
Albania		
Calories	2,340	2,503
Proteins	70.1	71.8
Fats	45.8	48.2
Bulgaria		
Calories	3,181	3,461
Proteins	94.9	101.1
Fats	77.5	97.5
Czechoslovakia		
Calories	3,371	3,489
Proteins	90.9	96.5
Fats	111.6	125.6
GDR		
Calories	3,217	3,463
Proteins	83.5	94.7
Fats	133.9	144.0
Hungary		
Calories	3,243	3,548
Proteins	82.7	89.0
Fats	110.4	135.6
Poland		
Calories	3,234	3,474
Proteins	97.5	104.4
Fats	89.3	110.5
Romania		
Calories	2,878	3,262
Proteins	84.9	96.7
Fats	65.8	82.8
Yugoslavia		
Calories	3,131	3,380
Proteins	92.0	94.3
Fats	66.7	92.3

Source: Paul F. Shoup, The East European and Soviet Data Handbook (New York: Columbia University Press, 1981), pp. 415-417.

also say nothing about quality. The fact of the matter is that the high quality produce and meat go for export, to eliminate the foreign debt, and second and third class produce is made available to the Romanian consumer in ever dwindling quantities. Thus, statistics are deceptive. Even the casual traveler in Romania can observe the long lines in front of bread and milk stores. The lesson is very clear: There is still milk, there is still bread, albeit in short supply, but still enough to warrant a visit (often of hours and hours duration) to the lines. There is virtually no purpose in looking for meat, however, so nobody wastes time this way. Meat is only obtainable through connections and bakshish.[17]

The widespread corruption surrounding the agricultural sector and the provision of foodstuffs to the population is amply documented by frequent and infuriated statements made by the RCP leader about the

TABLE 6.12   The Romanian "Scientific" Diet, 1985/86*

Commodity	Allowed Consumption/Year/Person
Meat and fish	54.88 kg
Margarine	1.10 kg
Edible oil	9.60 kg
Sugar	14.80 kg
Wheat and flour	114.50 kg
Potatoes	45.30 kg
Fruits and grapes	20.00 kg
Eggs	114 pieces

*Announced by Nicolae Ceausescu, in <u>Scinteia</u>, November 17, 1985. The RCP leader also announced that every Romanian is "entitled" to 1.1 kg of soap and 3.5 kg of detergent. See also Paul Gafton, "Romanian Food and Consumer Goods Program," <u>Radio Free Europe Research</u>, Romanian SR/1, 10 January 1986.

subject. Ceausescu has made it clear that the malfeasance of officials is considered the main reason for the admittedly serious situation in this sector. This problem has provided the General Secretary with ammunition and necessary leverage against parts of the nomenklatura, and he has used it to its fullest extent during the years of the deepening crisis by firing officials, recycling personnel, and hammering home his message on every conceivable occasion. The RCP leader has *not* been willing to accept the blame for the agricultural crisis, even though it is clear to every outside observer that *he* really is the culprit through his policy of two decades. Few failures can be expected to enrage the citizenry more than the lack of basic staples as well as the more advanced products of modern agriculture. In some other states, notably Poland, such scarcities have produced uprisings that shook the system itself and forced the recycling of political elites. So far in Romania the reaction has been cynicism, corruption, and occasional grumbling in the spirit of "every man for himself." But recent events, such as the massive demonstrations in Brasov last fall, show that even in Romania, abysmal failure in such a vital area as agriculture may trigger more forceful reactions. It is likely that there will be more such events in the future because the regime's policies continue unchanged—a sure recipe for further failures.[18]

The Provision of Services

All communist systems suffer from underinvestment and faulty performance in the field of services to the population. This phenomenon is a direct result of Marxist-Leninist ideology, which considers such activities unproductive and therefore unworthy of priority by regimes bent on industrialization. The retail trade network is woefully inadequate; goods are displayed in an unimaginative fashion, the system of purchasing goods is a nightmare, as experienced by any traveler to these countries. Furthermore, services such as dry cleaning, laundry, shoe repair, plumbing and electrical work are inadequate for the burgeoning city population and the enhanced expectations that have come with decades of rhetoric about the improved quality of life under socialism. There is now a clear recognition of these inadequacies throughout the region, especially as the regimes begin their quest for intensive economic development, perestroika, and glasnost in their local manifestations. A number of countries have taken serious steps to rectify the worst deficiencies, with Hungary leading the pack, but with all of the others following suit— all, that is, with the exception of Romania.[19]

The provision of retail trade and various other services is also abysmal in Romania, and it is declining, by private account and by the admission of the authorities. The lack of goods in the stores reduces any incentive for common courtesy among the sales help; the downtrodden masses waiting in despair for a loaf of bread or some wrinkled apples are hardly in a position to argue about surly sales personnel. The scarcity of skilled handicraft people of all kinds produces a similar kind of market in this sector. Only by offering something unusual, such as Western cigarettes, meat, or possibly "personal services" or large bribes, can the consumer hope to gain access to these small potentates who dispense with their services in a haughty manner commensurate with their scarcity. And even after the search for such service personnel has been crowned with success, and the "master craftsman" appears, his work is likely to be shoddy, with inferior material and workmanship. The Romanian press abounds with letters to the editor deploring such conditions, voicing both despair and outrage. Investigations and occasional firings occur, but the problem is simply one of market conditions, supply and demand, even in a tightly controlled system such as Romania.[20]

The woes described above are familiar ones in communist-ruled systems, although Romania represents an aggravated case. More serious are the deficiencies that pertain to this unfortunate country alone, because they are clearly the product of false policies on the part of the clan and the General Secretary, and as such they cannot be remedied without the removal of both of these preconditions. Particularly serious are the problems in the health and social sector. Here, Romania has taken a gigantic step backwards; the population is now experiencing conditions that are similar to those of wartime. Let us be specific:

The RCP, like all other communist rulers, emphasized early on the need for a significant strengthening of the health sector. This was particularly important in Romania, which had inadequate hospital facilities

TABLE 6.13   Hospital Beds in Romania, 1950-1985

	1950	1965	1975	1980	1985
Total number	69,221	144,054	196,236	208,213	211,842
Thereof in:					
Hospitals	53,889	114,338	174,696	194,845	201,263
Sanitoria	8,908	15,455	10,810	6,520	5,550
Birth clinics	4,873	8,927	7,307	4,602	3,168
Beds per 1000 inhabitants	4.2	7.6	9.2	9.4	9.4

Source: Anuarul Statistic 1985, p. 321.

and clinic space in the cities and only rudimentary health care in the countryside. A massive program of hospital construction was started, and the number of beds in health care facilities increased dramatically, as illustrated by Table 6.13. There was also considerable emphasis on training doctors and other medical personnel, as evidenced by Table 6.14. There was, furthermore, a concerted effort to construct and staff sanatoria, rest homes, and similar facilities throughout the country. Thus, by the beginning of the 1980s, Romania was relatively well-equipped in the health sector, at least in times of quantitative indices.[21] The decline has been precipitous, however, and it now appears that this basic sector is in deep trouble. Examples abound:

Most Romanian hospitals now operate on curtailed hours because of a lack of electricity and other utilities as well as a severe shortage of basic equipment, even bandages. Rooms are inadequately heated, and, since entire sections are closed down, the remaining wings are over-crowded in the extreme. Hygiene is deficient, the personnel are overworked and surly, and the training of doctors has declined considerably. Medicines are in short supply. There is a tendency towards more bribe taking than usual. Lest this sounds like an anti-Romanian diatribe, it should be noted that this summary is made on the basis of documented cases reported in the Romanian press. One can only assume that the reports merely represent the tip of the iceberg.[22]

The media reports do not supply enough evidence about the effects of these deficiencies to make generalizations possible, but, over a period of time such problems clearly have the potential of reducing life ex-pectancy, increase infant mortality, and otherwise impairing the health standards of large numbers of individuals. It is perhaps symptomatic that few systematic health statistics have been published in Romania in a long time.

Housing is another area that has been of concern to the Romanian leadership, again following the general pattern of the rest of Eastern

TABLE 6.14 Medical Education in Romania, 1950–1985

	1950/51	1955/56	1960/61	1965/66	1970/71	1975/76	1980/81	1984/85
1. Registered students			7,825	9,345	9,898	17,008	23,381	19,953
2. Graduates			1,786	1,473	1,569	1,978	3,822	3,722

Source: Anuarul Statistic 1985, pp. 302–304.

TABLE 6.15   Housing Construction in Romania, 1950–1985

Date	Number of Dwellings	Size (m^2)
1951–1955	433,061	
1956–1960	860,649	
1961–1965	905,624	
1966–1970	647,668	40,332
1971–1975	751,896	49,755
1976–1980	840,644	62,367
1981	161,391	12,442
1982	161,213	12,689
1983	146,615	11,502
1984	131,901	10,420

Source: Anuarul Statistic 1985, p. 230.

Europe. The housing shortages experienced by all East European cities are directly related to the massive industrialization and urbanization process undertaken by the communists from the beginning of the Stalinist era (1947–1948). To this day the massive building programs that have been undertaken all over this region have failed to catch up with demand, and Romania is no exception. Despite this deficiency, quantitative achievements have been impressive, as illustrated by Table 6.15. During the 1980s, the structural deficiencies of this housing program began to make themselves felt on a massive scale. The Romanians built fast and shoddily during previous decades, and this low quality construction is now falling apart all over the country. Furthermore, the quality of materials and workmanship utilized in the 1980s ensures the erection of instant slums, buildings that are crumbling even before the scaffolding is removed, plumbing that is not affixed to pipes, electrical wires that lead to nowhere or to hazardous conditions, plaster that falls off the walls and ceilings in huge chunks, etc. The litany is long and sad, and again, it comes from official Romanian sources, the press, and the other news media. There can be little doubt that the quality of life in this sector, too, has declined precipitously during this decade.[23]

The housing situation in Bucharest is now severely aggravated by the demolition of a substantial part of the downtown area and the construction of massive new public buildings in their place. The hastily erected apartments for those removed from the center of the city are of unusually low quality and represent a significant dislocation for the individuals involved. The artistic and cultural lessons resulting from the demolition cannot be measured. Even Mikhail Gorbachev pleaded for the preservation of historic Bucharest during his most recent visit to the Romanian capital.[24]

TABLE 6.16   Communist Education, 1950-1985

	1948/49	1965/66	1975/76	1980/81	1984/85
School population	2,203,728	4,103,082	5,087,917	5,584,821	5,588,059
Thereof:					
Preschool enrollment					
and "gymnasium"	157,934	353,721	812,420	935,711	886,199
Primary enrollment	1,791,182	2,292,802	3,019,776	3,308,462	3,035,209
Lycee enrollment	69,396	371,724	901,977	979,741	1,237,955
Higher education					
enrollment	48,676	130,614	164,567	192,769	166,328

Source: Romania Directia Centrala de Statistica, Anuarul Statistic al Republicii Socialiste Romania 1985, p. 290.

There is little doubt that education is one of the very highest priorities in communist-ruled systems, and Romania fits this generalization as well. The educational achievements of the communist order must be seen in the context of the state of education in the pre-communist system. Here, Romania ranked close to the bottom of all European states, with a very high proportion of illiterates, a weak general educational system (albeit topped by a good system of higher education, whose enrollment came primarily from the upper socio-economic strata of the population). Table 6.16 shows the achievements of the communist educational offensive since 1950.

Statistics are sometimes deceptive. The numerically impressive achievements have continued throughout the decade of the 1980s, but the Romanians themselves admit that qualitatively there is a considerable problem. As the energy crisis deepened, schools were closed for months during the winter. There was (and is) a shortage of basic school supplies, including paper, and laboratories are operating with outmoded equipment, with little prospect of new facilities. Broken pieces are hard to replace. Throughout the decade, the regime's emphasis on vocational training and the need to funnel skilled individuals into the work force has depleted the ranks of university students, shortened their curriculum, and reduced the time spent on basic research to a minimum. The politicization of the school system requires ever greater amounts of time spent on subjects such as Marxism-Leninism, the history of the RCP, and the works of the General Secretary, all of which are of little interest to the students and result in much boredom and cynicism. Some of the best academic personnel have left Romania during the last decade, and many others are awaiting an opportunity. The general "closing off" of the country from the rest of the world has caused immeasurable harm to the educational system, to research institutes, and to other institutions of higher learning. The atmosphere of despair and cynicism now so prominent among intellectuals and others is clearly detrimental to intellectual pursuits and academic achievement. All of this must be entered on the debit side of the ledger entitled "use of human resources."[25]

There are a number of other areas in the field of "services" that could be discussed for an assessment of achievements and failures, but it is not necessary. In all of these areas, the story is the same. There were impressive achievements up until the end of the 1970s, at least in quantitative terms, but a sharp decline subsequently. The decade of the 1980s must be seen as a turning point in the history of communist Romania, when the trends of general achievement but occasional failure turned to general failure with occasional achievement. Furthermore, the pace of decline seems to quicken as the crisis wears on, much like an avalanche that gathers momentum as it proceeds. Analysts and citizens alike wonder about the breaking point, the point of no return, when public patience and subservience finally turns to defiance, unrest, and overt challenges to an unpopular regime.

Conclusion

The multifaceted policies that the regime has produced over forty years have had profound effects upon Romanian society and its economy, its social structure, and ultimately, its political order. In the realm of socio-economic polity, the RCP, despite the many deficiencies of its policies, has industrialized the country to a point where we can now state that Romania is a mixed industrial-agrarian system, rapidly moving towards the status of being primarily an industrial economy. The output and mix of goods cannot be compared to the pre-communist era. Millions of individuals have become city dwellers and industrial workers, many of them right out of the village and a miserly existence as tillers of the soil. Many others are now, in fact, second generation proletarians, and their children will be the first full cadre of third generation industrial workers in Romanian history (with the exception of a few industrial pockets dating back to the era before World War I). Despite the failures of the service sector there are still services available that the average peasant from prewar Romania could not have imagined. The educational system, deficient as it may be, still has trained an entire population in the skills of a modern society. In fact, as we survey all of these changes and achievements, it is fair to say that the regime has produced a *societal revolution*. This societal revolution, in turn, has political effects. And these political effects help change the system further, in all its dimensions. Thus, Romania in the 1980s is experiencing the "feedback loop" of the system with full force. It is unlikely that the political order can ignore these factors indefinitely.

Notes

1. See, for example, Naum Jasny, *Soviet Industrialization, 1928-52)* (Chicago, IL: University of Chicago Press, 1961).

2. For an excellent analysis, see John M. Montias, *Economic Development in Communist Rumania* (Cambridge, MA: The M.I.T. Press, 1967), pp. 3–10.

3. I have discussed this process in my *Modernization in Romania since World War II*, ch. 5 (pp. 141–169).

4. This philosophy is evident in official Romanian publications of this era. See, for example, Academia Republicii Populare Romine, Institutul de Cercetare Economice, *Dezvoltarra Economica a Rominiei* (Bucharest: Edutura Academii Republicii Populare Romine, 1964), esp. pp. 16–81.

5. This commitment to extensive industrialization was reiterated by the General Secretary at the recent party conference, e.g. *Scinteia*, December 17, 1987.

6. For example, Nicolae Ceausescu signed a decree reducing already scarce energy consumption by 20 percent, (*ibid.*, February 7, 1987).

7. This point has been argued by a number of scholars and even Romanian observers. Mihai Botez made the point forcefully in an interview with the author in the fall of 1987.

8. This Western orientation is now supplanted by more intensive trade with the Soviet Union. See Vladimir Socor, "Romanian-Soviet Trade Surges Ahead," *Radio Free Europe Research*, Romanian SR/3, 22 April 1987.

9. E.g. Nicolae Ceausescu's speech to the tenth RCP congress, in *Congresul al X-lea al Partidului Comunist Roman*, pp. 42–44. This policy statement was subsequently implemented through massive efforts to attract Western trade and technology.

10. By now, Romanian policy is clearly aimed at autarky. Ceausescu defended the policy of autarky and austerity in a major speech in January 1987, published in *Scinteia*, January 27, 1987.

11. The National Council on Agriculture, the Food Industry, Forestry, and Fish Farming published a decree in February 1986 reemphasizing the increased use of horses in agriculture, (*ibid.*, February 27, 1987).

12. *Ibid.*, June 28, 1987, denounced the U.S. emphasis on most favored nation status connected with free emigration as unwarranted interference in internal Romanian affairs.

13. Botez is in fact in the West at the present time. For a discussion of Botez' removal from Bucharest, see Vladimir Socor, "Pressures on Mihai Botez Intensifying," *Radio Free Europe Research*, Romanian SR/7, 19 June 1987.

14. Ion Iliescu in *Romania Literara*, September 3, 1987.

15. Gilberg, *Modernization in Romania since World War II*, ch. 6 (pp. 171–188).

16. Ceausescu has now gone further by decreeing that food *consumption* must be controlled by the state. To this effect, cooking centers and canteens are to be vastly expanded, while private cooking is discouraged. See his speech to the

Congress of People's Councils, published in *Scinteia*, September 11, 1985. On rationing in Brasov, see *Radio Free Europe Research*, Romania/4, 4 March 1988.

17. This is so despite official programs allegedly established to improve the food supply. See, for example, the program adopted by the Grand National Assembly, published in *ibid.*, December 25, 1987.

18. For an account of the demonstrators in Brasov, see *Frankfurter Allgemeine Zeitung*, November 25, 1987, and *Die Welt*, November 26, 1987.

19. E.g. Nicolae Ceausescu in a major speech on February 24, 1987, published in *Agerpres*, February 27, 1987, in which he rejected "imitation" of foreign models.

20. The General Secretary denounced deficiencies in this and other areas in a speech published in *Scinteia*, December 23, 1986.

21. The party daily discussed the achievements of Romanian medicine under socialism in an article on August 20, 1985.

22. For a number of articles on the crisis in Romanian medicine, see *Flacara*, May 21, 1982; July 15, 1983 and June 7, 1985. The electricity crisis has deepened every year but Ceausescu continues to decree cuts in consumption. See, for example, his decree on reducing energy consumption by 20 percent in 1987 (*Scinteia*, February 7, 1987).

23. Again, *Flacara* has described the crisis in the housing section in considerable detail, e.g. November 30, 1984; December 7, 1984; January 11, 1985 and January 18, 1985.

24. *Pravda*, May 25, 1987.

25. Occasionally, writers and intellectuals courageously challenge the current system to be more open and willing to change. See, for example, Augustin Buzura in *Tribuna*, June 18, 1987 and *Tomis*, June-July 1987.

7

The Transformation
of the Social Structure

The Romanian regime, like all modernizing regimes, has made some progress in designated areas, as discussed above. In some instances, this progress has been spectacular, while in other cases it is less than planned and less than could be expected. The RCP leadership has also experienced a number of unintended consequences of the policies implemented. This is also a development that has a great deal of familiarity for modernizers everywhere. It should come as no surprise, therefore, that the Romanians are now also experiencing the *political* feedback of these developments, namely, the demand by some of the societal elites of modern Romania for greater political influence. What *is unique* in the Romanian case, however, is the regime's response to these demands, which differs fundamentally from the policies devised and implemented elsewhere in the region. More about this later.

The modernization process started by the RCP after its consolidation of power in 1947 occurred in a country which was characterized by a relatively undifferentiated social structure. The vast majority of the population was made up of peasants and landless laborers. There was a small but politically and economically powerful class of landlords, resembling the traditional boyar class, some of them, in fact, absentee landowners whose time was mostly spent in the pursuit of idle leisure in Paris and elsewhere. The distance between the peasantry and the landlords was therefore both economic and psychological, to the point where one can rightfully speak of two different cultures, indeed, two different worlds of existence.[1]

There was also an emerging industrial proletariat which was too small to make a real difference politically, but it served as the breeding ground for a number of revolutionaries and other personalities of great importance for the revolutionary movement. This social class served both as an example of the distance between city and village and as a bridge between them, because most of the workers were, in fact, peasant workers right out of the countryside and the villages with a strong emotional and cultural attachment to the latter. In any case, the Romanian proletariat lacked the traditions of occupation, residence, and shared experiences that were part of the lives of workers in the more highly developed central and northwestern Europe. In many respects, the Romanian proletariat resembled the "raw" proletarians of Russia in the years prior to the Revolution.[2]

The Romanian intelligentsia was small, but in some respects highly developed, both in terms of class consciousness and a shared cultural experience. The Romanians in this stratum considered themselves an integral part of the Latin heritage and derived their inspiration from Paris and Rome, with a strong tendency toward chauvinism and glorification of the past, with its Roman origins. This class had an ambivalent relationship with the other socio-economic classes of the country, not unlike that of the other intelligentsia of central and eastern Europe in the nineteenth and early twentieth centuries. Basically, the urban intellectuals of Romania had little in common with the workers and peasants; they were removed from them in culture, residence, income, and occupation. At the same time, the intelligentsia looked towards these classes, and especially the peasants, for inspiration and a dose of the "wholesome life" of the villages. This national romanticism created a false sense of togetherness, but it was held together by a common bond of nationalism, even as that nationalism helped separate Romanians of *all* strata of life from the numerous ethnic minorities of the country.[3]

The top of the Romanian social pyramid was made up of the descendants of the boyars, the landowners, and the industrialists. Small in number, but politically and economically powerful, these individuals ran the political and socio-economic order throughout the years after the establishment of independence. The system was primarily *their* system, and it was their legacy that the communists inherited in the immediate postwar period.[4]

The Civil Society and Its Eradication

As Romania established the formal structures and procedures of a parliamentary system, it also began the process of formulating a rudimentary civil society. The concept "civil society," I take it, describes a political and social order in which elite groups and organizations exist with some autonomy from the state and political authorities, with at least limited possibilities for some political action inside the parameters of the established system. This does not make the system a full-fledged democracy. For example, there may still be censorship, thus invalidating the notion of a free press. Furthermore, elections may be rigged, and the bureaucracy may be corrupt. Finally, there may be rather frequent executive interference in regular political procedures, thus "stacking the deck" in favor of this branch of government. Regular procedures of political and socio-economic decision-making and implementation may be violated in various ways. The main point is that there *is* a sphere of public life between the state and the individual, and this sphere has *some* autonomy and *some* opportunity for political activity.[5]

Romania gradually developed a limited form of such a civil society, although it was less advanced than was the case in some of the other East European societies of the late nineteenth and early twentieth centuries. A number of political parties were established, and they functioned like parties in other pluralistic societies, at least in part (despite their well deserved reputation for corruption and horse trading). Trade unions were also formed, and a number of peasants' organizations sprang up, some of them with clear-cut political goals, others with programs that had political implications. Literary societies and various other academic and intellectual groups functioned relatively free of interference. Sports clubs fostered the notions of organizational skills and togetherness. Last, but not least, there was a fairly substantial network of organizations for the ethnic groups of this multiethnic society.[6]

As the communists came to power, first in coalition governments and then in sole charge of the political order as of 1947/1948, the RCP leadership surveyed the existence of a limited civil society, reemerging from the ashes of the war. And, like all revolutionary regimes, the RCP faced the need to deal with this civil society and its organizational manifestations. The great societal revolution initiated in this period resulted in the destruction of this civil society and the establishment of an order of Gleichschaltung. More about this later.

Popular Attitudes and the Weakness of Communism

The RCP had to contend with the existing social structure of the country and the existence of a rudimentary civil society, but perhaps its greatest obstacle was the virtual absence of support for Marxism in any of its major manifestations in the population at large. Contemporary Romanian historiography to the contrary, there were few real communists in the industrial proletariat. Leftism usually took the form of socialism or social democracy. Radicalism among the peasantry had little to do with the Marxists and the latters' preoccupation with urbanization, industrialization, and the industrial proletariat. Marxism was only important in some limited circles of the intellectual community, where it was indeed, "Salonfähig." The masses of the population, regardless of social status or occupation, rejected Marxism as an alien idea, particularly obnoxious because, after 1917, it emanated primarily from Soviet Russia, thus feeding into the traditional hatred of things Russian so often found among the peoples of Central and Eastern Europe.

Popular attitudes, particularly among the peasantry, focused upon the local community, the village, the family, and the kinship circle. These attitudes and values, based upon paternalism and pastoralism, were singularly resistant to any radicalizing tendencies that might emanate from the cities. Instead, the peasant had developed a healthy skepticism against *all* political authority. Since their collective experiences for a long time had taught them that the representatives of political and economic power were rapacious, corrupt, and self-serving, primarily concerned with their own well being, but singularly lacking in any sense of community or noblesse oblige. The peasants, therefore, created their own version of civil society by focussing on the local setting and the mechanisms whereby they could reduce or eliminate their contact with the political order. This parochialism was well- suited to the preservation of village autonomy and the perpetuation of peasant society, but it was a most formidable obstacle to the revolutionary transformers who took power in 1947. In many respects, the party is still struggling with the resistance of this social stratum.[7]

The parochialism of the peasantry was offset by a sense of nationalism that was at once mystical, religious in nature, and all-pervasive in the masses of the population. This religious fundamentalism was anti-democratic, in that it rejected the notions of civil society and the concept of "unity in diversity." There was little respect for those who thought differently, acted differently, and were different. Indeed, some of the fundamentalist movements catering to the peasantry, such as the League of the Archangel Michael, were populist and anti-Semitic to a very large degree, emphasizing the organic unity between the Leader and the people, while decrying all intermediate structures.[8]

These movements and attitudes presented serious obstacles to the communist leaders who ascended to power after World War II. Many of them were clearly and virulently anti-communist, while others emphasized distance between the individual and his peer group and family, on the one hand, and the state and public authorities, on the other. Those groups that were dedicated to the organic unity of the mass and the political elite believed fervently in a society based upon religion, not upon "scientific Marxism." Thus, the RCP had a major task ahead of itself as it attempted to deal with the political system of societal values that it had inherited.[9]

A revolutionary elite that aims to maintain itself in power must deal with the elements of civil society that confront it upon the capture of power. The nature of the policies undertaken towards these elements will vary, depending upon the congruence of values between the elites of the civil society and the leaders of political organizations in the old order, on the one hand, and the ideological mind-set of the new rulers, on the other hand. Most likely, the revolutionary elite feels compelled to deal ruthlessly with the remnants of the old, for fear that the values represented there would subsequently rise again and become a focal point of demands on the established communist regime. The history of Eastern Europe up to the end of the Stalin era confirms this approach. And Romania was in the mainstream of such policies.

The rise of the RCP and its consolidation have been discussed in detail elsewhere and need no further elaboration here. Briefly put, the RCP leadership moved aggressively and ruthlessly against the established political parties, the organizations of established religions, the mass organizations of society, and the infrastructure of the civil society. By the mid-1950s, the RCP was clearly in full control, and those elements of civil society that had been permitted to survive were thoroughly infiltrated and turned into front organizations of the new order. Many organizations of various kinds had been established by the RCP itself to serve its goals of mass mobilization and societal control.[10]

There is a rather broad consensus among students of Eastern Europe as to what happened next in the region. As society developed rapidly on the dimensions of social mobilization, the political regimes of the area were compelled to accept the notion that the most important functional groups in society acquired a certain amount of autonomy in terms of their own functions and procedures, so that a limited form of civil society reemerged in those countries that had such an infrastructure prior to the establishment of communist power. In other systems without such a tradition, limited civil society may be in the process of emerging for the first time. Cultural, artistic, and literary groups have also begun to function in these systems with a certain amount of autonomy, thus adding to the movement towards civil society.[11]

It is clear that this trend does not amount to the emergence of real *political* pluralism (at least not yet). The communist parties of the region are clearly aware of the dangers associated with the possible move of civil society into pluralist society, and they have undertaken a number of important steps to prevent such developments and to restore their authority in those cases where it has been challenged. At the same time, there is growing awareness that civil society, interpreted in a limited way, is here to stay, and may indeed be beneficial for the smoother functioning of society under communist rule.[12]

Romania under "mature Ceausescuism" represents a major exception to the generalizations that are valid for the rest of the region. Since the early 1970s, the Romanian leader's tolerance for *any* kind of autonomy in society has diminished, (and in this decade it has vanished altogether). Instead, the RCP leader, through his rule by clan and by family, has reversed the trend towards civil society and is in the process of establishing a society of mass atomization and also mass alienation on a scale unknown elsewhere in the region. The establishment of such a society would be both a major political achievement and a massive tragedy. It is likely to come to pass in the next decade if the Ceausescus remain in power.

The Ceausescu quest for the fully controlled and synchronized society began in earnest in the early 1970s. Some analysts have even pinpointed it to the RCP leader's visit to China during the summer of 1971. At that time, Ceausescu became highly impressed with the goals, methods, and achievements of the Great Proletarian Cultural Revolution, and apparently decided to set out on a similar quest on his own. The result was the so-called "mini cultural revolution," which got underway in Romania during the celebration of the centennial of Romanian statehood in the period 1976 to 1978, and then, as a permanent feature during the decade of the 1980s. At the present time, it can safely be said that the processes of societal atomization and destruction of any vestige of civil society in Romania have no counterpoint anywhere else in Eastern Europe or the Soviet Union.[13]

The destruction of the last remnants of pre-communist civil society is complemented by the full synchronization and control with all societal groups and associations that may exist in the space between the individual and state power, in this case represented by the Ceausescus. Furthermore, such a process requires a system of supervision, observation of individuals and their behaviors, intrusion into the most private activities of individuals, fear, and insecurity. All of these ingredients are available in Romania in the 1980s, and they are becoming increasingly important in all individuals' lives. Some of these elements have become so prominent in the system that they now dominate it, making it increasingly difficult for "the man in the street" to escape into full-fledged apathy. The ensuing alienation is also becoming a factor of great political significance. At some point, one should expect these contradictory tendencies to clash and to produce significant political ramifications. Let us now examine each of these ingredients in some detail in the "epoch of Ceausescu."[14]

Synchronization of Organized Societal Activity

Since the early 1970s, rule of the clan and of the Ceausescu family has meant that the regime supervised all organized activity in Romania to an extent unknown elsewhere in the region since the Stalin period.

It is even possible to argue that modern techniques of supervision and communication have made it possible to go beyond Stalinist tendencies in this regard. All groups either have agents of the police as members, or the membership suspects that one or more of the group is an informer, thereby producing an atmosphere of insecurity and effective self-censorship. All major organizations are synchronized through the principles of overlapping membership and interlocking directorates. By all available accounts, the intrusion produced by these systems is major and enhanced by the zeal with which the job is pursued by the regime's controllers, since their own success or failure depends heavily upon finding culprits, whether they actually exist or not. The continuous dismantling of structures and construction of new administrative bodies under the Ceausescus' direction further enhance the sense of insecurity among subordinates and the sense of control and power among the clan.

The Ceausescu era is the era of mass supervision and the expanded use of informers in all walks of life. Exact figures are naturally difficult to obtain, but it is estimated that every fifteenth Romanian is a direct informer for the police. Many others probably engage in this kind of activity occasionally, for a variety of reasons. This is the kind of surveillance network that may exceed the system under Stalin's purges in the Soviet Union. It creates pervasive insecurity at all levels of society and reduces human interaction to a minimum, fundamentally impeding any kind of political dialogue, and thus also the possibility of forming counterelites.[15]

The insecurity produced by constant fear of surveillance and betrayal to the security police or other authorities is enhanced by the harsh methods employed against dissidents, demonstrators, strikers, and others who somehow challenge the regime and its policies. The Romanian dissident movement, always much smaller than its counterparts elsewhere in Eastern Europe, has been decimated through arrests, expulsion to other countries, and physical intimidation, including severe beatings. The extensive network of informers, discussed above, also impedes organizational capabilities, thus reducing the chances that individuals or small groups may go beyond the isolated position in society. One of the current jokes in Bucharest defines a Romanian dissident as an individual who resides in Paris. This is a good example of the cynicism and despair that engulf the movement in contemporary Romania. It is also an example of the political success of the Ceausescu clan in reducing the voices of opposition to impotence.[16]

The Ceausescu regime has also exhibited considerable skills in dividing the potential oppositionist groups according to ethnic background and religious affiliation, attempting to show that most of those who reject the regime's policies are non-Romanians and thus opposed to the ideals and goals of the Romanian nation. This kind of policy has had a certain amount of success because a number of earlier oppositionists were, in fact, Germans or Hungarians, reflecting the frustrations of the minorities with the nationality policies of the Ceausescus as well as the rejection by these individuals of specific regime outputs in other areas. Furthermore, Germans and Hungarians are products of political cultures that tend to be much less quiescent than the Romanian version. The factors combined have probably also helped reduce the likelihood of *Romanian* dissent becoming overt expressions on a larger scale. In any case, recent developments in this area have seen the emergence of a number of ethnic Romanians in the ranks of the dissenters, thus invalidating the regime's arguments on this score. And, in view of the dramatic events in Brasov in the fall of 1987, it is also likely that the submission of the Romanian masses is close to the breaking point. When that point is reached, the notions of divide and rule may no longer suffice, even in Romania.[17]

While the Ceausescu clan has been extremely active in destroying any development of autonomism in Romanian society, its members (and particularly the General Secretary himself and his wife) have worked ceaselessly to establish an "organic bond" between themselves and the "people" thus demonstrating at once that the Romanians have great political, socio-economic, and cultural capabilities and *only* the Ceausescus can realize this potential. Any failure or shortcomings, then, are the fault of the masses, and not of the leadership. This notion has been fostered and hammered home for so long that the General Secretary apparently believes it himself. In this regard he is clearly supported by his wife, Elena, who appears to be a singularly unlikable individual by most accounts, even those that attempt to be objective. The cult of the personality, which has reached unknown heights in Romania, further contributes to these attitudes among the top leadership. Furthermore, the cult isolates the top leaders from the rest of the world in a manner that is clearly detrimental to Romania's international standing and thus her national interest. All of this, however, appears to have no effect upon the actions, values, and attitudes of the top members of the clan, who continue to act in ways that appear irrational and distasteful to the rest of the world, including other communist regimes in Eastern Europe, the Soviet Union, and elsewhere.[18]

The notion of an unbreakable tie between the Ceausescus and the people carries with it the concept that there must be no intermediaries, no structures or organizations that interpose themselves between the Leader and the masses. It is also a notion of considerable arrogance, because the leading couple cannot conceive of "the people" having the capability of self-realization, or of generating its own leaders. The leaders are "set" and they are the only ones who can lead. Those who may emerge as major figures through semiautonomous structures and organizations cannot be trusted, because they would have achieved their successes apart from the top leadership, and thus not subject to their control. Since the Ceausescus apparently do not trust anyone, they cannot conceive of anyone else having motivations that go beyond the purely egotistical plane. Hence, there is constant need for vigilance, supervision, surveillance, and control.[19]

Any society which lacks certain basic levels of trust, cohesion, and acceptance of common values and goals has ceased to be a society in the sense of Gesellschaft, as the Germans conceive of it, and it does not come close to the idea of Gemeinschaft, "togetherness." In fact, such a society is not really a society, but rather an agglomeration of individuals who happen to live on the same territory, subject to the same regime, forced to seek a living in the economic setting in existence. It is fundamentally atomized; it is every man, woman, and child for himself or herself, with little notion of a commonality of goals, aspirations, values, or beliefs. This is the *ultimate* atomized political entity. It is seldom found in human history. I would contend that contemporary Romania is getting close to this stage.

Social scientists, philosophers, and those committed to the idea that a society, a nation, and a polity must have *some* common base, would find the Romanian case a tragic one in the annals of modern history. Those who are concerned primarily with power, its acquisition, maintenance, and expansion *for* the elites would consider it a singular achievement. An atomized society, in which intermediate structures and attachments are destroyed, leaves the individual adrift, personally bereft of support systems that may insulate him or her from the direct exercise of power upon him. It is much easier to *control* such a society. It is also much more difficult to get such a society to perform at maximum levels, because there is no discernable common ground, no all-encompassing passion except to stay alive as an individual; there is no collective spirit. Atomized societies maximize power and minimize performance, to the point where performance is barely sufficient to maintain levels of existence for the masses of the population. Hence there is constant pauperization at all levels below the very pinnacle of power, but continuous enrichment for those at that pinnacle. There is reverse social stratification because nobody outside the clan has much of anything, while the clan has more and more of the economic, political, and symbolic assets of the entire society. Elite, chasm, mass—that is all there is. There is no civil society. And because there is no civil society, the leadership can create its own. This, I take it, is "mobilization society," because all structures and agencies are there for the purpose of enhancing

TABLE 7.1   Occupational Development, 1950-1985

	1950	1965	1975	1980	1984
Work force total	100%	100%	100%	100%	100%
Percent thereof in:					
Industry	12.0	19.2	30.6	35.5	36.8
Construction	2.2	6.3	8.1	8.3	7.4
Agriculture	74.1	56.5	37.8	29.4	28.9
Forestry	0.2	0.2	0.3	0.4	0.3
Transportation	1.9	3.1	4.3	6.1	6.0
Telecommunications	0.3	0.6	0.7	0.8	0.8
Retail trade	2.5	4.0	5.5	6.0	5.9
Communal services	0.7	2.1	3.4	3.8	4.0
Education, culture and art	2.3	3.5	4.0	4.2	4.0
Science	0.2	0.5	0.8	0.9	1.2
Health services	1.1	2.0	2.6	2.7	2.7
Administration	1.7	1.0	0.7	0.6	0.5
Other	0.8	1.0	1.2	1.3	1.5

Source: Republica Socialiste Romania.   Directia Centrala de Statistica, Anuarul
Statistic al Republicii Socialiste Romania 1985, p. 60.

the power of the elite and carry out its will; it is a mechanism to mobilize *individuals.* In the rest of Eastern Europe, civil society is emerging or reemerging. In Romania, there has emerged Ceausescu's society.

Modernization and the Development
of Socio-economic Classes

While *political* development in Romania has acted as a powerful levelling influence, reducing everyone outside to the status of either political impotence or aspiration to membership in the clan, socio-economic development has created a number of classes which are different from each other in functional terms even as they exhibit similar aspects of pauperization and misery. In purely statistical terms, Tables 7.1, 7.2, and 7.3 illustrate this development over time. The tables above illustrate a process that is quite familiar in communist-ruled systems. The modernization process has created entire new socio-economic classes, notably a "socialist" proletariat, or "socialist" peasantry, and a "socialist" intelligentsia. As can be expected, the process is also characterized by increased functional specialization, and there has been considerable social stratification on indices such as prestige, acceptability of work, and preference of tasks. For most of the history of socialist Romania, there has been considerable social mobility and also spatial mobility.

Such mobility has manifested itself in a number of ways. First of all, the urbanization process has meant that literally millions of people have moved from the countryside to the cities, but they have also moved up

TABLE 7.2   The Dynamics of Occupational Development, 1950-1985

Percentage point increase/decrease of occupational categories in percent of total workforce:

	1950 -- 1985
Industry	+ 24.8
Construction	+ 5.2
Agriculture	- 45.2
Forestry	+ 0.1
Transport	+ 4.1
Telecommunications	+ 0.5
Retail trade	+ 3.4
Communal services	+ 3.3
Education, culture and the arts	+ 1.7
Science	+ 1.0
Health occupations	+ 1.6
Administration	- 1.2
Others	+ 0.7

Derived from: Republica Socialista Romania. Directia Centrala de Statistica, *Anuarul Statistic al Republicii Socialiste Romania 1985*, p. 60.

TABLE 7.3   Total Increase/Decrease in Occupational Categories, 1950-1985

	1950	1985
Total workforce	8,377,200	10,499,900
Thereof:		
Industry	1,000,700	3,865,500 (+2,864,800)
Construction	186,300	779,900 (+ 593,600)
Agriculture	6,208,700	3,032,600 (-3,176,100)
Forestry	17,600	35,300 (+ 17,700)
Transport	166,800	634,800 (+ 468,000)
Telecommunications	21,800	82,100 (+ 60,300)
Retail trade	205,800	617,000 (+ 411,200)
Communal services	58,500	414,800 (+ 356,300)
Education, culture and the arts	191,400	416,100 (+ 224,700)
Science	19,100	130,700 (+ 111,600)
Health occupations	90,800	280,900 (+ 190,100)
Administration	142,100	57,100 (- 85,000)
Others	67,600	153,100 (+ 85,500)

Derived from: Republica Socialista Romania. Directia Centrala de Statistica, *Anuarul Statistic al Republicii Socialiste Romania 1985*, p. 60

on the social and occupational mobility scale, because the move to the city entailed occupational change, from being a peasant to being an industrial worker. At the same time, this process set the stage for another form of upward mobility in that the new industrial proletariat now had access to goods, services, and the general ambience of the city which had not been available in the villages. And these possibilities, in turn, established the basis for education and functional specialization, first for the new proletarians themselves and then for their children. Upward mobility, then, came in waves from the village to the cities, from the peasantry through the proletariat and on to the intelligentsia. This form of mobility always represented a great safety valve in Romanian society, because it carried with it the hope of progress, without which legitimacy and the whole social fabric cannot be sustained over time.[20]

The urbanization/upward mobility process appears to have had two streams; first, the move of individuals directly from the countryside to the capital of Bucharest and, second, a spatial move from the village to some intermediate city, where the new proletariat settled for a period of time, perhaps permanently, while their offspring moved on to the capital as they became educated and acquired the functional skills of modern society. This tendency is consistent with evidence from other rapidly modernizing societies, in which the capital is the focus of all activity, be it political, social, economic, or cultural to an extent unknown in many modernized polities. The focus on Bucharest in Romanian public life is acted out daily in the proclivities of workers, intellectuals, and bureaucrats who may be employed elsewhere but find ways to spend long weekends in "the city," thus reducing further the already meager work output that they produce during their curtailed week at the place of employment.[21]

All modernizing societies sooner or later reach a stage of temporary or permanent maturation in terms of social mobility. This occurs when the rapid expansion of the economy slows down, thus limiting the need for new positions at the top of the socio-economic hierarchy. When this stage is reached, the chances of moving up are reduced, sometimes dramatically, because there is a glut of people on the top and at the intermediate levels of the social pyramid. Many educated and ambitious individuals are stymied in their career goals, and friction and animosity between social strata develop. Furthermore, the social pyramid "hardens," because there are fewer opportunities to move up and out. Socialist society begins to resemble the class society of old in that the sons and daughters of the peasantry and the industrial proletariat now find themselves confined to the class into which they were born. Their counterparts in the intelligentsia and in the social class of bureaucrats, on the other hand, enhance *their* chances for education and privilege, because their parents use their positions to ensure acquisition of this scarce commodity, education, for their children. This is a process of stratification that has been discussed by Walter Connor and others in considerable detail for the region as a whole.[22] While it applies in greater degree to some of the more highly developed systems, it is also increasingly relevant for Romania. And in Romania there are additional factors, based on idiosyncratic attitudes and policies, that aggravate this situation; these will be discussed below. In any case, there is no doubt that Romania is now experiencing the effects of slowed mobility in the socio-economic field. The political ramifications of this are sure to follow.

The socialist systems of Eastern Europe in the 1980s are also experiencing limited downward mobility. This is a process that will most likely be accelerated in the years to come for a number of reasons. First of all, the process of economic reform, sponsored in the Soviet Union and applied throughout the region with greater or lesser enthusiasm, is designed to stress efficiency and productivity. Given the nature of the economic system of socialism, large numbers of individuals are likely to experience various forms of dislocation, including unemployment, demotions, and loss of social privileges. These individuals will clearly suffer from the process, and they represent a significant political factor, precisely because of their numbers and their access to political power.

Secondly, the modernization process requires constant retooling and the acquisition of new skills. Those who cannot keep up in the race for these skills must, of necessity, fall from the ranks of the privileged into some other category of lower standing. These individuals, too, will experience downward social mobility, again with considerable political ramifications.

Thirdly, the attempts by the "apparatchik" intelligentsia to maintain its position in the political and socio-economic order may be crowned with temporary success, even though the long-range prospects are less bright for this stratum. During the period of such rearguard fighting, the apparatchiki (or those who are incompetent or resistant to change) may manage to force other elements into temporary downward mobility patterns. This is the most debilitating of all circumstances because it alienates precisely those elements that are needed by society in the modern and postmodern phase.

Other segments of society will experience this downward trend as well. In a period of economic change and a move towards a more achievement-oriented system of remuneration, the distance between those who have and those who do not will increase significantly. Prices are likely to rise, too, thus hurting those on a fixed income. Under these circumstances, pensioners, widows, and others dependent upon government rates of remuneration will fall behind, while the "entrepreneurs" of various kinds will move ahead. Much of Eastern Europe today is, in fact, beset by a social crisis that involves the increasing pauperization of the sick, the old, and the indigent. And because the regimes of the area have denied any existence of such problems in the past, there is no safety net to deal with such individuals or groups. This is significant downward mobility, indeed.[23]

The problems discussed above are present in Romania as well, but in a different configuration. In Romania, virtually *all* strata of society have experienced downward social mobility in the sense that the standard of living has declined drastically for almost all citizens, regardless of social standing, expertise, occupation, or education. Furthermore, the prolonged and deepening economic crisis has reduced any chance of upward mobility except in a few individual cases. All of society is undergoing severe pauperization, in which everybody who is not connected with the clan will need to stand in line for bread, milk, and other staples, and will need to battle erratic and overcrowded transportation systems and health services that function sporadically and at a low level of performance. This is, indeed, the most severe case of levelling that a society can experience, namely, that of equal *lack* of opportunity, goods, and services. Under these circumstances it is difficult to single out any particular social stratum as being favored or disfavored; everybody has great difficulty in getting by in a material sense. This, in turn, produces a society in which most individuals have lost hope and merely survive because that is the natural instinct for most human beings.[24]

As discussed above, the economic crisis in Romania has certain political benefits for the Ceausescus. It is clear that most people are simply too busy staying alive and providing for their families to engage in any form of meaningful political opposition. At the same time, the lack of opportunities for upward advancement through regular channels (and the meaninglessness of such movement, given the desperate situation in foodstuffs and consumer goods availability) provides the regime with added advantages insofar as it controls the availability of desirable positions inside the clan and its extended control areas. This is, indeed, the beauty of clan rule. It works like this:

Increasingly, the centralization of decision-making in Romania means that the nomenklatura is in the hands of a few individuals, in practice, the inner circle of the Ceausescu clan. Central interference in the process of personnel management and appointments has reached proportions unknown elsewhere at the present time, perhaps exceeding the historical precedent of the Stalin era in the Soviet Union. It is now literally true that advancement in one's profession largely depends upon one's relationship with Ceausescu cronies, perhaps the General Secretary himself, or his wife or favorite son, Nicu. The process of recruitment is not based upon special skills or the extent to which an individual is needed in society, but primarily on the personal connections mentioned above. Under these circumstances, the only way to advance is to maintain the correct political "profile," cultivate relationships, and hope for the best. And once an important position has been obtained, it is maintained on the same basis, through personal likes and dislikes, the whim of the proprietor, the extent to which sufficiently sycophantic behavior can be exhibited to satisfy the patron. Upward *and* downward social mobility is controlled by the same individuals. Normal measures of success or failure do not apply. Hence, it is futile to examine contemporary Romania on the basis of criteria utilized elsewhere. The serious analyst must establish criteria that are in conformity with the actual situation in this unique country. Nowhere is this more apparent than in the field of upward and downward mobility in the decade of the 1980s.[25]

Upward Mobility, Nepotism, and the Emergence of Opposition

It is clear that the strategy utilized by the Ceausescu clan to further its own power through control with upward mobility through nepotism is an effective weapon as long as it can "divide and rule" among those who have ambitions and hopes for a better life professionally and materially. It is also clear that it will inevitably produce criticism and demands for change among those elements of the population that the regime can least afford to alienate, namely the experts and managers, the intellectuals and artists. There is now emerging an opposition among precisely these strata of society in the second half of the 1980s. It is not yet broad enough to produce significant problems for the regime, and it has not yet consolidated itself to a point where it can be an articulate and effective spokesman and interest group. Its chief value lies in its potential as a support group for rival factions that may emerge after the death of the General Secretary or during a power struggle even before his departure. As such, this group has considerable political potential. It behooves us to discuss in some detail its main complaints and suggestions for change.

Intellectuals and Opposition: The Outrage of the "Sane" Society

Increasingly in the 1980s, intellectuals of all kinds have become more vocal in their denunciation of the Ceausescu regime and its policies in a number of areas, one of which is the area of social mobility and the access to positions of influence inside the socio-political order itself. The newly articulate intellectuals are often more impoverished than the workers themselves, and they have little prospect of improving their situation because the very nature of their work is such that the would-be omnipotent clan cannot possible accept its quest for freer discussion and the notion of differing views on a number of issues. The intellectuals are "stuck" in their social situation, unable to move ahead. At the same time, sycophantic individuals, often from the most mediocre of intellectual backgrounds, move rapidly into the ruling circle in which they function only on the basis of full submission to the clan and the General Secretary and his wife. Some of these individuals subsequently fall out of favor and reappear in their original social stratum (if they escape virtual oblivion in some manual labor position in a remote provincial town). In some ways, these individuals, if not effectively silenced, represent the potential for considerable ferment because they have seen the internal workings of the clan system and are presumably bitter about their own fall from grace. In any case, this process of political recruitment and the corresponding upward social mobility leaves the vast majority of the intelligentsia increasingly cynical and bitter. So far, this cynicism has taken on various forms of personal behavior, including personal pathologies such as alcoholism and psychological disorders. There is also an increasing tendency towards seeking emigration to the West, albeit in small numbers still. All of this represents little political threat so far because the solutions sought by individuals are escapism, whether physical or psychological, and not confrontation with the regime and its representatives. At some point, however, this may change. The security police, the eternally suspicious clan, and Western observers and scholars are all watching this problem with increasing interest, posing essentially the same question: When will this personal emigration and escapism turn to political rejection and confrontation?

The lack of physical and psychological mobility experienced by the intelligentsia is coupled with a powerful sense of disgust and contempt among these highly skilled individuals for the "peasants" that now run the country. The appellation "peasant" is highly significant because it reflects the attitudes and values of a citified intelligentsia that associates the countryside and the peasantry with lack of culture, coarseness, greed, and excessive preoccupation with material things and self-gra-tification. It is indeed the case in traditional peasant societies everywhere that the urban population (and particularly the urban intelligentsia) exhibits a sense of civilization and culture in a sea of "barbarianism." In the Romanian case, this sense is enhanced by the actual behavior of the rulers, which is nothing short of outrageous in many ways, especially in a society where most ordinary citizens constantly live on the margins of existence.

The Romanian intelligentsia's alienation goes much further than this, however; it focuses on the lack of "rational" behavior among the leaders of the country and their followers. The importance of the concept "rational" can hardly be overstated. The engineers, managers, social scientists, academics and artists are proud of their achievements in lifting this underdeveloped Balkan country out of its ruralism and joining it with the mainstream of modernity. They want to make decisions based upon modern scientific foundations, and thus to help the country achieve its rightful place among *modern* nations. In many ways they are the real patriots, and they are fully conscious of this fact. They despise the irrational, personalistic behavior of the Ceausescu clan; they are outraged at political and economic decisions that make no sense in terms of accepted notions of "rationality;" they are convinced that the present system is no better than those that preceded it, and probably a good deal worse than the inefficient but relatively tolerant autocracies of the interwar period. This is, indeed, a volatile and dangerous form of alienation that may have real political ramifications. What is needed is a catalyst that can galvanize this social class into action on a mass basis. Perhaps it also needs specific events that can trigger such action. Above all, such developments require the deterioration of the solidarity of the clan itself and a weakening of its hold over the security services and the armed forces.[26]

The alienation of the intelligentsia as a class cannot have significant political ramifications until this class begins to act as a collective entity. At the same time, however, the class may produce individuals who are capable of articulating the ideas, goals, and values of the whole social stratum, and perhaps also establish themselves as actual or potential counterelites. These individuals, then, may act as the catalyst necessary for collective action. And in any case, they will represent the individual expression of much more broadly held class views. Two such individuals are Mihai Botez and Ion Iliescu.

Mihai Botez has received a great deal of attention in the West during the last few years. It is generally recognized that Botez is a brilliant individual whose skills are needed by the Romanian system if it is ever to recover from the political, socio-economic, and psychological desolation of the Ceausescu era. It is also quite clear that the clan has no use for Botez and like-minded individuals. Botez was removed from his research institute, prohibited from working on matters in his own field of expertise, and eventually banished to the provincial city of Tulcea where the intellectual climate must have been singularly unattractive for a futurologist. Botez is now in the United States and may remain here, unless the political situation changes in his homeland.[27]

Botez personifies the alienated intellectual patriot described above. He would have been satisfied to live in an autocracy, provided it would be an *enlightened* autocracy. He pleads eloquently for a chance for himself and his colleagues to make a scientific contribution without constant interference from party hacks and the police. He feels strongly that contemporary Romania is not given the chance to make its rightful contribution to modern civilization because of the obscurantist and "peasant" orientation of the political leadership. Above all, he argues cogently that an entire class, the intelligentsia, is removed from the national fabric and prevented from making any kind of meaningful contribution. His analysis usually ends with the lament that Romanian society is in the process of falling apart, of losing its cohesion, of becoming completely atomized, as a result of the political mismanagement of the clan. Botez argues from the vantage point of a Romanian patriot, not a "Westernized renegade," which is one of accusations hurled at him by regime spokesmen. He rejects the notion that only the Ceausescus know what is good for Romania and hints broadly that the current regime has no real attachment to the country, its heritage, its culture, but only represents itself and its twisted understanding of society. You can be sane, skilled, patriotic, and dedicated to Romania without being a Ceausescu sycophant—this is really the individual expression of a widely held attitude in this crucial social class.[28]

Another individual has expressed his similar views with even greater political potential. In a recent article in a major journal (the publication of which is in itself a considerable achievement, given the vigilance of the real censorship that exists in Ceausescu's Romania), Ion Iliescu argues eloquently for important political changes that would leave the basic structure of the RCP's power intact, but would allow for much greater input into the decision-making process by all social groups, and especially the technical and managerial intelligentsia. Iliescu is interesting because he was once an important political figure, representing the "young Turks" of educated and hard-driving individuals who wanted a more open communist political system inside the parameters of RCP rule. He is, in fact, much like the technocrats who now dominate the political and socio-economic systems of the German Democratic Republic and Hungary and are increasingly coming to the fore in the Soviet Union itself. Iliescu would be the kind of modern, "rational" leader who could win the respect of the intelligentsia and reestablish a modicum of positive regard for Romania inside the socialist commonwealth and more generally in the concert of nations.

Ion Iliescu is of interest not only because of his message but because he is "around." His rapid political demise did not result in physical harm or liquidation. Furthermore, he clearly still has access, as the publication of his semi-heretical piece in an officially sanctioned journal shows. Does this mean that influential elements allowed the publication of the piece as a trial balloon, to see what the reaction would be in the clan and indeed beyond, in other political circles? Could this be the beginning of the *political* upward mobility of the long-suffering intelligentsia? Only time can tell. But the Iliescu case is important because it reveals the possibility that there is, indeed, a future beyond the clan, beyond the Ceausescus.[29]

The Stagnation of the Industrial Proletariat and Its Political Consequences

As discussed above, the upward social mobility of the industrial proletariat in Romania has slowed down considerably, partly because of the general pauperization of the country, but also because the socio-economic system has reached a stage of development where extensive industrialization now must give way to intensive modernization. This modernization process creates fewer jobs at higher levels of skill, thus stunting the rapid upward mobility of unskilled and semi-skilled individuals from the peasantry into the proletariat and then upwards inside this class. From now on, each generation of young people entering the work force must assume that increasing proportions of their cohorts will remain inside this socio-economic class, at least until the post-industrial revolution takes off in Romania. Consequently, improvement in the conditions of the proletariat must come about as improvement for the *whole class.* In other societies, this realization has resulted in greater group consciousness and more political assertiveness. It is possible that this tendency will also manifest itself in Romania, with considerable political consequences.[30]

The Hopelessness of the Countryside

The peasantry still represents a substantial proportion of the population of Romania, despite the rapid urbanization process that has taken place in the country since the advent of the communists to power. One of the major side effects of this rapid development is the formation of a hybrid class, that of "peasant-workers," who reside in the villages and spend considerable time commuting to the cities and the construction sites. These individuals are really peasants in outlook, attitudes, and values, and for them, the notion of urbanity is far removed from real life experiences. As a political and psychological element, then, this class should be considered as part of the peasantry. And as such, they share in the hopelessness of this least advanced social class. The only advantage of the worker-peasant is the limited social mobility experienced by the daily or weekly commute to the workers' hostels and temporary living quarters in the cities. [31]

For the "real" peasants, the mobility available through urbanization is slowing down. In fact, most of the enterprising individuals have left already, and the villages are full of older men and women as well as the children of the intermediate generation. There are also a relatively large number of unproductive elements in the village who further reduce the possibility of rural rejuvenation and increased production. All of this adds up to a depressing atmosphere of stagnation, hopelessness, and idle time filled with alcohol and other unproductive pursuits.

The depressed state of the peasantry as an economic class bodes ill for Romania as the system moves from extensive to intensive development, because the provisions of foodstuffs is a crucial element in the process of increasing labor productivity. As a *political* actor, however, the peasantry probably represents no real challenge to the regime because it is insufficiently developed in political terms to act collectively for the enhancement of its interests, (or even to perceive a collective interest). Thus, the clan can continue its rule with little danger emanating from this particular element of the population, at least for the time being. At the same time, it is fair to remind politicos and analysts alike about the capabilities of sudden jacqueries among the Romanian peasants, as witnessed by the uprisings of the eighteenth century and the great peasant revolt of 1907. The revolt shook the entire political system to its foundations and still represents the most extensive event of its kind in the history of Europe in this century. Where is the breaking point of this class in the late twentieth century?[32]

The Ethnic Minorities and Socio-political Mobility

The ethnic mosaic of Romania represents an added problem for any regime, particularly one as nationalistic (or chauvinistic) as the Ceausescu clan. Briefly put, the policies of the Ceausescu era have been hostile towards all minorities, particularly the Magyars, and these policies have now become an international issue of considerable magnitude as well. Herein lies one of the greatest potential problems for the clan in the near and intermediate future.

Upward social mobility is a great asset to any regime, because it provides avenues for the most enterprising individual in any class or ethnic group to advance economically and thus acquire positive attitudes about the system in which he or she lives. This has been true to some extent for the ethnic minorities of Romania, particularly the Germans and the Magyars. (The Jews of the country have been allowed to emigrate in large numbers, and this group now constitutes a very minor population element). Most of the upward mobility generated by the economic development of Romania has, nevertheless, benefitted the ethnic Romanians most because this group had the largest reserve of peasants who could be mobilized for urbanization and industrialization. Thus, the perception always existed among the minorities that the modernization program was developed primarily by and for the Romanians. There was great resentment over the steady influx of Romanians into traditional German and Magyar territories, and this feeling deepened as more and more Romanians became supervisors and factory managers over predominantly German or Magyar workers.

Despite this resentment, there was always an opportunity for enterprising Germans and Magyars who were willing to accept the prevailing political and managerial order. These individuals could experience upward mobility and even prosper to a limited degree. Now, those opportunities have dwindled, as the socio-economic system begins to slow down in extensive development. The attitudes and values of these individuals now turn to the injustices of the policies perpetuated upon them. Instead of "getting out" through upward (and sometimes spatial) mobility, these individuals now become the catalyst for increased nationalism among their own ethnic group. Relations among the various nationalities deteriorate as a result. The polarization process now underway in ethnic relations in Romania is potentially very dangerous.[33]

This process is fueled by actual regime policies, discussed earlier. These policies are clearly chauvinistic and have been criticized as such by elements in the ethnic Romanian population itself. They represent the epitome of the personal attitudes and values of the Ceausescu clan. Given the shrinking opportunities for individuals inside the Magyar national group to advance in the socio-economic realm, these policies have become a major catalyst for increased group awareness and cohesion. During the last few months, the desperate economic conditions and the paranoid and exploitative policies of the clan towards this group has resulted in the unprecedented emigration (presumably mostly illegal) of thousands of Magyars, now increasingly joined by ethnic Romanians as well. The pressure of resentment and despair builds up constantly inside this oppressed element. Perhaps emigration is being allowed to relieve this pressure. But there are still two million Magyars in Romania, and the problem will require a much more comprehensive solution before it erupts in a more dangerous way.[34]

By comparison, the ethnic Germans represent much less of a problem. Considerable out-migration has already taken place, and the West German policy of providing economic aid in return for a steady flow of ethnic Germans from Transylvania is likely to remain very successful because the clan desperately needs this infusion of funds and technology. Furthermore, the Federal Republic is a major international actor who can become a considerable problem for Bucharest, should the need arise.

All of this points to continued (and orderly) out-migration of ethnic Germans. This process is a form of upward mobility that reduces the political risk of emanating from the minority problem. The departure of so many individuals with needed skills and attitudes akin to the work ethic is clearly a considerable *economic* problem, however, and it adds to the sad state of affairs in contemporary Romania on this dimension. The clan has demonstrated in the past that it will accept economic costs if political rewards can be achieved. The out-migration of large numbers of Germans represents this kind of trade-off. On that basis alone, it is likely to continue.[35]

Conclusion

The present political and socio-economic situation in Romania is fraught with potential dangers, both because of systemic problems and disequilibria and also because of specific policies produced and implemented by the Ceausescu leadership. The internal pressures that build under such circumstances can no longer be alleviated by extensive socio-economic development. The student of political instability must, of necessity, examine the extent of this pressure as well as its intensity, and then measure it against factors that would tend to produce equilibrium. This "correcting mechanism" is mass political culture. In Romania, there are, in fact, a number of different political cultures, based upon ethnicity and national consciousness. They all warrant a more detailed examination.

Notes

1. The official Romanian literature on this subject is rather biased, but it still contains much valuable information. See, for example, Constantinescu, *Istoria Romaniei*, esp. pp. 576–593.

2. Many of them were peasant-workers. For a discussion of the process of industrialization and the creation of a class of peasant-workers see Arthur E. Adams, "The Peasantry in Russia, 1900–1917," in Volgyes (ed.), *The Peasantry of Eastern Europe*, ch. 1 (pp. 1–15) and Samuel L. Sharp, "The Peasantry of Eastern Europe under Communism," in *ibid.*, ch. 12 (pp. 213–219).

3. E.g. Otetea, *Istoria Poperului Roman*, pp. 487–505.

4. *Ibid.*, esp. pp. 530–560.

5. "Civil society" in communist systems may resemble some of the ideas of Gorbachev on glasnost and perestroika, concepts well known in the West.

6. For an examination of the party system in Romania in this period, see my "Romania" in McHale (ed.), *Political Parties of Europe*, Vol. II, pp. 774–810.

7. The latest figures on party membership were provided by Nicolae Ceausescu at a Central Committee plenum in March 1988. His discussion was printed in

Scinteia, April 1, 2, and 3, 1988. The social composition of the RCP at the time of the thirteenth congress was discussed in detail by Ceausescu in *ibid.,* November 19 and 20, 1984.

8. Fischer-Galati, "Fascism in Romania," in Sugar (ed.), *Native Fascism in the Successor States,* pp. 112–123.

9. King, *History of the Romanian Communist Party,* ch. 1 (pp. 9–39).

10. Ionescu, *Communism in Rumania, 1944–1962,* ch. 6 (pp. 126–144).

11. For a good overview of recent developments in the region, see Volgyes, *Politics in Eastern Europe,* esp. ch. 12 (pp. 285–311).

12. In contrast, Nicolae Ceausescu's proclamations of "socialist democracy" (e.g. *Scinteia,* December 17, 1987) sound hollow.

13. The Ceausescu leadership is clearly gearing up for another ideological campaign, this time centered around the notion of "socialist patriotism," which is directed against the ethnic minorities. See, for example, *ibid.,* March 6, 1988, and also *Era Socialista,* April 10, 1984.

14. The synchronization is occasionally resisted, particularly by intellectuals and artists. See for example, an article by Octavian Paler on the relationship between politics and literature in *Revista de Istorie si Teoriei Literara,* January–February, 1987.

15. An exaggerated but still basically accurate account of this system is provided by Pacepa, *Red Horizons.*

16. Under these circumstances, any kind of dissident activity is an act of extreme courage. See, for example, Vladimir Socor, "Prospects for Reform and Appeals to Gorbachev from Romanian Dissidents," *Radio Free Europe Research,* Romanian SR/11, 15 October 1987; and "National Peasant Group Silenced After Human Rights Initiative," *ibid.,* Romanian SR/1, 6 February 1987. A Romanian dissident group, Romanian Democratic Action, has had its manifesto published in Western news media (e.g. *Neue Zürcher Zeitung,* March 19, 1987).

17. Many Western papers reported the disturbances in Brasov. The most detailed accounts are in *Frankfurter Allgemeine Zeitung,* November 25, 1987 and *Die Welt,* November 26, 1987.

18. By now, the cult clearly has religious overtures. For an especially striking example of this, see Nicolae Stoian in *Informatia Bucurestului,* January 24, 1986.

19. This is one of the reasons for Ceausescu's constant criticisms of the party apparat, which "interferes" with his relationship with the people. See, for example, his concluding speech criticizing shortcomings in the nomenklatura at the recent RCP national congress in *Scinteia,* December 17, 1987.

20. E.g. Gilberg, "Ceausescu's Romania," *Problems of Communism,* July-August 1974, pp. 35–38.

21. Ingenious ways are found to reside in Bucharest despite the restrictions established by the regime. For an account of such efforts by the man and woman in the provinces, see *Scinteia,* April 16, 1988.

22. E.g. Walter Connor, "Class, Politics, and Economic Stress: Eastern Europe after 1984" in Jeffrey D. Simon and Trond Gilberg (eds.), *Security Implications of Nationalism in Eastern Europe* (Boulder, CO: Westview Press, 1986), ch. 4 (pp. 49–69).

23. Remarkably frank discussions about these problems appear in the Romanian press with some regularity. See, for example, *Flacara*, October 9, 1987. On the region as a whole, see Volgyes, *Politics in Eastern Europe*, pp. 307–311.

24. The economic crisis has produced a great deal of unemployment, which results in bribery and extortion by individuals who hire workers. For a sharp denunciation of such practices, see *Flacara*, March 28, 1986. *Munca*, September 18, 1986, discussed the monthly "protection fee" for workers in certain jobs.

25. I have discussed this in "Romania's Growing Difficulties," *Current History*, November 1984, pp. 375–389.

26. E.g. Mihai Botez in *Financial Times*, April 8, 1986.

27. I interviewed Botez at length in the fall of 1987. Similar views were also expressed by Ion Iliescu, once a rising star in the RCP, in *Romania Literara*, September 3, 1987.

28. *Ibid.*

29. *Ibid.*

30. The eruption of workers' protests in Brasov in the fall of 1987 may be an omen of things to come. There are also other activities protesting the actions of the clan, and the regime is clearly cracking down. An underground publication, *Hungarian Press of Transylvania*, has reported on a number of strikes in that region in the fall of 1986, and on regime reactions and policies. For an analysis, see Vladimir Socor, "Transylvanian Hungarian Underground Press on Social Problems and Strikes," *Radio Free Europe Research*, Romanian SR/2, 6 March 1987.

31. Against such a backdrop of hopelessness and despair, the regime's recent plan to increase food production and supply is utterly unrealistic. The plan was unveiled in *Scinteia*, December 25, 1987.

32. The peasant revolt is discussed in great detail in Andrei Otetea, et. al., *Marea Rascoala a Taranilor din 1907*, esp. ch. II (on the preconditions for the revolt).

33. The treatment of ethnic Hungarians has prompted a major dispute between Hungary and Romania. Ceausescu strongly rejected Hungarian interference in Romanian domestic affairs in a speech to the Council of Working People of Hungarian Nationality and the Council of Working People of German Nationality (*Scinteia*, February 28, 1987). One of the representatives on the Council who is an ethnic Hungarian criticized Hungary in the strongest terms in *ibid.*, February 27, 1987. Karol Kiraly, an ethnic Hungarian who was once a high party official, sent a letter protesting regime policy to Ceausescu (*Neue Zürcher Zeitung*, January 10/11, 1988).

34. Ceausescu has escalated the tension in this field by his plan to "reorganize" a large number of villages with German and Hungarian populations in Transylvania. See also the chauvinistic article by Corneliu Vadim Tudor in *Saptamina*, February 13, 1987.

35. On the plight of the Germans in Transylvania, see *Der Spiegel*, March 2, 1987.

8

The Mass Culture
of Ethnicity and Nationalism

One of the main problems confronting the Ceausescu clan at the present time is the conflict between its own nationalistic and chauvinistic program, on the one hand, and the existence of well developed ethnic cultures among the national minorities, on the other hand. This tension is most dramatic at the elite level, but the views and arguments of political and cultural elites normally reflect deeply held values of the masses from which these elites emanate. Thus, the question of mass political cultures and their relations with other such cultures becomes crucial for an understanding of the political dynamics of contemporary society.

The Hierarchy of Ethnic Perceptions

Romania has the misfortune (not unlike other multiethnic societies in Eastern Europe) of a "skewed distribution" of ethnic groups in the political, socio-economic, and cultural realms. Specifically, since the achievement of national independence in the late nineteenth century, the political system has been controlled by the ethnic Romanians, but significant areas of the socio-economic system and the cultural realm have been dominated by others, notably Germans, Jews, and Magyars. This produced an ethnic "map" in which the Romanians were relatively privileged politically but disadvantaged in terms of economic development. At the same time, other groups were relatively advanced in the socio-economic and cultural arena, but lacked the political access necessary to make them feel part of the larger political system.

This complicated mosaic of relationships and hierarchies among the various ethnic groups of Romania had the potential of establishing various "models" of political interaction. There was, first of all, the model of assimilation, in which the politically dominant Romanians, through various control mechanisms, would attempt to force (or encourage) assimilation of the ethnic minorities into a predominantly Romanian culture. Such a policy would have required specific policies, determination, and relative success of the "assimilators" in the socioeconomic and cultural realms. It would also require willingness on the part of the minorities to be so assimilated. For a variety of reasons (to be discussed later) the most important ethnic groups in the country were not so inclined. Assimilation was therefore not attempted in any major or serious way by the Romanian elites before the advent of communists to political power.[1]

The second model would have been "unity in diversity." Unity in diversity presupposes not only a considerable amount of socio-economic, cultural, and linguistic autonomy for the various national groups in the system, but devotion to a common goal of politics and society as well. Perhaps the United States is an example of such a system, where the great diversity of ethnic groups and manifestations has produced a common political framework and acceptance of *American* institutions and political procedures and processes.

Unity in diversity presupposes the acceptance of goals and structures that stand above the parochialism of an ethnic group and also a certain level of performance in various realms by the structures and elites that represent the notion of a united system above the parochial interests of such a single group. It also assumes a certain amount of tolerance and willingness to accommodate (or at least accept) the goals, attitudes, and values of others. Perhaps the most important element in such tolerance is the notion that one must leave old animosities and hatreds behind and move to a new stage, a new life. Emigration to a new country makes such a psychological break possible.[2]

Romania did not possess these conditions for assimilation or the acceptance of unity in diversity. The ethnic groups on her territory had lived there for a very long time and had not chosen the form or the ethnic composition of the regime that was established upon independence in 1878. There was no voluntary association with the new state because this political structure had been established as the result of great power maneuverings and not because of any real mass participation. There were no overriding goals to which *all* ethnic groups could subscribe; on the contrary, the Romanian state was basically perceived as the political expression of the interests of the Romanians, with little regard for other groups. Unity in diversity could not be achieved under these circumstances.[3]

Assimilation was also unfeasible. The Romanians in charge of the political system were not inclined to attempt to incorporate the Magyars, Germans, Jews, and assorted others into a state that was perceived as the long overdue achievement of state and nationhood for the suffering Romanians. The minorities, for their part, had no intention of accepting the notion that the model to which they must assimilate would be the Romanian nation, which they had traditionally looked down upon as the despised "Vlachs," (or, in some cases, "Gypsies"). There emerged, instead, a system of relative autonomy for each group inside the parameters of the Romanian state. In this autonomy, each major ethnic group continued its life, with strong emphasis on national traditions and ethnic separatism. Old attitudes, values, and prejudices continued and were occasionally reinforced by behavior and policy on the part of the ruling Romanians. A hierarchy of ethnic preferences developed in which each group rated itself first and best on a number of dimensions, with others ranked according to perceived assets and deficiencies. Quite frequently, the Romanians ended up in a rather inferior position in this hierarchy. Thus emerged a political culture among the ethnic minorities in which the political rulers of the country were considered inferior, something to be avoided. At the same time, group cohesion inside each nationality solidified as a natural response to the unpalatable political conditions prevailing in the system.[4]

Another problem of major proportions was the fact that wars and diplomatic politics changed the boundaries of Romania quite frequently. In 1918, territories which had been part of Hungary inside the Austro-Hungarian Empire were incorporated into Romania, providing a considerable ethnic minority of Magyars and an irredentist cause on both sides of the new border. These territories were, by and large, reincorporated into Hungary in 1941, but reverted to Romanian control at the end of World War II. Bessarabia was ceded to the Soviet Union in 1940, not to return to Romanian jurisdiction, thus establishing a Romanian irredenta there. All of this is well known and requires no further elaboration here, except to stress that constant territorial adjustments gave the ethnic minorities even less of a reason to become assimilated or accepted by the political order in which they found themselves. Furthermore, historical memories of the "glory days" of existence inside the boundaries of the ethnic home fanned the flame of resentment and conflict. Harmony between ethnic groups could hardly be expected under such circumstances.[5]

Early Communist Nationality Policies

At the end of World War II, therefore, the Romanian state found itself in a difficult situation on the dimension of ethnic relations. The country was defeated, severely depleted of resources, and under Soviet occupation. The new leadership, consisting of a series of coalitions with increasing communist participation, faced the multiple problems of reconstruction, economically and politically. There was little choice for the leadership but to take a strongly nationalistic stance on the many issues that related to territorial adjustments and the reincorporation of Transylvania into the Romanian state. Thus, in the period 1944–1947, even the communists loudly proclaimed the need for reestablishing "Romania mare" and for an assertive stance in the concert of nations. The communists clearly advocated national reconstruction if not full reconciliation with other political elements, and they folded their economic program into the need for economic development at the national level. As time wore on, the nationalistic message began to fade, but it remained an important part of the RCP political platform until the onset of full-blown Stalinism towards the end of the decade.[6]

The political stance of the RCP was not unique in Eastern Europe or elsewhere on that continent. Throughout the region, nationalistic attitudes prevailed, partly because many of the local communist leaders and most of the rank and file believed in the need for national reconstruction, and partly because it was tactically wise to do so under unsettled political conditions in which the communists represented a mere minority (and, in some cases, a small one at that). Furthermore, the Kremlin counseled caution during this period and looked askance at any party or leadership group that attempted to move too rapidly on the path of socialism. Thus, one could be loyal to the Kremlin and to the national cause at the same time.[7]

It is ironic that the RCP leaders who attempted to carry out such a policy of national reconstruction and achievement of national goals were, to a considerable extent, non-Romanians, or at least of mixed parentage. There were a number of Jews among them, and also individuals of Bulgarian background. The ethnic Romanians in the leadership were less prominent during these early years, but, as is known, they clearly came to the fore after the death of Stalin, and have dominated the RCP ever since. That aside, the RCP leadership, despite its policies (or established goals) was less "national" in composition than most of the other elites of Eastern Europe during this period.

This fact led to added mistrust among the masses of the population. The Romanian masses had never exhibited any real interest in Marxist doctrine, in part because of the peasant nature of most of this population, but also because of the fact that this doctrine had been implemented in Russia, a traditional hegemon in the Balkans whose interests were considered detrimental to Romania. There was also the fact that most Romanians considered themselves culturally and ethnically superior to the Russians. Now, in the immediate aftermath of World War II, there were Jewish Marxists in important positions of leadership, and they all talked about the need for *national* reconstruction. The Romanian masses distrusted such individuals and programs on the basis of ethnic prejudice. They also distrusted them because they felt alienated from *all* political authority, regardless of the ethnic origin of the political leaders.[8]

The fact that Jews, some Germans, and an occasional Magyar held high political positions in the postwar governments of Romania did not endear them to these ethnic minorities, despite the common heritage and language. First of all, the political and economic programs of the Marxists, despite their emphasis on national economic development, did not correspond to the interests of most of the ethnic minorities, especially their socio-economic and political leaders. Furthermore, these RCP leaders still represented *central* power, which, by definition, meant the power of the *Romanian* state. This affiliation with Romania heightened the mistrust of the Germans and Magyars and produced considerable resentment against individuals of their own group who had "sold out" to Marxism and the Russians.[9]

These first few years were formative and fundamental for an understanding of the relationship between ethnic groups in socialist Romania during the last few decades. They also help explain current nationality policies formulated and implemented by the Ceausescu regime. It was in the period 1944–1947 that the old intersected with the new in "the national question" of Romanian politics. This represents the roots of one of the most fundamental problems facing this beleaguered system today. And, unfortunately, it is a problem that will remain even after the Ceausescus.

Stalinism, Nationalism, and Modernization

Once the fury of Stalinism broke upon the landscape of Eastern Europe, there was a temporary reduction of ethnic animosities and nationalistic fervor. Stalinist political and economic policies had a massive levelling effect upon *all* individuals and groups in Eastern Europe, regardless of ethnic background. Furthermore, the policy of economic and political synchronization that now emanated from the Kremlin reduced or eliminated the opportunities for national policy in all areas. Now, the states and parties of the entire region were forced to act in the same manner, produce the same slogans and goods, and maintain the same subordinate position vis-a-vis Moscow. Under these circumstances, there could be no national economic policy and no deviations from the established political line, assiduously supervised by the Kremlin. During this period, then, the RCP leadership, controlled by "Muscovites," slavishly followed the dictates from the Soviet capital. And these Muscovites, most of whom were not ethnic Romanians, made sure that the

TABLE 8.1   National Composition of Romania, 1930-1977

	1930	1956	1966	1977
Total population	18,057,028	17,489,430	19,103,163	21,559,416
Ethnic affiliation (%)				
Romanians	71.9	85.7	87.7	88.1
Hungarians	7.9	9.1	8.5	7.9
Germans	4.1	2.2	2.0	1.7
Jewish	4.0	0.8	0.2	0.1
Gypsy	1.5	0.6	0.3	1.1
Ukrainian/Ruthenian	3.2	0.3	0.3	0.3
Serb, Croat, Slovene	0.3	0.3	0.2	0.2
Russian	2.3	0.2	0.2	0.1
Czech		0.1	0.1	0.0
Slovak		0.1	0.1	0.1
Tatar	0.1	0.1	0.1	0.1
Turk	0.9	0.1	0.1	0.1
Bulgarian	2.0	0.1	0.1	0.0
Other	0.5	0.6	0.0	0.1

Source: Paul Shoup, The East European and Soviet Data Handbook (New York, NY: Columbia University Press, 1981), p. 139.

"locals" (leaders who had spent the war years in Romanian jails) were controlled, and in some cases liquidated.[10]

For the masses of the population, the Stalinist years constituted a period of extreme hardship, with severe economic and social dislocations. Life was too hard and too controlled for nationalistic expression, even if the yearnings were still there. Still, the socio-economic policies of the rapid and forced industrialization produced massive population movements which gradually shifted the ethnic balance in a number of areas which had hitherto been rather homogeneous in composition. The most important of these developments was the in-migration of large numbers of ethnic Romanians into territories inhabited primarily by Magyars and Germans. Table 8.1 shows the ethnic composition of the country as a whole during the decades of communist rule. Table 8.2 examines the ethnic composition of each county (judet) in the same time frame. By the end of the Stalin era, then, considerable changes had taken place in the population structure of Romania. This trend continued unabated during the era of Gheorghe Gheorghiu-Dej and Nicolae Ceausescu, as illustrated by Tables 8.1 and 8.2. By the late 1980s, the ethnic Romanians have become ensconced in traditional minority areas, thus fundamentally changing the ethnic balance there. This development has considerable political ramifications as well, as we shall see below.

The modernization process has also changed the characteristics of each ethnic group in various and crucial ways. All groups have benefitted from the process of urbanization, educational development, and functional specialization and stratification. Table 8.3 examines the occupational

TABLE 8.2 Ethnic Composition of Romanian Administrative Units, Census of 1966
(The complete census figures for 1977 have not been made available in
the West).

	Total Population	Romanians	Hungarians	Germans	Gypsies
R. S. Romania	19,013,163	16,746,510	1,619,592	382,595	64,197
Judets:					
Alba	382,786	339,545	26,989	12,823	2,811
Arad	481,248	344,302	75,445	43,874	2,645
Arges	529,833	528,439	397	103	292
Bacau	598,321	590,259	5,193	194	321
Bihor	586,460	337,837	192,948	1,106	3,678
Bistrita-Nasaud	286,600	236,789	22,358	6,102	3,023
Botosani	452,406	448,998	92	36	104
Brasov	442,692	331,007	65,326	40,857	3,405
Braila	339,954	335,865	294	81	439
Bazau	482,784	479,979	145	37	2,261
Caras Severin	358,726	295,879	9,175	23,882	2,132
Cluj	631,100	457,169	164,768	1,738	4,322
Constanta	465,752	421,486	923	494	252
Covanta	176,858	34,099	140,472	277	1,465
Dimbovita	421,557	420,505	142	56	601
Dolj	691,116	687,687	322	210	1,768
Galati	474,279	470,160	720	163	450
Gorj	298,946	279,279	267	47	1,013
Harghita	282,392	31,272	248,886	237	1,390
Hunedoara	474,602	423,128	40,047	6,671	730
Ialomita	363,075	361,998	164	37	296
Iasi	617,397	612,192	490	198	141
Ilfov	576,622	754,621	183	74	1,241
Maramures	427,645	339,984	53,583	2,993	899
Mehedinti	309,457	304,305	589	560	778
Mures	561,598	278,386	249,675	20,625	11,402
Neamt	471,836	469,372	774	123	239
Olt	476,513	475,969	105	35	195
Prahova	699,224	695,835	862	436	971
Satu Mare	359,393	203,780	147,594	4,427	1,750
Salaj	263,103	194,790	63,850	72	1,179
Sibiu	414,756	293,282	20,139	96,882	3,037
Suceava	572,781	550,196	608	2,830	203
Teleorman	521,478	519,180	91	27	1,952
Timis	607,596	378,183	76,183	109,315	4,637
Tulcea	236,709	201,510	130	105	126
Vaslui	431,555	430,478	40	24	244
Vilcea	368,779	368,172	190	76	145
Vrancea	351,292	350,364	146	35	165
Municipiul Bucuresti	1,451,942	1,421,211	9,287	4,733	895

(continues)

TABLE 8.2 (continued)

Hungarians Ruthenians 54,705	Serbs, Croats, Slovenes 44,236	Russians 39,483	Jews 42,888	Tatars 22,151	Slovaks 22,221	Turks 18,040	Bulgarians 11,193
35	25	66	267	--	64	2	14
259	2,850	164	1,862	2	7,317	5	1,683
39	10	50	46	2	19	13	8
23	6	86	1,461	1	13	7	9
63	114	147	1,798	1	7,813	9	85
102	7	36	102	1	12	--	5
192	--	122	2,494	--	14	3	6
59	73	251	862	13	24	21	43
20	24	1,154	301	3	6	147	65
18	15	48	143	1	5	16	12
3,647	15,826	142	190	7	1,292	25	108
70	73	151	2,011	4	101	16	46
93	33	4,062	251	21,538	25	14,118	304
4	5	39	37	--	2	2	7
2	38	55	21	1	7	6	22
8	38	57	130	4	14	7	23
16	23	451	1,365	15	9	58	63
130	15	30	16	4	9	6	2
263	9	133	98	1	9	--	1
505	149	259	510	3	296	17	131
11	12	73	17	1	9	293	34
46	7	281	3,719	17	15	18	9
14	16	79	20	3	10	117	37
29,060	30	161	763	2	28	2	3
14	1,517	40	58	2	12	460	31
30	18	98	1,053	2	41	4	25
18	22	52	1,015	4	9	10	17
2	8	13	14	--	12	3	12
73	43	202	294	4	11	13	34
905	15	100	573	1	142	5	13
16	12	19	88	1	2,357	1	5
90	57	152	407	6	41	23	29
11,568	6	1,917	2,314	--	10	3	8
16	12	37	15	4	23	6	20
1,780	22,709	342	2,209	4	2,300	37	7,509
5,061	15	26,447	154	401	10	2,091	220
5	2	41	649	--	7	4	8
75	4	14	2	--	11	1	5
9	6	61	372	--	7	2	11
364	392	1,851	14,487	98	115	469	526

(continues)

Czechs	Greeks	Poles	Armenians	Others	Undeclared	
9,978	9,088	5,860	3,436	4,681	2,309	R. S. Romania
						Judets:
56	6	21	8	38	16	Alba
407	10	141	21	139	122	Arad
5	224	26	31	65	64	Arges
8	522	35	12	109	62	Bacau
63	581	68	7	80	62	Bihor
9	5	17	1	11	20	Bistrita-Nasaud
3	285	20	5	6	26	Botosani
189	198	146	25	131	62	Brasov
8	1,417	16	40	52	22	Braila
5	36	18	4	21	20	Buzau
5,858	12	223	1	258	69	Caras-Severin
106	69	115	173	107	61	Cluj
24	669	54	998	356	72	Constanta
4	292	14	1	129	9	Covasna
7	32	12	3	27	20	Dimbovita
14	605	26	17	79	107	Dolj
10	598	37	51	69	21	Galati
17	4	7	1	16	65	Gorj
10	2	31	10	15	25	Harghita
484	709	539	5	384	35	Hunedoara
--	21	20	3	28	58	Ialomita
7	76	56	13	44	68	Iasi
5	27	12	10	40	113	Ilfov
35	8	41	7	17	29	Maramures
953	20	17	1	41	59	Mehedinti
54	13	68	20	50	34	Mures
8	19	31	8	39	76	Neamt
5	16	9	3	13	99	Olt
44	120	61	35	142	44	Prahova
27	1	10	1	19	30	Satu Mare
57	6	6	1	6	37	Salaj
116	105	223	15	105	47	Sibiu
38	195	2,830	13	24	18	Suceava
5	13	5	5	10	57	Teleorman
971	50	220	60	288	99	Timis
1	239	12	30	134	23	Tulcea
1	23	4	--	9	16	Vaslui
4	5	2	2	25	46	Vilcea
1	21	14	46	17	15	Vrancea
359	834	653	1,749	1,538	381	Municipiul Bucuresti

Source: Republica Socialista Romania, Directia Centrala de Statistica, Recensamintul Populatiei si Locuintelor din 15 Martie 1966, p. 153.

TABLE 8.3   Occupational Statistics, Census of 1966

Nationality	Total Population	Workers	Intellectuals Functionaries	Collective Farmers	Individual Farmers	Crafts and Trades
Total	19,013,163	7,624,981	2,356,082	7,365,179	996,600	614,659
Romanians	16,746,510	6,507,669	2,065,083	6,646,623	926,911	479,537
Hungarians	1,619,592	742,623	188,215	533,724	32,063	89,168
Germans	382,595	224,264	52,028	75,478	3,772	22,531
Gypsies	64,197	30,362	324	19,501	1,670	10,427
Ukrainians, Ruthenians	54,705	22,583	2,392	10,007	18,433	1,151
Serbs, Croats, Slovenes	44,236	14,173	3,989	19,291	4,577	1,938
Russians	39,483	23,639	3,762	10,186	233	1,166
Jews	42,888	12,440	25,496	142	71	3,200
Others	106,648	46,497	14,467	29,669	8,788	5,467
Undeclared	2,309	767	326	558	82	74

Source: Republica Socialista Romania, Directia Centrala de Statistica, Recensamintul Populatiei si Locuintelor din 15 Martie 1966, p. 153.

structure of each major ethnic group in 1966 (the last census for which we have complete figures). Table 8.4 examines occupational development in each county over time, thus providing indirect evidence of occupational development for *all* ethnic groups. For the ethnic Romanians, modernization, communist-style, has meant massive improvements in all categories of social mobilization, especially since this group was heavily rural and undereducated at the start of the communist era. For the other groups, and particularly the Magyars, Germans, and Jews, the undeniable overall improvement in their social mobilization is offset by the fact that the Romanians have developed even faster, thus catching up with the more highly developed groups which, in turn, lost the privileged status that they had acquired over the centuries that preceded communist rule. This trend in itself heightened the feeling among these ethnic minorities that they were actually the victims of discrimination. While this may have been inaccurate in purely statistical terms, the political importance of perceptions, mistaken or not, must not be overlooked. The three more highly developed groups *did* perceive discrimination, even if none was practiced as official policy during the early part of the post-Stalin period.

The rule of Gheorghe Gheorghiu-Dej, while increasingly nationalistic and autonomist in foreign policy, maintained a certain amount of tolerance for the needs and wishes of the ethnic minorities. During the Hungarian Revolution of 1956, the Romanian leadership dealt with its large Magyar minority by means of the carrot and the stick, but largely kept the notion of some cultural and national autonomy for the minorities intact. Thus, the Autonomous Magyar Region was maintained throughout the

TABLE 8.4   Occupational Structure of Romanian Judets, 1984

	Total	Industry	Con-struction	Agri-culture	Forestry	Transport
Total	7,585,000	3,523,500	710,500	604,200	55,000	592,400
Judets:						
Alba	143,900	76,700	14,400	8,800	1,200	11,000
Arad	175,500	78,900	10,700	23,000	1,900	14,100
Arges	230,600	115,600	23,700	13,500	1,500	16,400
Bacau	214,600	101,700	26,100	13,100	2,000	15,800
Bihor	214,300	100,600	18,200	18,500	1,700	16,200
Bistrita-Nasaud	83,100	38,200	6,700	7,700	1,500	6,100
Botosani	97,500	42,400	7,500	11,000	700	5,600
Brasov	295,900	178,800	20,500	10,300	1,300	19,300
Braila	138,400	57,000	13,800	23,100	500	9,700
Buzau	140,400	68,600	10,900	13,200	1,100	11,200
Caras-Severin	147,300	70,800	18,900	6,300	3,100	14,000
Calarasi	103,400	28,800	15,200	29,300	500	6,400
Cluj	274,300	133,400	25,600	14,100	1,700	24,200
Constanta	280,100	67,600	48,600	35,600	1,000	47,100
Covasna	76,600	39,900	6,000	4,900	1,200	5,100
Dimbovita	166,000	92,200	14,100	10,300	1,100	10,400
Dolj	226,200	92,400	23,000	29,400	1,200	19,600
Galati	210,000	91,400	24,100	18,600	800	25,800
Giurgiu	85,000	21,800	11,200	19,100	800	9,500
Gorj	136,100	68,000	19,200	5,100	1,200	12,000
Harghita	116,700	63,400	8,400	5,800	1,800	8,600
Hunedoara	218,800	116,000	27,500	6,100	1,600	17,300
Ialomita	81,500	19,100	8,100	23,500	500	8,300
Iasi	220,300	97,300	20,200	16,600	1,600	17,300
Maramures	159,000	82,100	14,000	7,100	2,000	10,200
Mehedinti	98,900	35,400	19,100	11,200	1,200	8,300
Mures	205,800	104,800	12,600	16,400	1,300	14,200
Neamt	156,900	89,100	8,700	8,300	2,100	9,600
Olt	139,100	55,100	17,000	18,900	900	11,100
Prahova	323,500	182,200	26,800	15,200	1,300	23,600
Satu Mare	120,400	61,600	5,600	11,300	1,000	7,200
Salaj	70,200	33,200	6,000	6,100	1,300	4,500
Sibiu	197,000	118,900	8,500	13,500	1,200	11,500
Suceava	177,600	87,700	15,100	10,000	3,200	14,900
Teleorman	116,700	45,600	7,900	19,000	700	10,200
Timis	282,200	128,900	19,700	34,900	1,000	21,700
Tulcea	90,100	31,900	8,600	19,400	900	7,700
Vaslui	109,100	51,900	6,400	14,300	1,800	6,000
Vilcea	121,700	49,100	18,600	6,400	1,800	10,500
Vrancea	93,400	38,200	6,800	12,300	1,400	9,500
Municipiul Bucuresti	1,046,900	467,200	86,500	13,000	400	60,700

(continues)

Table 8.4 (continued)

Telecom- munication 81,899	Retail Trade 621,500	Communal Services 361,900	Education, Culture, the Arts 406,400	Science 145,700	Health Services 277,100	Adminis- tration 54,100	Others 150,800
1,800	9,100	5,200	7,200	900	4,600	1,000	2,000
2,100	16,100	8,000	7,500	3,600	6,400	1,100	2,100
2,000	17,100	10,100	11,800	6,700	6,900	1,300	4,000
2,500	15,300	9,400	12,600	1,400	8,100	1,200	5,400
2,100	19,700	9,600	11,700	1,800	9,700	1,200	3,300
1,000	6,800	3,900	5,600	500	3,200	700	1,200
1,500	8,200	4,200	7,700	400	5,900	900	1,500
2,300	23,200	11,600	11,400	5,400	7,600	1,000	3,200
1,200	10,600	5,000	6,200	2,700	4,600	700	3,300
1,700	10,400	4,800	7,800	2,300	5,400	1,000	2,000
1,700	11,300	6,400	5,900	1,200	5,000	1,000	1,700
1,000	7,400	2,700	4,400	2,900	2,500	700	1,600
2,700	20,600	12,200	17,900	6,100	10,600	1,300	3,900
2,400	37,500	13,700	11,100	2,600	9,300	1,000	2,600
900	6,300	2,800	4,300	300	3,200	600	1,100
1,600	10,700	5,200	8,300	1,100	5,500	1,000	4,500
2,100	17,900	9,500	12,900	5,300	8,200	1,300	3,400
1,700	15,500	9,000	10,200	2,300	6,700	1,000	2,900
1,100	5,900	3,200	4,400	2,200	2,800	800	2,200
1,200	8,100	7,300	6,000	900	3,700	900	2,500
1,300	9,700	4,500	6,400	100	4,400	800	1,500
2,100	17,500	8,800	8,700	1,300	7,700	1,200	3,000
1,200	8,000	3,300	4,700	200	2,800	700	1,100
2,100	17,500	8,900	18,700	3,800	11,300	1,200	3,800
1,900	12,500	8,200	9,600	1,500	6,700	1,000	2,200
1,300	7,500	3,700	4,800	600	3,700	800	1,300
2,100	16,800	10,600	12,000	1,900	8,500	1,200	3,400
1,600	11,600	6,100	9,300	1,600	5,900	1,000	2,000
1,500	10,700	5,100	8,100	2,400	4,800	1,100	2,400
2,900	23,800	11,500	13,700	5,200	9,300	1,400	6,600
1,500	10,100	6,000	7,800	1,600	4,300	800	1,600
1,100	5,900	2,700	4,700	100	2,700	700	1,200
1,800	13,200	7,600	9,400	2,000	5,800	1,000	2,600
2,200	15,100	7,100	11,100	1,100	6,600	1,200	2,300
1,500	11,100	4,400	6,600	900	4,300	1,100	3,400
3,000	20,800	14,700	16,400	4,500	10,800	1,300	4,500
1,300	8,200	2,500	4,400	400	2,900	700	1,200
1,500	7,900	3,500	8,300	600	4,600	900	1,400
1,500	10,600	5,800	7,300	1,400	5,300	1,000	2,400
1,300	8,000	3,200	5,800	1,400	3,500	800	1,200
12,600	97,300	89,900	53,700	62,500	41,300	14,500	47,300

Source: Republica Socialista Romania, Directia Centrala de Statistica, Anuarul Statistic al Republicii Socialiste Romania 1985, pp. 64-65.

entire period of Gheorghiu-Dej's rule, and it was Nicolae Ceausescu, his successor, who began the process of dismantling this region and then administratively incorporating it into the territorial scheme of counties (judets) with some gerrymandering included. In the period 1956–1968, the large ethnic minorities continued to enjoy a certain amount of religious, social, and even economic autonomy.[11]

Ceausescu and Chauvinism

Gheorghe Gheorghiu-Dej was clearly a Romanian nationalist; after all, the celebrated "Romanian declaration of independence" in economic development occurred in April 1963, two years before Gheorghiu-Dej's death. The regime, intrusive as it was, lacked the will and the resources to control all aspects of its citizens' lives. Thus, a relatively benign balance between center and periphery was maintained.

The situation of the ethnic minorities changed drastically under Nicolae Ceausescu, even if it took a while for his policies to mature and reach their full fruition as they now appear at the end of the 1980s. Nicolae Ceausescu's policies can only be understood in the context of the complicated interethnic situation as it existed right after World War II. At the same time, one must also attempt to fathom the change that has occurred within the mind of the General Secretary himself (as well as his close associates) on this issue. Taken together, these elements allow us to construct a more detailed picture of actual regime policies on the national question as well as the political and socio-economic ramifications of such policies.

When Ceausescu came to power after Gheorghe Gheorghiu-Dej's death in 1965, the autonomist policy of Romania inside the Comecon and the Warsaw Pact was already launched, apparently with considerable internal support in the party apparat and in the general population itself, especially the ethnic Romanians. It was therefore likely that the new leader would continue a policy which enjoyed such support. In fact, it was clear that greater legitimacy in the elite structure, as well as the population itself, could only be achieved through the vehicle of nationalism. Here, then, was a case where the "objective conditions" of society outlined the path which must be travelled during the new leadership's tenure, much as it had been during the reign of Ceausescu's predecessor. And it was even likely that this policy would be expanded, for greater public support for the foreign relations offensives contemplated by the ambitious new leader, as well as the accelerated economic development he envisioned.

For a period of time this policy worked. After a suitable interlude of power consolidation, Ceausescu had an opportunity to demonstrate his allegiance and devotion to Romania and Romanian nationalism during the crisis over Czechoslovakia (in the spring and summer of 1968). In this crisis, Ceausescu demonstrated firmness and a great ability to communicate with the Romanian masses, as evidenced by the popular meeting in Bucharest at the height of the crisis, where genuine enthusiasm was displayed for the cause of the republic and the stance taken by the leadership. This was, indeed, a time when nationalistic policies and statements served the purpose of engendering mass support and enthusiasm among the societal elites, even those outside the formal party structures.[12]

After 1968, there were other policies as well that helped bolster the regime's image and standing in the Romanian mass public. During the celebrations of the centennial of Romanian independence in the second half of the 1970s, mass patriotic manifestations of various kinds reflected at least partial success in the regime's attempts to utilize historic events to enhance its stature. And there can be little doubt that the continued emphasis on foreign policy autonomy and an orientation towards the West, to Latin and Central Europe, helped in this regard as well. Thus, Ceausescu cleverly utilized the nationalism of Romanian masses for maximum benefit in his quest for mass support.

The other side of this policy had to do with policies towards the ethnic minorities. It is generally recognized that any attempt to enhance the stature and self esteem in an ethnic group may have negative connotations for other groups, thereby widening the chasm that exists between them. This was clearly the case in Romania throughout the entire era of Ceausescuism, both because of the general tone of regime policy and also because of specific policies undertaken. By the end of the 1970s, there could be no mistaking the fact that the Ceausescu era had become one of ethnic chauvinism rather than just nationalism.

A number of specific policies were carried out during the early years of the Ceausescu era that presaged the approaches utilized subsequently. In 1968 the Magyar Autonomous Region was dissolved, and its territory divided and incorporated into the reconstituted counties (judets) in a territorial reorganization that clearly enhanced Ceausescu's control of the regional party apparatus. This development also made it possible for the new leader to staff the new party bodies on the same level with his close associates, most of whom were ethnic Romanians. Even in areas with heavy minority concentrations many of the key party positions were now staffed with ethnic Romanians.[13]

The next step in the synchronization process was taken with the advent of the so-called "little cultural revolution," which began in the summer and early fall of 1971, and continued unabated throughout the decade, only to be further enhanced during the 1980s. The "little cultural revolution" was not specifically directed against the ethnic minorities, but it emphasized the importance of ideological orthodoxy, greater political control with all aspects of societal life, and the elimination of all group autonomy, thereby reducing the few opportunities for ethnic self-expression that still remained. Throughout the decade of the 1970s, the ideological emphasis of the regime became more and more personalized, reflecting the tendency of the General Secretary and his close associates to define both ideology and politics in terms that gradually shifted the focus from Marx and Engels to Ceausescu and Petrescu, and made nationalism into chauvinism. As discussed above, this chauvinism spelled increasing trouble for the ethnic minorities, since the Ceausescu vision was heavily colored by a rather unsophisticated notion of Romanian history. Particularly important was the Ceausescus' claim to represent the tradition of Stephen the Great and Michael the Brave, two kings whose fame and fortunes were made in the struggle with outside forces, especially the Turks, but also others. Increasingly, Vlad Tepes was also upgraded to a national hero, especially as a strong ruler who kept law and order in the land and ensured the continuity of the Romanians as a nation and as a power to be reckoned with in the annals of European history.[14]

By the middle of the decade the chauvinistic tendencies of the regime had become conscious policy. The celebrations of Romanian independence unleashed a torrent of books, plays, movies, historical findings, and even anthropological works that harked back to the glory of the Romanians and emphasized the historical continuity and unbroken bond between the historical figures of the Middle Ages and the current leadership. Much of this research was of rather questionable quality and credibility, but the regime continued to emphasize and encourage it. There were also thinly veiled attacks on those who failed to understand the greatness of the Romanian nation and its heritage—a message clearly aimed at the larger ethnic minorities, particularly the Magyars. Increasingly, Nicolae Ceausescu and his wife considered themselves the embodiment of this national heritage, and thus, any criticism of it was interpreted as a personal attack on the leading couple.[15]

A number of other events helped sharpen the relationship between the ethnic groups in Romania. During the 1970s, there were occasional controversies between Budapest and Bucharest about the treatment of Magyars in Transylvania. Some prominent Romanian citizens of Magyar origin openly protested the policies of the regime on this issue, and the fledgling dissident movement was heavily populated by minority figures. Ceausescu railed against such behavior and such attitudes, emphasizing that people who had lived on Romanian soil for hundreds of years could not possibly claim a home anywhere else (an argument aimed primarily at the ethnic Germans who now sought emigration in increasing numbers). The General Secretary also emphasized that other groups (primarily the Magyars) must accept the notion that the national interest of Romania supersedes anything that could be considered "national" in the more limited, ethnic sense. Throughout, his notion of the "organic society" became more and more developed as an analytical tool and as a guide to policy. By the end of the decade, it had become a full-fledged concept that dominated all political discourse in Romania.[16]

The emphasis on the organic society deepened during the 1980s, and it was mixed with advanced paranoia, which changed Ceausescu's views on the nation and Romanian nationalism in a major way. The General Secretary continued to emphasize his close connection with the glories of the Romanian past, and he continued to deliver speeches that extolled this heritage and the role of contemporary Romania in the world. In fact, his claims to achievements in the Romanian nation became more and more exaggerated and became the laughingstock of most of the scientific community. Examples of those claims include the notion that archaeological digs had revealed the first human-like skeleton on Romanian soil. There was also the contention that the political and social organizations of the kingdoms of Benebista and Decebalus were superior to that of the Romans and thus helped advance the level of the Roman Empire after Trajan's conquest of Dacia. The General Secretary also discussed many other alleged scientific achievements by the Romanians throughout the centuries, especially in the Middle Ages.[17]

These claims on behalf of the Romanian nation clearly relegated all others to a position of secondary or tertiary rank. For the Germans and the Magyars, this was indeed heresy, insofar as these ethnic groups possessed a proud heritage of their own, while at the same time denigrating the achievements of the Romanians. The intellectual and emotional climate of interethnic relations declined markedly during the decade of the 1980s precisely because of the messages emanating from the General Secretary as he continued his odyssey towards even greater paranoia and megalomania. In addition, the court poets and scribes surrounding the clan added much inflammatory material by producing books, plays, and movies that were frankly chauvinistic and often anti-Semitic. The tone of this production was so heated that most members of the ethnic minorities assumed that they had official sanction, which may indeed have been the case. Thus, the chauvinistic tendencies of the Ceausescu era came to a peak during the decade of the 1980s.[18]

Specific policies added to the problems experienced by the minorities. The regime began to assess emigrants high fees, allegedly to compensate the state for educational expenses incurred; in fact, much of the added fee usually ended up in the pockets of officials. This policy caused a serious rift with the Federal Republic, because it had a detrimental effect upon the out-migration of ethnic Germans. After a considerable period of political controversy the Romanians again eased the restrictions imposed. The flow of Germans out of the traditional homeland of Siebenbürgen then continued unabated.[19]

The controversy over German emigration was but the most visible of the policies that Ceausescu perpetuated upon the ethnic minorities during the apex of his rule, the decade of the 1980s. There were many restrictions on educational opportunities; place names were changed to reflect the Romanian heritage while removing the historical facts of German and Magyar influence; officials allegedly changed birth certificates to reduce the number of ethnic Germans and Magyars born in Romania. Myriads of little annoying practices took place at the regional and local levels, again reflecting a general climate of discrimination which must have had the general blessing of the political leaders at the center even if they did not specifically order all of these measures of harassment.[20]

All of these policies, together with the steadily worsening conditions of the economy, made the physical and psychological conditions of the minorities intolerable, particularly in the case of the Magyars. In 1987 and 1988, large numbers of individuals of Hungarian ethnic background began to cross the border into Hungary. By the summer of 1988, there were at least one hundred thousand such individuals in refugee camps in Hungary. An increasing number of ethnic Romanians began to join them during the first months of the year 1988, possibly reflecting a policy change in Bucharest to allow such troublemakers to leave the country. At the time of this writing, the flow of desperate individuals, Magyars and Romanians, across the heavily guarded border into a neighboring socialist state represents the most obvious illustration of the failures of the Ceausescu era in human terms.[21]

During the decade of the 1980s, the General Secretary's views on the nation began to change, subtly at first, then more drastically. The Leader began to define the nation only in terms of the great men who had been the chieftains. Implicit in this argument is the idea that the nation *as such* cannot produce greatness, but must be led by individuals who can mobilize the innate resources in the mass for the fulfillment of potential. It is doubtful that Ceausescu has read Nietsche or others who advocate the "big man in history" theory, but his ideas are very much in the line of argument advanced by these philosophers. (It should be noted that Lenin also advocated top-down leadership and expressed his belief that the masses are only capable of trade union consciousness. Furthermore, Stalin's policies, which were very much akin to those of Ceausescu throughout the last two decades, was also a firm believer in such policies and values). Whatever the intellectual inspiration for Nicolae

Ceausescu, he is now utterly convinced that the Romanian nation can only be "activated" through great leaders.[22]

The logical conclusion to such attitudes is rather clear, and the General Secretary has now made it. Only he (and, presumably, his consort) can be that leader. This attitude has emerged more and more clearly as the second half of the decade wears on. Some of these views may have been fostered by the Byzantine personality cult fostered by the politics surrounding the leading couple, as well as the many sycophantic elements who make a living out of flattery at the margins of power. Some of it clearly originates with his wife, who is at least as ambitious and self-centered as the General Secretary himself. But much of this comes from the Leader himself, who appears more and more preoccupied with his place in history as he ages. His illness, which is reportedly prostate cancer, must also make him concerned with the need to establish himself in the annals of mankind before his physical demise.[23]

As of now, the General Secretary appears to be distrustful of *all* nations, including his own. True, the Romanians represent the best and the brightest, and they are endowed with the greatest of all assets, a leader who is the only one to activate them, but the nation is not performing up to a level worthy of the leadership, just as individual Romanians are seriously in default in their own tasks and performance. This is, of course, an important defense mechanism for an individual whose leadership is clearly faulty on most ordinary dimensions of measurement, and it might be sufficient to simply consider it as such, except for the fact that the General Secretary persists in expressing his conviction about the need for great leaders in history. This is clearly more than just a defense mechanism for poor performance. And because it is so much more, it is going to remain a permanent fixture of Romanian politics until the end of the Ceausescu era. Indeed, if dynastic succession is achieved, it may go on for a long time even after the departure of Nicolae and Elena.[24]

The disturbing developments in the General Secretary's mindset about the nation and its faults bode ill for *all* Romanians, regardless of their ethnic background. It is, nevertheless, most troublesome for the non-Romanians, because the Ceausescus have retained a mystical affection for their own collectivity, despite its faults (as perceived by the leading couple). This affection will ensure preferential treatment for the Romanians in cases of choice. It will also ensure the continuation of discriminatory policies towards all minorities. The most obvious target is the Magyar group, because it is the largest, and because it has the longest history of adversary relations. Furthermore, the Magyars have no protectors other than Hungary, a fellow socialist state whose economic capabilities are insufficient to ransom ethnic Hungarians. (In fact, Budapest does not want a population movement, but rather hopes to influence the Bucharest regime to improve its treatment of the Magyars inside Romania. Nationalistic elements in Budapest have begun to demand territorial adjustments as the only way to ensure proper treatment of the Transylvanian Magyars).[25]

In comparison with the Magyars, the Germans are in a much better position, and the out-migration of this group continues. It is therefore merely a matter of time before the "German problem" is solved. The Federal Republic, with its considerable economic resources and political clout, will make every effort to ensure the continuation of this emigration.

Ethnic Relations and Instability

The reemergence of Romanian nationalism and chauvinism as legitimizing devices for the political regime made a great deal of sense originally, because it clearly helped bolster the political system in the minds of the ethnic majority of the country. It was also in line with Romanian traditions and the aspirations of many individuals and groups in this society. Such policies and statements, coupled with a stance of foreign policy autonomy, produced some mass support at critical times in the history of communist-ruled Romania, most notably during the Prague Spring and the subsequent Soviet-led invasion, now two decades behind us in history. The mass support engendered through such policies and such a political climate clearly offset the resentment produced among the ethnic minorities; after all, they constitute less than ten percent of the population, and thus carry little weight politically.

All nationalism must sooner or later produce practical political and socio-economic results; otherwise, slogans, banners, and symbolic rewards lose their meaning. This is indeed the case with Romania towards the end of the 1980s. There are still elements in the ethnic Romanian population who are intrigued and pleased by the chauvinistic statements and policies that emanate from the Ceausescu clan, and these elements nowadays represent the strongest supporters of the General Secretary in the mass population. Furthermore, they are the direct political and psychological descendants of the followers of the League of the Archangel Michael, who also worshipped mystical nationalism, chauvinism, anti-Semitism, and the belief in great leaders and "organic" causes. But they are increasingly in a distinct minority, removed from the realities of Romanian political life, somewhere in a twilight zone of faith where political facts do not intrude. Outside, in the daylight of political reality, the demise of Ceausescu's nationality policy can be clearly seen in two major groups, the general Romanian population and the ethnic Romanian intelligentsia.[26]

The ethnic Romanian masses are now clearly too downtrodden and too cynical to believe in nationalistic slogans and chauvinistic demagoguery. The most obvious change in Romania during the last three to four years is the loss of spirit among the general population. While this cannot be measured in any scientific way, it is a palpable fact for any experienced visitor. People straggle from empty stores to dispirited queues, their faces closed, their eyes averted (except for those who want to exchange money, provide goods and services, or offer their loved ones to Westerners with hard currency). There is no ambience, no Latin esprit, which always made Bucharest such a fascinating city, even under communist rule. People are atomized, subjugated, listless. This is not the stuff from which causes are made and furthered, or enthusiasm produced for "Romania Mare" or "Ceausescu and the people." For these bedraggled masses, a regime, *any* regime, must provide a minimum of goods and services before it can lay claim to affection. In fact, there may emerge a sense of betrayal among these masses, a feeling that the clan has no right to drape itself in the Tricolor and speak about its national mission, its glorious heritage, its shining path to the future and its place in history. The Ceausescus may feel that the nation has failed them; the nation may now begin to feel that it is, indeed, the other way around. In any case, there is little payoff in nationalism under these circumstances. *Any* leader with *any* kind of sense for mass attitudes would perceive this. The General Secretary and his clan, shielded by self-serving Praetorian guards, either cannot or will not understand this elementary fact.

The alienation among Romanian intellectuals of all kinds is much more fundamental, and occasionally rather outspoken. As discussed above, the General Secretary and his family are despised and quietly ridiculed because of the irrational and erratic behavior they display, and because of their ostentatious lifestyle and obvious contempt for the suffering masses, as well as their distrust of intellectuals. The chauvinistic statements and falsification of history and contemporary reality produced by alleged "scholars" engenders nothing but cynical contempt among the real intellectuals of the country, many of whom are ethnic Romanians. It is quite clear now, at the end of the 1980s, that nationalism and chauvinism cannot possibly restore the support that Ceausescu once may have had in this social stratum. Thus, chauvinism has now backfired, and the General Secretary has been deprived of the essential skills that the intellectuals represent. It is likely that this mutual alienation has reached a point where it cannot be remedied. Thus, the performance of the system in all areas of activity will decline further. The intervening variable of nationalism and chauvinism has become largely irrelevant in the question of regime maintenance and transformation.

The loss of the support mechanism represented by nationalism would normally spell great trouble for the regime, and this may yet be the case. At the same time, the very fact that the clan is totally isolated from political and socio-economic reality may help it disregard even this debilitating handicap. As discussed above, the General Secretary and his wife have already accomplished this in their minds by dismissing the nation as irrelevant as an independent political variable—an astonishingly arrogant attitude for *any* political leadership. This insularity may allow the clan to survive even the loss of nationalism as a support mechanism, provided that the agents of coercion remain loyal, and the clan retains its internal solidarity. Analysts, political decision-makers, and oppositionists are back at *the* fundamental question of contemporary Romanian politics: How long can this regime survive?

The nationality policies of the clan, together with the utterly dismal performance in the economy, in the social sector, and in human rights, have made Romania the pariah of the so-called "socialist commonwealth." In this context, the clearly discriminatory policies produced against Magyars and others may represent the trigger mechanism that forces increased political pressure on the Ceausescus. Furthermore, such pressure may galvanize oppositional elements into action disguised to salvage the *Romanian* nation from the debacle of the Ceausescus. The current controversy with the Hungarians over ethnic relations and overt discrimination represent a potential threat to the clan chauvinists, but only if it leads to greater pressures from Moscow. And herein lies both an opportunity and a liability for Nicolae and Elena Ceausescu.

The liabilities are, certainly, clear enough. Increased pressure from elements inside the Warsaw Pact and the Comecon, especially the Soviets, will represent a major challenge to the clan and its present policies. It may be sufficient to topple the regime. But it may also have the opposite effect, because overt pressure, particularly from the Kremlin, may rekindle the innate nationalism of the Romanians and reestablish mass support for the Ceausescus. This would indeed be the supreme irony of the present predicament of Ceausescu's Romania. If it comes to pass, it will demonstrate, again, that passion often supersedes reason in this most human of endeavors, politics.

Notes

1. For an analysis of some of these concepts, generally and in the Soviet context, see John A. Armstrong, "The Ethnic Scene in the Soviet Union: The View of the Dictatorship," in Eric Goldhagen (ed.), *Ethnic Minorities in the Soviet Union* (New York, NY: Frederick A. Praeger, Inc., 1968), ch. 1 (pp. 3–49).

2. Many sources have been examined in this context. One of the most important books is still Karl W. Deutsch, *Nationalism and Social Communication* (Cambridge, MA: The MIT Press, 1966).

3. The ethos of Romanian nationalism is well described in Pascu, *Marea Adunare Nationala de la Alba Iulia,* esp. ch. IV (pp. 99–125) and ch. V (pp. 125–160).

4. See Gilberg, *Modernization in Romania since World War II,* ch. 8 (pp. 207–241).

5. These historical memories are utilized in the current conflict between Hungary and Romania over the treatment of ethnic Hungarians in Transylvania. See, for example, the resolution of the Council of Working People of Hungarian Nationality, published in *Scinteia,* March 4, 1987.

6. E.g. Dinu Giurescu, *Illustrated History of the Romanian People,* pp. 578–593.

7. Brzezinski, *The Soviet Bloc,* esp. ch. 3 (pp. 41–67).

8. Ionescu, *Communism in Rumania, 1944–1962,* ch. 6 (pp. 126–147).

9. Robert R. King, *History of the Romanian Communist Party,* esp. ch. 5 (pp. 99–120) and ch. 6 (120–135).

10. Brzezinski, *The Soviet Bloc,* ch. 5 (pp. 84–104) and ch. 6 (pp. 104–138).

11. Gilberg, "Ceausescu's Romania," *Problems of Communism,* July-August, 1974, pp. 30–31.

12. *Ibid.*

13. This process was further accelerated at the tenth RCP congress in the fall of 1969, through consolidation of Ceausescu cadre at the judet level. See *Congresul al X-lea al Partidului Comunist Roman,* pp. 751–758 (membership list for the top RCP bodies).

14. See, for example, Dan Zamfirescu in *Luceafarul,* December 1, 1976 and Constantin Giurescu in *Magazin Istoric,* March 1974.

15. E.g. speech by Nicolae Ceausescu to the Council of Working People of Hungarian Nationality, March 15, 1978 (*Scinteia,* March 16, 1978). See also Dumitru Berciu and Constantin Preda on the continuity of the Romanian nation, *Contemporanul,* February 10, 1978.

16. This emphasis has continued to the present time. See his speech to the thirteenth party conference, printed in *Scinteia,* December 17, 1987.

17. This claim was made earlier as well; see Berciu and Preda in *Contemporanul,* February 10, 1987.

18. One of the most chauvinistic statements on this issue was made by Corneliu Vadim Tudor in *Saptamina,* February 13, 1987.

19. *Der Spiegel,* March 2, 1987.

20. See statements made by Karoly Kiraly in a letter to Ceausescu, published in *Neue Zürcher Zeitung,* January 10/11, 1988.

21. The Romanian authorities dismissed the news about the mass flight across the Hungarian border, blaming "hostile elements" inciting to desertion (*Agerpres,* June 27, 1988).

22. This attitude is being fed by the sycophants who extol him in the press, in films, and in plays. See, for example, Gehorghe Iordache in *Scinteia Tineretului,* March 22, 1985.

23. One of the latest statements on this topic occurred in a major speech by the General Secretary at a recent Central Committee plenum; see *Agerpres*, June 28, 1988.

24. See, for example, Ceausescu's speech to the Central Committee on October 5, 1987 (*Scinteia*, October 6, 1987) in which the General Secretary blamed others for the problems in the economy.

25. In June 1988, a large crowd of Hungarians demonstrated outside the Romanian Embassy in Budapest to protest Ceausescu's nationality policies—the latest dramatic event in the conflict between the two socialist states. See *Radio Free Europe Research*, Romanian SR/8, 23 June 1988.

26. Important elements of the Romanian intelligentsia now rejects the sloganeering of Ceausescu and demand performance in the economic sector. See, for example, Mihai Botez in *Financial Times*, April 8, 1986.

9

Societal Change and Instability

As history marches on, and the societal crisis of contemporary Romania deepens, analysts and policy-makers alike increasingly concern themselves with the question of a possible breakdown of political authority and a corresponding challenge to law and order and the capability of the regime to rule. This problem is, indeed, both theoretically and practically interesting, because it poses fundamental questions that are quintessential *political* questions: At what point will *power* be transferred, changed, or altered? Under what circumstances will the modicum of stability necessary for the operation of the political and socio-economic order become instability? At what point will instability become crisis, and when will that crisis become regime-threatening? These are the questions that have been posed by political scientists and practitioners for a very long time. Romania in the 1980s provides us with a laboratory in which these questions can be tested.[1]

A political system may experience stability for a number of reasons, and that stability may be interrupted or changed into instability in a number of ways. First of all, I take it that "stability" in the political sense means that the political process flows routinely; that the system includes in its established procedures and rules various mechanisms for the alteration of these procedures to accommodate new entrants, new problems, and new conditions; finally, that the institutions, those structures tasked with the arduous activity of making binding decisions, are flexible enough to cope with the demands made upon them by society, and, if they are not so flexible, that they have self-correcting mechanisms that can adjust and cope. If any one of these elements is missing, the procedures and structures of the political order itself break down and may cause instability.[2]

Stability also depends upon regulated and predictable relations between polity and society. Thus, the political order must be able to deal with significant changes in that society, be it in the economic, social, or cultural realms or in countless other conditions of interaction and

185

interdependence. Drastic changes in socio-economic relations tend to produce stresses and strains that demand political response. By the same token, the political order is the chief guiding mechanism for economic and social activity, thus itself producing change and stress in the economy and the social order. There is always tension between these crucial elements of society. Stability requires that this tension is productive, not debilitating or so controversial that procedures and communications patterns are disrupted.[3]

Stability also requires that the political order must deal creatively with the existence of religion and the practical manifestations of belief in God. History has decisively demonstrated the remarkable staying power of religion regardless of the nature of the political order. This is particularly relevant for communist-ruled systems, which are doctrinally dedicated to the destruction of religion as a guiding experience in human life. The regimes so doctrinally committed without exception have had to coexist with religious persistence and have been forced to devise creative ways of dealing with this persistent phenomenon of the human condition.[4]

The complex relationships that exist between society and polity are in constant change and flux, demanding flexibility on the part of both elements. This interrelationship may be threatened whenever one element changes faster than another, thus producing demands which are difficult to accommodate or regulate. In revolutionary systems, the political order early on changes faster than society and makes demands upon it that the old order cannot easily deal with, thus creating a crisis of full-blown societal proportions. If the revolutionary order is successful in maintaining itself in the political realm, it will also eventually manage to implement some of its goals, thus likely changing the society over which it presides in a fundamental way. The societal order, then, may acquire a self-sustaining momentum, eventually threatening to upset the balance between society and polity. The political order, by contrast, may become ossified, bureaucratized, and sluggish in its handling of changed societal conditions. When this happens, instability will naturally occur, and it represents the most fundamental of crises because such instability forces *political* change, whereas the demands made upon society early on in the revolutionary process "only" demanded *societal* change. Assuming, as one must, that political change is, ultimately, the most fundamental of all, the challenge from society to polity is the kind of challenge that calls for "sea-change" in the history of a nation.[5]

Stability depends greatly upon the "profile" of the political order in society. Assuming that societies in change create a great deal of pressure on institutions and decision-making procedures, it becomes clear that no political system is equipped to handle all of these problems with equal capability and equal success. Furthermore, successful resolution of certain problems most likely will upset other areas, generating other problems there. Thus, no societal-political system can be in perfect equilibrium in all areas of interaction. Under such circumstances, the political order is incapable of commitment to all areas at once, and leaders must choose which areas are, indeed, crucial, and which may be neglected for the time being, or perhaps even permanently. There are areas of societal activity that the "state" may choose to leave completely alone for the simple reason that it may become overextended through overinvolvement. Thus, a low "profile" is required.[6]

Instability, then, may arise from conditions inside the polity itself, or within the socio-economic or cultural sphere. The more complex society is, the more possibilities exist for instability to develop; conversely, in "simple" societies, the likelihood of instability in subsections of society or societal-political relationships is reduced. In "simple" societies, however, the lack of dynamism in relations between elements of society and the polity results in stagnation and the consequent building up of pressures for change that may eventually produce upheaval or political revolution. Thus, the continued and partial instability always present in complex and dynamic societies may be preferred to the stability of stagnant societies in which pressures for fundamental change may eventually produce revolution and thus the transformation of the political order itself.[7]

As discussed elsewhere, communist systems are particularly prone to the kinds of stresses and strains that eventually produce instability. They compensate for this by means of greater application of coercion or the threat of such application. Thus, communist-ruled systems possess their own equilibrium function. This makes them both stable and unstable at the same time. Many analysts have contended that the systems of Eastern Europe have reached a stage where the equilibrium cannot be maintained, thus posing the question of basic *political* change. Let us now turn to an examination of the nature of the developing disequilibrium of communist-ruled systems in Europe, with a special focus on Romania.[8]

The Dynamics of Instability in Political Systems

"Instability" carries with it a pejorative connotation in most Western usages. We talk about countries in which there is political, socio-economic, religious or ethnic trouble as "unstable countries" and assume that these systems must find their way back to equilibrium, to stability. There is also a tendency in social science literature to prefer stability and to examine those conditions that are conducive thereto.

The fact of societal reality is different. Instability, defined as dynamic interaction and change, is a necessary condition if stagnation is to be avoided. And, as discussed above, stagnation is ultimately conducive to much greater instability, because it will result in uncontrollable pressures for change on a more massive scale, thus threatening the very nature of the society itself as well as its key element, the political order.

Instability is required in a number of key areas of analysis. First of all, the political order must be able to change itself and to produce dynamic interaction among the participants in the system. It must allow for the entry of new political actors in the system, and to integrate these new actors in the processes as established, or develop new processes to deal with them. A political system must be in constant change in order to maintain its *basic* equilibrium, its basic stability. "Instability within stability" is the characteristic most illustrative of successful political systems.[9]

The successful political system must also have multiple communications channels and the ability to deal creatively with the many messages which are transmitted through these channels. In any society (and particularly a modern, stratified, and heterogeneous society) there is bound to be a great deal of controversy in these communications. This amount of controversy represents the differing ideas, goals, and aspirations of the various activated elements of the political order. Such communications patterns produce initial controversy and therefore a measure of instability, as the communicators attempt to influence decision-makers to act on their behalf, or as they react to policies already undertaken. But such instability is the lifeblood of decision-making. It produces the "raw material" of political choice, and it provides the safety mechanism represented by political communication. Above all, it helps decision-makers acquire a realistic knowledge of real concerns and goals in elements of the population. Instability as dynamic interaction is a fact of modern political life. It is also beneficial and indispensable.[10]

Instability also arises in relations between polity and society. Any society with any kind of dynamism has a number of disequilibria which produce controversy. These controversies, in turn, must be settled by some mechanism, often political. Again, it is indispensable that the dynamic interaction in the economy, in the social sector, in the cultural realm, and in other areas of human endeavor has a political avenue for conflict resolution through the political order.

Instability and Communist Systems

Communists are uniquely vulnerable to the kinds of instability discussed above, even as they deny such political manifestations doctrinally.

It is ironic that Marxism in its various manifestations relies heavily upon the dialectic instability of the interaction of thesis, antithesis and synthesis as the vehicle of historical (and necessary) change, while denying its validity once communist power has been established and the stage of socialism has been reached. Insofar as the doctrine has not been changed, all systems run by self-proclaimed Marxists assume that socialism means creative interaction among individuals and social strata, and that this interaction is devoid of controversy and thus the detrimental effects of instability. The end goal of communist power is the communist society, in which harmony prevails and creative energies are released through the harmonious interaction of all individuals against a backdrop of material plenty.[11]

Political and socio-economic realities in communist-run societies are quite different. This has been openly admitted by social scientists and theoreticians in a number of the East European states, and there is even a willingness to discuss such matters among the political leaderships of the region. In the era of glasnost, the Soviet leadership is engaged in a far-ranging debate about the notion of contradictions in socialism and the effects of such manifestations on stability and political and social harmony. Instability is admitted, controversy is accepted, and "antagonistic contradictions" are seen as a side-effect of the developmental process undertaken and conducted by the Marxist-Leninist system itself. In fact, Gorbachev and his associates wish to use these controversies and contradictions as the vehicle for rejuvenation of the Soviet system. There is a realization here that controversy is necessary and beneficial because it produces the dynamic force for change and revitalization needed in any society.[12]

The Soviet Union is but the most dramatic example of the growing awareness of political and societal realities and complexities in the communist-ruled societies of Europe in the 1980s. In Hungary, a rather sophisticated discussion of such matters has been conducted for at least two decades. In Poland, detailed analyses of societal and political relationships constitute the hallmark of some of the best sociologists anywhere. There is increasing awareness of this phenomenon and the need to study it everywhere in the region. The one exception is Romania, where early promising attempts to understand societal dynamics in the late 1960s were snuffed out by the ideological and personalistic policies of the Ceausescu clan. Ironically, then, the society which carries in it many of the known elements of controversy and instability has the least knowledge of it, and certainly the least amount of willingness to understand it and utilize it creatively.[13]

Communist-ruled systems are revolutionary in nature during the early stages of the establishment and maintenance of power. The communists came to power through the process of political upheaval; in Europe there are no communist regimes that have been established and maintained as a result of free elections under conditions of political and societal stability and equilibrium. The communists are also doctrinally dedicated to fundamental change in the polity, in the economy, in the social order, and in the cultural sphere. In those areas of Europe where this political party has established power there have been fundamental changes, initiated from the top of the political pyramid and enforced downward into all area of societal activity. Thus, the early stages of communist rule have produced instability because of the programs and policies of the regimes themselves. Briefly put, the communists were revolutionaries and modernizers who came to power in stagnant and traditional societies, and then proceeded to change them in a fundamental way. Many analysts have discussed this process in considerable detail, and there is no need to examine the details here. Suffice it to say that the revolutionary programs were successful in the sense that they *did* fundamentally change much of society in Eastern Europe. In many ways, the instability produced thereby was creative, perhaps even necessary.

There is also a considerable literature on the results of the societal transformation initiated and conducted by the East European communists. By the end of the 1980s, all of these societies have become industrial rather than agrarian. They are characterized by social stratification and functional specialization and no longer resemble the relatively simple peasant societies that existed in the area before World War II. New socio-economic classes have been established. The political and social "horizon" of millions of people has been expanded to include "modernity" in all its manifestations. This is indeed a societal transformation because it has changed *people*, not merely the physical and productive landscape of Eastern Europe.

It is clear that the primary vehicle for this transformation has been the communist party. In retrospect, the policies and coercive capabilities of the communists were uniquely suited to the relatively underdeveloped societies upon which power was exercized, because these programs had the ability to produce rapid and fundamental change throughout all of society. It is equally clear that these agents of transformation, as presently constituted, are ill-suited to the management of *modern* societies. There are two basic reasons for this: First of all, the communist parties have changed but little in their organizational structure, operational form and operational characteristics, while society has changed fundamentally. Secondly, communist parties, for reasons to be explored below, have displayed little ability to deal with the existence of creative instability and incremental change based upon that instability. In the meantime, the societies over which they presided (and whose transformation they engineered) have changed so much that the polity can no longer be expected to maintain a reasonable dialogue with it.

As the problems associated with such "cognitive dissonance" between society and polity multiply, the various communist parties of Eastern Europe (and now increasingly the Soviet Union as well) have taken a number of steps to combat it. In Hungary, the political leadership has long relied heavily on the expert advise of technocrats and social scientists in the decision-making process. A number of individuals in leading political positions are, in fact, technocrats, and they have had a great deal to do with the greater openness that has long characterized the political discourse in this country.[14] In Poland, the post-martial law period has been remarkable for the multifaceted discourse that has taken place on a number of issues, even though this form of advanced communication has not resulted in greater trust among the masses of the population.[15] Even in systems normally considered ideologically orthodox and resistant to change, such as the German Democratic Republic, Czechoslovakia, and Bulgaria, there has been a conscious effort to deal with the multivarious societal problems that have developed through modernity. Part of that coping process has been the willingness of political elites to listen to others, to broaden the base of recruitment, to expand the flow of information available for decision-makers, and to examine other elements of the problems and the possible solutions, even outside the established parameters of Marxist-Leninist ideology.[16] All of this represents a welcome, if belated, realization that the old approaches and established screens of perception are no longer sufficient.

It is unlikely that the piecemeal approaches to the new societal-political relationships will change the fundamental problems of a contemporary communist-ruled system in any major way, but they represent at least a recognition of the need for new thinking, new openness, and new criteria of political behavior.

Aberrant Romania

In the context of contemporary Eastern Europe, Romania is an aberrant case. Few, if any, of the conditions that lead to relative political stability exist in that unfortunate country. There is little of the creative instability that helps ensure basic political stability. The political elite refuses to recognize the need for discussion, discourse, and controversy. In short, Romania in the late 1980s is a politically stagnant system with a number of destabilizing elements and developments in the wider society. It should therefore be a prime candidate for instability, perhaps even upheaval. That this is not taking place requires a serious effort of explanation.

First let us examine precisely *how much* Ceausescu's Romania fits the blueprint for instability as established above.

To begin with, there is no real political willingness to produce change in the system itself. The Ceausescu clan is not interested in institutional or structural change designed to admit new political entrants or to listen to the expressions of goals, aspirations, or concerns that important elements of society have. The creative instability that comes from more openness, more discussions, and a broader base of information is anathema to this region. There is a great deal of structural change, to be sure; Nicolae Ceausescu routinely establishes new committees, revamps others, and habitually recycles the personnel in existing structures. This is not genuine change, however. It is undertaken with a view towards *reducing* discussion and eliminating the possibility of competing power centers being developed. Institutional and structural change is mere tinkering with the mechanisms of the system without creative renewal. In the end, it signifies nothing, except to illustrate that the "sound and fury" really represents mere cosmetics. In the meantime, power becomes more concentrated in the hands of even fewer individuals.[17]

The institutional flexibility so much needed for systemic stability is also lacking, for much the same reason. The flexibility that is manifestly present in the Romanian political order is not based upon the need to accommodate a variety of ideas and political preferences (which exist in all political parties, even the other communist parties of Eastern Europe) but rather to reduce all political participants to a residual status of manipulation. The constant recycling of elite personnel is designed to accomplish just this. Even the recruitment patterns into leadership positions display the same amorphous quality of personal choice, indeed personal whim. Major trends and tendencies in the polity may go totally unrepresented, while other, insignificant elements are elevated to positions of temporary power and influence. The only thing that is predictable is the unpredictability of the top clan members in personnel and policy matters.

A third element of political stability, namely the predictability of the behavior of individual leaders and some procedural constancy, is also fundamentally missing in Ceausescu's Romania. The system is characterized by unpredictability in all areas of activity, including recruitment, decision-making (and the criteria for making decisions), and the goals of the regime. It is impossible to predict what will happen next, and it is also impossible to foresee what political, economic, and managerial structures will be like, because the General Secretary's leadership style (as pointed out earlier) is predicated upon the extreme instability of cadre, thus preventing the development of counterelites and their institutional power base.

The result of all this is a political leadership that is characterized by extreme centralization and rigidity at the top of the political pyramid, but extreme fluidity at all levels below that small inner circle of oligarchs. No one can make decisions with any certainty that they will be backed up by higher authority; a much more likely scenario is the blaming of mistakes on subordinates rather than the top individuals who made the faulty decisions. Structural changes and reorganizations occur with dizzying speed, making orderly procedures even more difficult, if not impossible.[18]

Political leadership, then, is marked by both rigidity and drift, personalistic determination and extreme fluidity. Nobody wants to make decisions, and all problems are either left to fester or referred to the very top of the political pyramid. Much is left undone, and much that has been done is changed shortly thereafter. This is not creative instability; this is debilitating drift and chaos.

Relations between the polity and Romanian society also lack the creative tension and interaction that characterize dynamic and successful systems. The political system is removed from the rest of society by a widening chasm, and the very top of the political pyramid is separated from the rest of that order by a yawning abyss that is growing wider all the time. The areas of societal activity that require the attention and respect of the Ceausescus but receive none are legion. For example, the General Secretary in his megalomanic quest for recognition as the greatest of all leaders in all areas of human endeavor accepts (even fosters) a personality cult that has religious and mystical overtones to it, while at the same time denigrating the faith of real believers and persecuting some of them (notably Baptists and Uniates) both physically and in words and spirit. There is a steadfast refusal to accept the notion that anyone can believe in anything but the organic unity of the people and the state, the latter represented by Nicolae Ceausescu and his inner circle. Religion becomes treason in the General Secretary's mind. This precludes rational and cooperative arrangements with the existing church structures in the country, as found elsewhere in Eastern Europe. The Orthodox Church of Romania only survives because it is submissive and because it helps lend a legitimizing aura to the present political leadership.[19]

There is no doubt that the current political system is incapable of relating to contemporary Romanian society in a constructive way. A society which is becoming modern in the sense of functional specialization, structural differentiation, and inbued with the ideals of technology and communications requires multivariate access to political decision-makers as well as vehicles for self-expression. Furthermore, the various societal elites that have emerged require respect for their views and a sense that they will be listened to, that they are accorded a stake in the quests and achievements of their society, and thus a sense of shared destiny. There is no such sense in contemporary Romania. Instead, there is mutual distrust, disdain, even hatred, between societal elites, on the one hand, and the Ceausescu clan on the other. Above all, there is fear—fear that the unpredictable hand of the dictator will reach down and identify *you* as the culprit in the latest economic fiasco, fear that the newest elements of the chauvinistic campaign will affect *us* Magyars in even more palpable ways, even fear that the "Leader" may choose *me* as an inductee into the clan, because such a position, even with its perquisites, is extremely exposed and subject to the whim of the fickle leadership, especially Nicolae, Elena, and Nicu. Thus, even those who *are* picked through this personalized process fail to respond in a way that would help bridge the chasm between society and polity.

The picture that emerges out of this analysis is complex and frightening in its implications. There is tension inside the political system and very little rational and meaningful communication and interaction between levels inside the structures and institutions. There is also a great deal of tension in society, between various elements, strata, and ethnic groups. At the same time, there is little if any meaningful communication between society and polity, or even inside society itself, because pervasive fear has shut down such horizontal communications channels as may have existed, or the channels have all been directed vertically, towards the pinnacle of power, where all *safe* decisions are made. Thus, there is no creative instability, no controversy that helps resolve problems, no understanding that problems must exist in order for decision-makers to deal with issues that arise, and must arise, in any dynamic society. This is a society of stagnation. More importantly, it is a society in which people have turned inwards. It is a society of despair.

The "Alternative Society" and Its Atomization

A repressive regime that does not encourage communication inside the parameters of power invariably fosters an alternative society, in which individuals ban together for mutual protection and communication, and for the purpose of economic survival in a situation that has become critical during the last three to four years. This kind of society provides individuals and groups with human and physical needs in an environment that can only be characterized as hostile to all but the most highly placed.

The alternative society takes many forms. There are close friends, with whom one gets together occasionally or regularly, to enjoy each other's company, to drink, to tell stories, and to escape. All communist-ruled societies are characterized by this kind of defensive mechanism against the outside world. In Romania, such a network exists, innumerable in its individual manifestations and permutations. And in such a multiethnic society, there are groups and informal associations that help individuals of the same ethnicity weather the adversities of the outside world. None of this is strange or unexpected. What is definitely worthy of notice is the intensity of life inside such groups, and the distance between each such minicollectivity and the wider society and the political order. The chasm is widening, and society is beginning to resemble an atomized agglomeration of isolated and inward-directed "islands," collectivities that have no overarching unity.

A regime can, conceivably, survive the atomization of the ordinary citizenry, because their skills are not necessarily crucial to the survival of the political order or the performance of the economic and managerial systems of the country. It can ill afford the development of such islands of autonomy and rejection among the societal elites whose skills are indispensable for the continued performance of the system, let alone any prospects for improvement. Yet this process is clearly underway in Romania in the second half of the 1980s. Where it will end, nobody knows, but there are important implications for the continued existence of the regime as presently constituted.

The development of detached groups and individuals with special skills has already progressed rather far. There are important elements of the artistic intelligentsia who refuse to publish the kind of regime-commissioned literature that glorifies the Ceausescus and the RCP. In fact, some of these individuals have on occasion written thinly veiled fables and allegories designed to ridicule or criticize the current regime and its most important personnel. There are also occasional voices of opposition in the theatre, in cinema production, in music, and in sculpture and other forms of "plastic arts." More important than the openly expressed dissatisfaction, perhaps, is the growing tendency to privatization and withdrawal among the artistic intelligentsia, in which plays and novels are written "for the drawer," and the talents of other artists are simply withheld from the regime's programs. Assuming that these talents are considered important by the political elite, at least for its glorification, this development is noteworthy indeed. It produces an underground of creative individuals who are keeping themselves "in reserve" for another day and a more receptive leadership.[20]

The technical and managerial intelligentsia is also clearly disgruntled and elements of it have begun to "withdraw" in the sense that they only work at a minimum level, and spend much of their spare time in pursuit of other activities, some of which are centered around their professional goals and aspirations and their frustrations with the political order in which they find themselves. At times, articles and pamphlets emerge from such gatherings, expressing the need for more rational, predictable, and "businesslike" decision-making, but most of the time there is simply an outwardly silent network of skilled individuals whose energies are focused upon survival and the hope for a better day.[21]

The ethnic minorities, as mentioned above, are also increasingly concerned with the need to conserve their capabilities and energies for the future, since the present is simply too bleak to contemplate as a way of life. Again, energies are focused inward, thus withdrawn from society as a whole, which surely could use the skills and talents of these groups. This kind of withdrawal will last beyond the Ceausescus, producing a void for years and decades to come, representing perhaps the widest and least bridgeable rift in the societal order.[22]

There are other formations as well which have grave political potential for the current regime if they should become politically activated, alone or in combination with others. There are persistent rumors that elements of the professional military are upset over the low level of funding accorded this group. Furthermore, many important officers of high rank feel that the pseudo-autonomous policy of the Ceausescu clan in the Warsaw Pact and the Comecon has deprived the Romanian armed forces of much needed technology and professional development. These officers also realize that the pauperization of the economy and its people is a most dangerous development with dire consequences for the capability of the armed forces to acquire the wherewithal to do their job in a professional manner. All in all, the dissatisfied elements of this crucial regime support factor are important, and they may be getting stronger.[23]

There remain the party apparat and the security police. There are clearly elements in the RCP ranks at various levels who feel that the policies of the regime are disastrous and must be changed. At times, these kinds of attitudes surface in the policy debates that are published in organs of the press and other media; one can only assume that the debate that takes place behind closed doors is more heated, more outspoken. There have also been unexplained cases in which a Ceausescu initiative has been delayed, changed, or disappeared altogether, probably as a result of opposition in various sectors of the RCP apparat, possibly at the very top, in the Political Executive Committee. For example, some recent changes in the first secretaryships of judet party organizations took a great deal of time to implement, and in one case, the General Secretary announced such a change without a corresponding endorsement by the PEC. The constant criticism that emanates from Nicolae and Elena Ceausescu about malfeasance in the RCP is a further indication of the level of political disgruntlement found in the apparat. Veiled references to "activities incompatible with RCP guidelines and theses" also indicate factional infighting at various levels. Unfortunately, we do not know the *extent* of this opposition inside the apparat.[24]

Even less is known about the attitudes of the security police. There have been instances of plots in this vital service, as indicated by the firing of several important officials during this decade. The defection of Ion Mihai Pacepa is another example of problems in high places in this sector. On the other hand, Ceausescu clearly has important support in the police, and he has "eyes" that can spot any plots or serious disaffection rather quickly, as evidenced by the personnel changes discussed above. Furthermore, rapid recycling of personnel at most levels of this service helps reduce the formation of factions and their solidifying into counterelites. All in all it must be assumed that the clan could not possibly survive with the increased disaffection of so many elements in the polity and the society without continued strong support from most of the security apparat.[25]

Options, Coalitions, and Outcomes

Given the existence of several groupings of individuals who have expressed misgivings about the current regime and its policies, the analyst must examine the various coalition possibilities that exist, as well as the policy ramifications that stem from the formation of such coalitions and the possible political program that they may establish. There are a number of such possibilities, as follows:

1. Elements of the military, the managerial and technical intelligentsia, and segments of the RCP apparat, particularly those that represent some of the younger and better educated apparatchiki, with some support from older elements now in contention with the clan, ban together in opposition to the current leadership.

This coalition would be a formidable political entity, because it would span the kind of generational and educational spectrum that is so fundamentally wanting in contemporary Romanian society. It would have the advantage of representation close to the top of the present power structure and would command the kind of technical and managerial expertise that Romania so sorely needs in the protracted period of reconstruction that must follow the end of the "Ceausescu epoch." Furthermore, it would be acceptable to many individuals and groups in the wider society and would certainly expand communications with these groups, thus enhancing the informational base upon which decisions are made. Such information and political communication, then, would help to revitalize the societal and political order and begin to formulate the "creative instability" that exists in dynamic societies. The coalition would also increase its capabilities in the coercive sector by including those elements of the military who have a vested personal and doctrinal interest in a more modern and rational political leadership. This faction would, presumably, include the more technically oriented and better educated officers, but it excludes the average field officer who is mostly tasked with the need to command low-grade troops in policy activities, in construction, harvesting, and other very mundane matters.

2. The artistic and cultural intelligentsia splits, and the more independent-minded elements join the coalition outlined under 1 above, to lend their considerable capabilities to the cause.

This development would not have a direct impact on the political fortunes of the established coalition in the short run, but it would help mobilize others who are also upset about the anti-intellectualism of the Ceausescu regime. If the artistic intelligentsia is added to the military-technological group early, it will help marshal added firepower for the cause and may have a significant effect in bridging the gap between the societal elites represented in coalition 1 and the general public. Ultimately, then, it would help mobilize those elements of the general public that are not already completely demoralized or depoliticized. Such a development would add a dimension of mass support necessary for the success of any anti-clan coalition.

3. Elements of the RCP apparatus join hands with mobilized segments of the proletariat, with secondary support from various elements of the technical and managerial intelligentsia and perhaps some of the artists and writers.

Coalition 3 is significantly different from the other two constellations discussed above. In option 3, the emphasis is on the working class, not on societal elites. Furthermore, the elements in the RCP who might be the leaders of such a formation are not necessarily the same as those involved in option 1 (in fact, it is unlikely that the two factions would be the same). The RCP leadership elements who would most likely team up with the workers are the *general* apparatchiki, responsible for supervision of production as well as troubleshooting at the plant level. Such individuals are not particularly enamored of the more technically trained and oriented people in the apparat but do have concerns that are similar to those of the workers themselves (wages, production quotas, working conditions, job security, and output).

Coalition 3 would focus on *economic* reform, but may not consider *political* changes to be fundamental. The assumption here is that the working class will be "conservative" rather than "liberal" in matters of personal freedom, civil rights, and a local version of glasnost. Autocratic, perhaps even ideologically oriented policies would be acceptable, as long as the ostentatious consumption and irrational behavior of the clan had been removed.

4. Dissident individuals from all strata of society join hands with those who have the most fundamental grievances, namely the ethnic minorities (and particularly the politicized elements among the Magyar population). In this coalition one would most likely find individuals from the artistic intelligentsia, some of whom have already spoken up against discrimination and excessive chauvinism.

Coalition 4 would run up against basic nationalism among the ethnic Romanian masses and would experience great difficulty in obtaining support from the technical and managerial intelligentsia and the military establishment, which is overwhelmingly Romanian in ethnic background. Its chances of success are therefore severely weakened.

5. Elements of the RCP and the proletariat (discussed above as option 3) add politicized individuals and groupings from the peasantry to their list, thus strengthening the mass aspect of this coalition. At the present time, the level of political consciousness in the peasantry is probably so low that it is hard to mobilize any segment thereof for political affiliation, let alone meaningful action. At the same time, no analyst can afford to disregard the traditions of jacquerie in the Romanian peasantry. In the past, this downtrodden mass has occasionally risen up in elementary rage and afflicted massive damage upon repressive authorities. Perhaps the depoliticization process under the Ceausescus has gone too far for this to be a possibility. Perhaps the repressive mechanism and the information-gathering capabilities of the clan are too strong. But there is at least the historical memory of jacqueries and the mythomoteur thereof in the oral traditions of the villages. Thus, we cannot ignore this possibility. It all depends upon the trigger mechanism for such behavior (on this, more below).

The coalition possibilities discussed above all exclude the security police or elements of this structure. The main reason for this is the fact that the police have more to lose from any anti-Ceausescu coalition than any other group because the security forces have prospered more from the existing order and thus are more thoroughly pro-Ceausescu than any other actor. Most of the personnel in this category have few skills that would be meaningful outside of existing structures. Their skills are not appropriate for other kinds of activities, and this makes them uncompetitive in any other system other than that of the police state. Consequently, a coalition that would include these elements must promise similar conditions and perquisites as the ones already enjoyed. And this, again, requires an autocratic regime, not a more pluralistic one. Thus, the peculiar Romanian catch-22 continues: It may be necessary to have elements of the security police on board any coalition that has a realistic chance of toppling the Ceausescus and Petrescus, but these very elements will ensure that the liberalization process is very limited indeed. And this, in turn, may not be sufficient for the rejuvenation that is necessary in the post-Ceausescu era.

Maximizing Coalitions:
Is There a Winning Combination?

Any of the possible coalitions discussed above has serious weaknesses and may need added elements to succeed in the political quest for a regime change. The first coalition has skills, expertise, and coercive capabilities, but it lacks mass support, and may find itself faced with the popular attitude of rejecting *all* elites, regardless of political goals, regardless of personnel make-up. The Romanian masses, after all, have a great deal of experience with elites that establish honorable goals but end up selling them (and thus their mass support) short for some other kind of gain. This kind of attitude, which is based on centuries of collective experience, cannot be shaken easily, and counterattitudes at the very least take a long time to mature. In the meantime, the Ceausescu clan may succeed in launching countermoves that effectively eliminate the coalition as a meaningful political actor.

For the elite coalition to succeed, it needs the support of the artistic intelligentsia, whose writings and opinion-formation techniques can help guide public opinion or focus the diffuse anger that now exists in much of the proletariat and perhaps even elements of the peasantry. But that may not in itself be sufficient, and so there is a need for a trigger mechanism that can activate these elements. Such a mechanism may be a sudden downturn in the economic crisis (which would be hard to envision given the current abysmal performance of the economy). It could also be a specific act by the leadership or external events (more on the latter later in this chapter).

By contrast, the third coalition discussed above has the potential of considerable mass support, but it lacks the kind of coercive capability that makes grouping one above a potentially formidable formation. At the very least, coalition three must secure some assistance from elements within the armed forces. In addition, the proletariat must exhibit much greater willingness to become involved than has hitherto been the case. Such willingness may be bolstered by more forceful leadership than was the case in the past, but it is likely to be hampered significantly by the innate caution of the masses so frequently disappointed by their leaders.

By comparison, a coalition of disparate dissident elements, particularly from the ethnic minorities, would have little chance of success unless it could attach itself to one or more of the other possibilities discussed above. The same can be said for a coalition that includes the peasantry;

such a group needs important elements of strength from other areas of society, given the low level of political consciousness in this socio-economic stratum.[26]

Trigger Mechanisms and the Potential for Success

A number of "trigger mechanisms" may develop with the capability to produce political action by one more of the configurations discussed above. The most important of these mechanisms are listed below.

The Present Socio-economic and Political Crises Worsen

Despite the dismal conditions prevailing in contemporary Romania, there are possibilities for even further decline in economic performance, particularly in the agricultural sector. This kind of decline would result in a worsened supply situation for most foodstuffs, and the conditions for consumers, now very difficult, could become desperate. At the present time there are still some food reserves, and there is food available if one has connections. There is no real starvation (even though the supply deficiencies have resulted in undernourishment and, presumably, increased infant mortality and increased death rates for the sick and the elderly).[27] But people are clearly living on the margins, and even a relatively mild downturn in economic performance may have political repercussions in a situation that is already tense for other reasons.

Since the present crisis is a societal phenomenon, exceeding the parameters of the economy, other elements may also experience deterioration and thus help trigger political responses of a scope, magnitude, and direction not easily foreseen at the present time. One area of political trouble would be in interethnic relations, where the chauvinism of certain Romanian elements (urged on by the statements and policies of the regime itself) is met by increasingly assertive attitudes by the minorities. Excessively chauvinistic acts or statements by the Romanian "court scribes" may help trigger more forceful responses.

There is also the possibility that some of the writers and artists who have hitherto voiced their views in the form of allegories and symbolism may choose to become more outspoken in their rejection of failed policies. Such boldness may be associated with signs of weakness in the top leadership on one or more issue. The same effect could be expected if the alleged health problems of the General Secretary were to become exacerbated. Needless to say, a serious, debilitating development of the "Leader's" health would have a trigger effect for a number of actors who may be waiting for just such a development to take place. The intellectuals may well be the elements that would grasp such an occurrence with the greatest alacrity.

Specific Acts by the Regime

The worsening of the socio-economic crisis on the confluence of several other aspects of the societal crisis may represent one of the scenarios that could lead to increased (perhaps decisive) action by one or more of the coalitions that have been outlined above. It is also possible that specific acts by the top leadership could occur, with such effects in one or more of the political constellations that have formed in recent years. For example, the razing of much of downtown Bucharest triggered fairly outspoken opposition by a number of individuals representing different political and cultural interests.[28] Renewed and costly foreign policy initiatives, designed to shore up Ceausescu's flagging reputation as a major statesman, could have similar effects. Further examples of ostentatious consumption of scarce resources in a pauperized nation may well galvanize individuals or groups into action. This is especially likely if the excesses are directly attributable to Elena or Nicu, whose reputations are much more negative than that of the General Secretary himself.

External Pressure

The most potent trigger mechanism for political action by disgruntled elements would be external pressure, both generally from developments in the rest of the region, and especially (and most effectively) from the Kremlin. Such pressure could be subtle or more direct; it could take the form of signals sent to the Ceausescu clan itself, or even communications with one or more of the identifiable groups discussed above. Such communications would signal concern from important forces in the "socialist commonwealth" and would represent encouragement, perhaps even tacit offers of assistance in the reconstruction period, post Ceausescus. In the present dire economic situation, offers of aid would indeed represent a powerful incentive for an exhausted population whose vision has been reduced to mere survival for the short term.

The most important of these outside influences would, of course, be forceful statements by the leaders in the Kremlin. Under present Soviet circumstances, such pressure could be forthcoming from two camps, the reformers and the hardliners. The supporters of Gorbachev, as well as the Soviet party leader himself, have sent signals about the need for reform in all of Eastern Europe, and these communications continue even as Gorbachev struggles to manage his own reforms. The signals emanating from the Soviet capital are clearly amenable to the technical intelligentsia and the managers; other academic and artistic personnel are also excited by these signals. It is, furthermore, likely that the technically oriented elements of the officer corps are favorable to such reform signals and policies, even if they emanate from Moscow. This is indeed the kind of external encouragement that the potentially most powerful coalition presently in existence (or in the making) in Romania needs.[29]

Mikhail Gorbachev may not succeed in his quest for reform in the Soviet Union, and he may fail even in his attempt to stay in power. But even a more orthodox, hardline leadership in the Kremlin would be interested in serious political change in Romania. A more rational, technically based RCP leadership might be less chauvinistic than the Ceausescu clan, and would therefore represent less of a nuisance factor in Soviet-East European relations. A more orthodox leadership in the Kremlin is likely to demand greater integration in the Comecon, greater subordination to the ideological line of Moscow, and more coordination inside the Warsaw Pact. All of these aspects have been resisted by the Ceausescus, and this will most likely continue if there is dynastic succession in Bucharest. The Moscow "hardliners" would therefore welcome changes in this recalcitrant ally and could be expected to argue their case rather forcefully through a number of channels. In fact, it is likely that such elements in the Kremlin would be more forceful than Gorbachev, who has his hands full internally at the moment and can be expected to remain preoccupied in this fashion for a considerable period of time to come.[30] Thus, the greatest chances for serious Soviet pressure for change in Romania may paradoxically lie in the demise of the Gorbachev regime. This is indeed one of the paradoxes that continue to haunt the forces for change, reform, and a measure of liberalization inside contemporary Romania.

The Long Road to Success:
Factors Limiting Reform Possibilities

The coalitions discussed above are potentially powerful, but they must be reified and activated. It is not enough to have an agglomeration of individuals with common interests; they must also organize their activities, establish mechanisms for program implementation, and find ways to act in a hostile environment. As pointed out above, it may be necessary to have a trigger mechanism of events or happenstance that will activate such political configurations. By the same token, there are a number of factors that tend to limit the possibilities for groupings such as these, particularly in systems as closely controlled as contemporary Romania. All in all, the prospects for success, then, may not be good.

There are a number of factors that would tend to limit the chances of any coalition working toward the unseating of Nicolae Ceausescu and his clan at the present time. The most important of these are the Romanian political culture; the lack of coordination among the oppositionists, and the occasionally contradictory aspects of their political platform (if any such word can be used for the relatively vague policy statements that have been produced at times by these groupings); the repressive capabilities of the Ceausescu *apparat*; and the contradictory signals from external forces, especially the Kremlin.

Romanian political culture has certain characteristics that militate against early political activism on the part of the unofficial actors. Towards the end of the 1980s, these characteristics have been exacerbated by the policies of the Ceausescu clan over a protracted period of time. Taken together, these factors are likely to inhibit political activity by oppositionists, be they groups or individuals, in a major way.

Specifically, Romanian political culture is characterized by submission, quietude, and a tendency to subvert the existing order rather than to confront it directly. Throughout the centuries of foreign rule, the Romanian peasant learned to withdraw from political concerns and to concentrate on the life of the village, the extended family, and friendship circles. As mentioned above, excessive repression would occasionally produce outbursts in the form of jacqueries, but in between these events there were long periods of submission, withdrawal, and political quietude. This made it difficult to organize underground movements and parties, and mass actions against established authority were rare (again with some spectacular exceptions, such as the great peasant rebellion of 1907). Mass movements in Romania were associated with nationalism and the quest for national liberation; in these circumstances, the peasantry joined hands with the intellectuals and the religious structures of Orthodoxy and produced formidable coalitions that helped bring about the desired objective. Mass movements *against* nationalistic leaders, however corrupt and rapacious, did not develop among the Romanians. This is an important fact, because Nicolae Ceausescu has draped himself in Romanian nationalism and made it the mainstay of his regime. To act against the Ceausescus may be perceived as acting against the traditions of the Romanian nation. For this to happen, the political and socio-economic situation must become truly desperate. It is questionable if the situation has become that difficult as of this writing.[31]

Acts against professed nationalists may become possible when the masses of the population share the view of the counterelites that the regime is, in fact, acting in ways that are contrary to the interests of the nation, and has actually subverted those interests for personal gain and power. Should such perceptions develop, the sense of betrayal that would naturally follow might produce *greater* likelihood of political activity designed to punish the usurpers. This may not have occurred yet in Romania. While many certainly consider the regime, as such, corrupt (especially Elena and Nicu), there is apparently still a residue of respect for the General Secretary, who is perceived as the Vozhd who is misled by his rapacious subordinates. The "little Father" syndrome thus works to the benefit of the present leader.[32]

Other factors aid the present regime against potential moves to unseat it. The alienation of many in Romania has produced the time honored phenomenon of political parochialism and privatization, not counter-regime activism. The repressive capabilities of the regime have instilled almost palpable fear among many potential oppositionists. Society has become so atomized that individuals are afraid to share their views and hopes with others, preferring instead to suffer in silence and expanding their energies in the quest for the material essentials of life. Under these circumstances, organized opposition cannot be established easily, but would require unusual leadership figures. These have not yet emerged in contemporary Romania.

The inability of the scattered spokesmen for oppositionist views to coordinate their activities stands in sharp contrast to the successes scored by KOR and other organizations in Poland. In Romania, there is as yet no national coordinating body that attempts to aggregate the interests and demands of the groups and individuals who have a commonality of interests in changing the regime, or at least its chief actors. Scattered outbursts of worker discontent appear to take place in response to local conditions, not as a result of coordinated acts designed to deal with a common, national, set of problems. The vigilance of the security police and the lack of solidarity across regions, classes, or limited concerns have prevented the establishment of a Romanian equivalent of KOR or Charta 77. The traditional submissiveness of the Orthodox Church has made organizations such as the peace movement in the German Democratic Republic impossible. All in all, the factors hindering organized and nationally coordinated opposition in Romania are formidable.

In addition to the factors discussed above, it should be noted that the various groups that may form a meaningful opposition to the clan have somewhat contradictory goals and aspirations. The technical and managerial intelligentsia may make a coalition with elements of the military, but there are surely other factions in the military establishment that oppose such a coalition, because their role would be reduced in a system emphasizing technical prowess. The regular line officers and those in charge of the militia-type formations which have developed as a result of the change in military doctrine (adopted in the late 1970s) would represent such a force. Furthermore, the industrial proletariat is not likely to accept the reforms envisioned by the technocrats, because that would mean greater differentiation in income and harder work, with an emphasis on labor productivity. In this regard, developments in Poland and in the Soviet Union represent illustrations of what might transpire under a reform-oriented leadership.[33]

Even within the technical and managerial intelligentsia there are divisions. There *are* technocrats who benefit from the Ceausescu policy of gigantomania and continued emphasis on capital investment rather than consumption. These individuals have profited from existing policies and cannot be expected to aid in the dismantling of such an approach. By the same token, there are elements inside the artistic intelligentsia who have benefitted greatly by the cultural policy of the Ceausescu clan; they are not likely to dismiss the policy of chauvinism and accept a new artistic climate in which quality and not sychophantism is rewarded.

The forces that divide the political opposition to the Ceausescus and the Petrescus are formidable indeed. They can only be overcome if a number of factors come together in an auspicious manner. First of all, there is a need for a strong leader who can emerge as the catalyst for commonality, bridging the gaps that now exist between the scattered and somewhat parochial interests of various potential oppositionists. Secondly, the individuals and groups with grievances must decide to challenge the regime rather than making separate deals with it. Thirdly, there must be solid support for such actions from the outside, both from other states and parties in Eastern Europe and from the Soviet leadership as well. These are formidable conditions indeed. Perhaps their confluence is too much to be expected. Perhaps the success or failure of change must await the demise of the General Secretary. For the beleaguered Romanian people, that is a painful hiatus.

Notes

1. On the notion of the political system and its capabilities (including the capability to maintain itself through stability), see, for example, Karl W. Deutsch, *Politics and Government: How People Decide Their Fate* (Boston, MA: Houghton Mifflin, 1980), ch. VI (pp. 132–152).

2. E.g. Gabriel A. Almond and G. Bingham Powell, Jr., *Comparatice Politics: System, Process, and Policy* (Boston, MA: Little, Brown and Company, 1978), ch. XI (283–322).

3. *Ibid.*, ch. I (pp. 3–25).

4. This is particularly important in the case of communist-ruled systems, where the ruling elites are doctrinally committed to atheism. See, for example, Alan Scarfe, "National Consciousness and Christianity in Eastern Europe" in Pedro Ramet (ed.), *Religion and Nationalism in Soviet and East European Politics* (Durham, NC: Duke University Press, 1984), ch. 2 (pp. 31–41).

5. E.g. Samuel P. Huntington and Clement H. Moore, "Conclusion: Authoritarianism, Democracy, and One-Party Politics," in Huntington and Moore (eds.), *Authoritarian Politics in Modern Society* (New York, NY: Basic Books, 1970), ch. 17 (pp. 507–518).

6. The current Romanian regime stands in sharp contrast. Nicolae Ceausescu is determined to control all aspects of human life. See his speech to the recent RCP national conference, published in *Scinteia*, December 17, 1987.

7. Huntington, "Social and International Dynamics of One-Party Systems," in Huntington and Moore (eds.), *Authoritarian Politics in Modern Society*, ch. 1 (pp. 3–48).

8. E.g. Volgyes, *Politics in Eastern Europe*, ch. 5 (pp. 107–127).

9. This notion is crucial to the concept of the self-regenerating system. See the classic on this topic, David Easton, *The Political System* (New York, NY: Knopf, 1953).

10. This is indeed one of the weaknesses of communist systems, because the information flow is restricted. I have disucssed this in a manuscript entitled "Nationalism and Communism," to be published in a volume edited by David Mason and Bogdan Szajkowski (Westview Press).

11. Nicolae Ceausescu is a firm believer in this thesis, but he has added the un-Marxist touch of self-glorification and belief in rule by great men. See his speech to the RCP national conference, in *Scinteia*, December 17, 1987.

12. This was indeed one of Gorbachev's main themes at the CPSU congress; see *Pravda*, February 26, 1986.

13. Romanian policies are now coming under criticism even in the most conservative circles in Eastern Europe. See, for example, *Rude Pravo*, June 24, 1988.

14. Alfred Reisch, "Nonparty Academician Elected Head of State," *Radio Free Europe Research*, Hungarian SR/11, 5 August 1988. Other important changes also took place during the summer of 1988 in the wake of the party congress that replaced Janos Kadar. See Reisch, "Other Changes in Official Personnel," *ibid*.

15. For a good analysis of Polish conditions, see Kristian Gerner and Stefan Hedlund, "Die polinische Dauerkrise," *Osteurope*, May 1988, pp. 369–385.

16. The Bulgarian Communist Party held a much heralded national conference to deal with the need for change. For main themes, see Todor Zhivkov's speech, published in *Rabotnichesko Delo*, January 29, 1988. The East Germans, while conscious of the need for change, consider Soviet-style reforms to have little relevance for the GDR; see, for example, Otto Reinhold in the SED theoretical journal *Einheit*, June 1988. For a thorough discussion of the need for reform in Czechoslovakia, see Zdenek Haba in *Rude Pravo*, June 23, 1988.

17. Ceausesce has now made himself the chief planner. See *Scinteia*, December 24 and 25, 1987.

18. Trond Gilberg, "Leadership Drift in Romania," (paper presented to the annual convention of the American Association for the Advancement of Slavic Studies, Boston, MA, November 1987. to be published by *Comparative Communism* in 1989).

19. Despite its submissiveness, the Romanian Orthodox Church lives under difficult conditions. The new patriarch, Teoctist Arapasu, elected to the post in November 1986, has joined the chorus of uncritical praise of Ceausescu. See *Frankfurter Allgemeine Zeitung,* August 22, 1986.

20. Occasionally some of these intellectuals and artists speak out, albeit in an elliptical way. See, for example, Augustin Buzura, *Tribuna,* June 18, 1987.

21. Pamphlets now circulate in Romania discussing the need for such change. For a discussion, see Vladimir Socor, "Proposals for Reform and Appeals to Gorbachev from Romanian Dissidents," *Radio Free Europe Research,* Romanian SR/11, 15 October, 1987.

22. A number of Romanians have left Romania and are now living in exile in Hungary, where they publish an exile newspaper. For reports on this, see *Süddeutsche Zeitung,* June 29, 1988.

23. There is no direct evidence of organization among these individuals, but they have on occasion resisted decisions by Ceausescu, thus indicating their opposition. An example of this is the refusal of the Political Executive Committee to expel Gheorghe Stoica despite Ceausescu's demand that it do so. See *Scinteia,* October 6, 1987, which listed the actions of the PEC.

24. Ceausescu again criticized such elements in his speech to the RCP national conference, (*ibid.,* December 17, 1987).

25. In October 1987, the leadership of the Security Service was changed. For the announcement, see *Agerpres,* October 3, 1987. Constantin Olteanu became the new ideological chief in May or June 1988. For the latter development, see Michael Shafir, "Former Defense Minister Appointed Ideological Chief," *Radio Free Europe Research,* Romanian SR/8, 23 June 1988.

26. There are occasional rumblings of dissent in the peasantry, but they are quickly squashed. See, for example, *Le Figaro,* January 7, 1987, on the treatment of a dissident who argued for the resurrection of the National Peasant Party.

27. And plan targets are not met; this is partly because of unrealistically high targets, partly because of faulty performance, as admitted by Ceausescu himself (*Scinteia,* February 6, 1988).

28. E.g. Dan Ionescu, "Historians Protest Against Church Demolitions," *Radio Free Europe Research,* Romanian SR/1, 10 January 1986.

29. The Soviet press is highly critical of Romanian developments. See, for example, *Komsomol'skaia Pravda,* August 23, 1987.

30. For an overview of Soviet-East European relations, see J. F. Brown, *Eastern Europe and Communist Rule* (Durham, NC: Duke University Press, 1988), ch. 2 (pp. 30–62).

31. "Socialist patriotism" is emphasized with increasing frequency and vehemence in the Romanian press. See, for example, the theoretical monthly *Era Socialista,* April 10, 1988.

32. This perception may change, however, as Ceausescu continues to castigate the performance of cadre and refuses to accept responsibility for failures. See the General Secretary's speech to the RCP Central Committee plenum in June 1988, published in *Agerpres,* June 28, 1988.

33. For an analysis of the Polish crisis, see Gerner and Hedlund, *Osteuropa,* May 1988.

10

Romania and the World

During the Ceausescu era, the foreign policies of "maverick Romania" have received much greater attention than the aberrant domestic decision-making processes and the peculiar implementation of policy conducted in the "epoch of Ceausescu." Much of this attention has been focused upon the nationalistic and autonomist foreign policy of the clan. It has been commonly accepted in the West that Nicolae Ceausescu, through his occasional criticism of the Kremlin, has become an element of autonomy inside the Soviet "bloc" and hence an individual worthy of our attention and our sympathy. Consequently, Western leaders have been willing to accept a number of unpalatable features of the domestic regime, because that very regime was perceived as a thorn in the side of the Soviets. "The enemy of my enemy is my friend" is a crude way of expressing this Western mind-set, but it is not widely off the mark as a brief characterization of Western assessments as they pertained to Romanian foreign policy and hence the nature of the regime responsible for that foreign policy.[1]

The Romanian emphasis on foreign policy autonomy in ideological matters as well as state policies represents not only a genuine concern, but also a well conceived set of imagery that appears to represent more independence than actually exists. Western analysts and policy makers alike have tended to assume that deviation from established and expressed Soviet goals and policies ipso facto represents an element of advantage for the U.S. and other Western powers. This may or may not be so, depending upon the specific goals pursued by Bucharest in each individual case. We should keep in mind the possibility that Romanian goals, while deviating from specific *Soviet* objectives, may also be detrimental to *Western* interests. In fact, a number of specific policies pursued by the Ceausescu regime during the last two decades have been contrary to the interests of both global powers. Thus, Romania has been a maverick in this area of activity, in much the same manner as it has pursued a distinctly national path in political and socio-economic development at home. It is now time to examine the specifics of this foreign policy.

The Symbiotic Relationship
of Domestic and Foreign Policy

Romanian foreign policy is intimately tied in with the main aspects of domestic policies. It is always true that there is a strong relationship between these two sets of political behaviors, goals, and objectives, but in the case of Ceausescu's Romania, the correlation is stronger than usual. In short, Romanian foreign policy during the last two decades revolves around nationalism, indeed chauvinism, the notion that history is made by great men, and Ceausescu's personal vision of Romania's rightful place in the concert of nations. It is also a serious attempt by the Ceausescu regime to maximize Romania's influence in the world beyond the scope of available resources. Such an achievement is sought through an extremely active diplomacy and a policy of visibility through carefully timed acts and statements. The greatness that Nicolae Ceausescu perceives for *his* Romania, obtainable only through the policies produced by the General Secretary himself, is only worthwhile if it is recognized by the rest of the world. In this sense, Ceausescu's domestic and foreign policies are symbiotically related in the General Secretary's quest for personal power.[2]

The nationalistic element in Romanian foreign policy has other important connotations as well. The recognition accorded this medium-sized European state is an important legitimizing factor at home, especially since there are few other areas of performance that can be utilized for the establishment and maintenance of legitimacy and mass support. A chauvinist is not satisfied with the demonstration of his superiority at home; he must also act out his values in relations with others. This has increasingly become a hallmark of Ceausescu's relations with other states and communist parties, as we shall see below.

During part of the Ceausescu era, foreign policy has had important economic connotations as well. The regime, bent upon "an opening to the West," utilized foreign policy autonomy as a vehicle for expanded trade with the capitalist economies, especially for the purpose of import of technology and the establishment of hard currency credits. Such benefits were thought to be more easily obtainable by means of a foreign policy that would please the most important leaders of the capitalist world, and autonomism was the most likely manifestation to produce the desired result. As it became clear that Romania was a rather difficult system in which to do business, with exceedingly slow bureaucratic procedures and an inefficient industrial plant with low productivity labor,

Western interest in the alleged maverick waned, and it became necessary for Bucharest to turn its attention to the Third World for expanded markets and sources of badly needed raw materials. During the decade of the 1980s, the Ceausescu regime returned to the fold of socialist economies in many respects, perhaps more out of necessity than of conviction and choice.[3]

This short survey will be discussed in greater detail below. The main point to be made here is that Romanian foreign policy has always been an integral part of the economic development program of Bucharest, and as such has been crucial to the fortunes of the political leadership itself. The quest for economic development at home demanded steady sources of raw materials, capital, and technology, and the increasing output from the Romanian industrial plant needed markets. The essence of extensive, rapid, and forced economic development depended upon this confluence of domestic and foreign policy. The legitimacy derived from socio-economic development, communist-style, depended upon this interaction. It is a measure of the decline of both that legitimacy and the vitality of the Romanian system itself that this nexus between domestic and external policy is broken. Romania flounders in increased isolationism and internal stagnation, as the system spirals downwards into ever-deepening levels of crisis.

Romania and the Socialist Commonwealth

Upon the advent of Nicolae Ceausescu to power in 1965, it became clear that the autonomist policies initiated by his predecessor, Gheorghe Gheorghiu-Dej, would be continued, perhaps even expanded. The new RCP leader soon became embroiled in a number of controversies with the Soviet Union and the CPSU, especially over the issue of ideological orthodoxy and the question of centers of world communism. As the Sino-Soviet dispute heated up during the latter half of the 1960s and into the 1970s, the RCP increasingly pictured itself as the mediator in the struggle between the two communist giants, and Nicolae Ceausescu constantly hammered home this idea in his speeches and writings. As pointed out by a number of scholars, this emphasis on mediation allowed Bucharest much greater autonomy inside the "socialist commonwealth," because Ceausescu could lend a sympathetic ear to both sides without being accused of treason to either camp. It was also in this context that the General Secretary began to develop his ideological notions that soon took on rather idiosyncratic connotations and became known as "Ceausescuism" to many analysts. Ceausescuism was Marxism with a special national and personal twist, and the Romanian leader, careful not to commit the "Titoist" sin of billing it as an alternative model, nevertheless emphasized its validity for Romania, as well as the principle of *national* socialism and national communism as the leading guidelines of interstate and interparty relations among communists. Later, during the 1980s, the megalomania of the RCP leader has also spilled over into foreign policy and ideological attitudes. Now, the General Secretary is wont to discuss the "Romanian way" as both superior and possibly relevant for other communist leaders as well.[4]

The evolution of Romanian autonomism in ideological matters had its important counterpart in interstate relations. Here, the RCP leader steadfastly emphasized the need for all actors to respect the principles of noninterference in domestic affairs, relations based upon mutual advantage, reciprocity, and respect for national sovereignty. This principle is still touted as the key to socialist interstate relations, and the General Secretary is adamant that it should in fact be made the guiding principle for *all* interstate relations, regardless of the ideological nature of each state. These principles of national sovereignty are, of course, fundamental to any kind of autonomist foreign policy and must remain as the basis of Bucharest's relations with all other systems. They are also increasingly accepted by the other states and parties of Eastern Europe as the Soviet grip on the region is modified.[5]

With these principles of party-to-party and interstate relations as the general backdrop to its foreign policy, Romania has developed a set of regional and bilateral relations that testify to the skill of Bucharest's diplomacy. It is only during the paranoic decade of the 1980s, particularly the second half of it, that the General Secretary has begun to violate his own successful formula—a topic to which we shall return below.

As the Ceausescu era wore on, there gradually developed a *regional* policy which Bucharest has pursued with a great deal of persistence but with varying degrees of success. Briefly put, the Romanians divided the Comecon into two subcategories, the developed North and the developing South. In the former category Ceausescu put the GDR, Poland, Czechoslovakia, and Hungary. In the developing South, Bucharest placed Bulgaria, Yugoslavia, Albania, and Romania. The developed socialist systems have higher levels of industrial development, urbanization, and technological sophistication; the southern societies are still mixed industrial-agrarian in nature. Under these circumstances, it is the duty of the more highly developed systems to aid the less advanced in their development, through loans, technology transfers, and bilateral relations designed to advance industrialization and the diffusion of technology in the southern tier.

The themes of "socialist duty" and the idea of developmental aid to the southern states represented a demand for assistance in the autarkic quest for industrial development, and it ran counter to the notions in the rest of the Comecon that greater specialization and functional integration must take place if the socialist systems were to establish competitiveness with the EEC and the United States and Japan. It has been vigorously resisted by the northern tier states, especially the GDR and Czechoslovakia, whose leaders are struggling with a multitude of problems on their own and thus show little inclination to aid the Balkan states in their quest for development.[6]

Bucharest also increasingly emphasized the notion that the states of the southern tier have common interests and should take a regional approach to matters of economic development, environmental issues, and even security. These policies have been pursued with great vigor, particularly in relations with Bulgaria and Yugoslavia, while approaches to Albania were habitually rebuffed (it remains to be seen if the "opening" of Albania to the outside world since the death of Enver Hoxha will result in greater activity in relations between Bucharest and Tirana).

The regional approach to the Balkans has actually extended beyond the boundaries of socialism and has included Greece and Turkey. The ambitious plans for such regional cooperation are, in fact, a Ceausescu hallmark and illustrate his refusal to be hemmed in by ideological boundaries in his quest for greater influence and economic benefit for Romania.[7]

Relations with the Soviet Union and the CPSU are clearly different from regional or bilateral policies established toward other systems. The Soviet Union is the military, economic, and political hegemon of the entire region, and it stands to reason that all actors in the area must relate differently to such a power. Throughout the Ceausescu era, the RCP leader has struggled to maintain Romanian foreign policy autonomy, both in matters of state relations and in ideological questions pertaining to relations among communist parties. At the state level, the principles of national sovereignty and mutual advantage have been reemphasized repeatedly during the last two decades. Bucharest has opposed Soviet policies on a number of issues such as the Kremlin's aid to Vietnam during the invasion of Cambodia, and also in matters such as the stationing of troops and missiles on foreign soil. The RCP leadership did not join the chorus of support for the Soviet invasion of Afghanistan and has discussed the pull-out of troops from that war-torn country in tones that smack of "I told you so" wisdom. The emphasis on autonomy from the regional hegemon continues, as it has become a staple of Romanian foreign policy.[8]

Despite this continuity, it should be pointed out that there has been a toning down of Romanian rhetoric during the last few years. The RCP leader is now more wont to discuss the need for unity of socialism in the face of increased aggressiveness from imperialist forces. This noticeable turn in rhetoric may be purely tactical, as Romania finds itself more and more dependent upon the Comecon for economic survival. It may also be part of the changing nature of Ceausescuism, which is markedly more orthodox ideologically and outwardly anti-Western than was the case ten years ago. Whatever the reason, Bucharest has clearly returned to the fold of the "socialist commonwealth" on a number of issues lately. This is a development that must be welcomed in part by the Kremlin, despite the fact that Moscow is clearly embarrassed by the Byzantine intrigues and irrational behavior of the Ceausescu clan and would like to see considerable changes in the leadership, to fully integrate Bucharest into the commonwealth of glasnost and perestroika.[9]

Bucharest's relations with Moscow in economic matters have changed as well. The Ceausescu regime emphasized the need for economic autonomy as well as relative political independence, and to this end relations were expanded with the West and with the resource-rich countries of the Third World, with which a lively barter trade of finished goods in exchange for raw materials and fuels was conducted. As mentioned above, the unreliability of Romania as a partner soon scared away a number of Western investors and banks, reducing this connection considerably. The low quality of Romanian goods also made them uncompetitive on the Western markets. Increasingly, then, Bucharest was forced to rely on its trade with the Third World. But, as discussed elsewhere,[10] the changes brought about by the oil crisis of the 1970s forced Romania out of these markets as well, and, during the latter part of the 1970s, Bucharest increasingly relied on the poorest developing nations, the so-called Fourth World, for the needed raw materials and fuels. Since this was a costly policy with little prospect of success, Bucharest was gradually forced back into the Comecon for its foreign economic relations, and a substantial part of this redirection came in the form of increased trade and cooperation with the Soviet Union. At the present time, Romania buys oil and other fuels from the Soviets in considerable quantities, presumably paying for these commodities with finished products. There are at least 1200 Soviet inspectors in Romanian plants attempting to ensure high quality production for export to the USSR at the present time. This is but the most visible sign of increased Romanian dependence upon its eastern neighbor—a far cry from the heyday of economic autonomism a decade ago.[11]

The course of Soviet-Romanian relations has also changed in matters of security. An integral part of the quest for national sovereignty is the ability to defend one's own territory and to conduct security policy with a modicum of independence. The Ceausescu regime has been adamant on this issue for a long time, and its reputation in the West as a maverick stems primarily from such policies. Romania has demanded the dismantling of military blocs, the expansion of relations between all states, regardless of political and socio-economic system; greater multilateral activity among all small and medium-sized states, presumably in defense against the machinations of large powers; the need for all states to defend their own territory against *all* aggressors (a tacit acknowledgement that, for autonomous Romania, the greatest security threat stems from the fraternal states of the Warsaw Pact and not from the capitalist imperialistic powers). Throughout the period of Ceausescu rule, Romania has been marginally integrated into the Warsaw Pact at best, never permitting pact exercises on its soil and mostly contributing staff officers to map exercises rather than actual troops. Bucharest has not participated in joint operations of the Pact such as the invasion of Czechoslovakia in 1968.[12]

The security field has experienced the least important changes in Romanian foreign policy during the 1980s. Nicolae Ceausescu still emphasizes national sovereignty, and there has been no marked increase in Bucharest's willingness to integrate into the Warsaw Pact. The RCP General Secretary still occasionally launches into tirades about autonomy and national sovereignty. Bilateral relations with the Soviet Union have remained stagnant in the security field. But Ceausescu's increasing alienation from the West (to be discussed below) has had the indirect effect of reducing the allure of autonomism. There is no place to go for Romania in security matters towards the end of the 1980s. Isolationism reigns. And an isolated Romania is an irrelevant Romania in the security schemes of Gorbachev's Kremlin.[13]

In ideological matters, the Romanian quest for autonomy and a national road to socialism and communism has been successful. The post-Brezhnev leaders, especially Mikhail Gorbachev, have accepted the notion that national conditions will demand specific national solutions to political and socio-economic problems, albeit within the parameters of basic aspects of socialism, most notably the continued monopoly of power for the local communist party and an economic structure in which the most important means of production remain public, even if greater private enterprise is allowed on the margins of the economic order. This increased Soviet willingness to accept diversity in Eastern Europe has been utilized by the Ceausescu clan as it rejects Moscow's insistence on change and reform in each of the systems of the region. Thus, the paradox exists that Soviet reforms themselves make it possible for repressive regimes such as the Ceausescu clan in Romania to act with relative impunity in the face of criticism emanating from all quarters, some of which comes from other socialist states and communist parties.[14]

Since the advent of Nicolae Ceausescu to power, Romania has developed good relations with Beijing. This has manifested itself in ideo-

logical matters, where the RCP leader early on accepted the Chinese
contention that there can be no center of international communism and
hence no heretics; the Romanian leadership has steadfastly supported
the right of the Chinese (or anyone else) to maintain a "national road"
to socialism and communism. Furthermore, Nicolae Ceausescu was
personally impressed with the achievements of the Great Proletarian
Cultural Revolution and launched his own "mini-cultural revolution"
after a visit to China in the summer of 1971. Since then, the notions
of revolutionary elan, anti-intellectualism, and mass mobilization that
represented the driving force of the Proletarian Revolution have largely
been abandoned by the Chinese, but increasingly influenced the RCP
leader up to a point where they clearly dominate his current thinking.
This is one of the main aspects of Romania's anachronism at the present
time.

Ceausescu's support for "national roads" also had direct connotations
for Romania's own policy, as pointed out by many analysts. His argument
on behalf of Beijing on this issue, therefore, was self-serving and tactical,
even as the General Secretary apparently accepted certain elements of
Maoist doctrine and practice. These tactical and strategic relations with
the Chinese Communist Party (CCP) then grew into substantial economic
relations and regular exchanges of military personnel as well as discussions
on matters of security. Romania never abandoned its place in the Warsaw
Pact, and never challenged the Soviet Union and the CPSU in an overt
and provocative manner, but the "China card" was played with a great
deal of skill to enhance autonomist aspirations in Bucharest.[15]

It should be pointed out that Nicolae Ceausescu has maintained strong
relations with North Korea during much of his rule. These relations are
ideological, economic, and strategic in nature. The RCP General Secretary
has openly voiced his admiration for the leadership style of the North
Korean elite, and he has argued the notion of the "organic link" between
people and Leader in a way that strongly resembles the ideas of Kim-
il-Sung and his dynasty in Pyongyang. In this respect, Romania deviates
sharply from the practices of the other East European regimes.[16]

Relations between Romania and the other states and parties of Eastern
Europe vary greatly, from very friendly to icy. Bucharest and Belgrade
have had a long-standing relationship based on shared perceptions of
national security, foreign policy autonomy, relationships with multilateral
blocs, ideological positions on sovereignty and development, and relations
with the developing countries. This continues, albeit with less outward
warmth and coherence than during the Tito era in Yugoslavia. There
are still a number of vehicles for bilateral relations, and there is still a
limited form of security cooperation, for example, in the production of

a jet fighter and in tactical matters. Economic interaction also continues at a relatively brisk pace.[17]

In sharp contrast to the friendly ties with Yugoslavia, Bucharest's feud with Budapest continues, indeed deepens as the treatment of the Transylvania Magyars worsens and Hungarian assertiveness on this issue increases. The polemic between the two capitals has heated up considerably during the last two or three years. It is likely to become even more sharply defined as the political reform process continues in Hungary, thereby expanding the role of public opinion as a factor in the decision-making process of Budapest. That public opinion is now inflamed to a considerable extent on the Transylvanian issue, and it is likely that it will continue in this direction for a period of time. For its part, the chauvinistic Ceausescu clan has done little to dampen the views of the anti-Magyar elements inside Romania, because this kind of chauvinism is seen as a vital ingredient in public support for the regime. In this field, then, deterioration, and not improvement, can be expected.[18]

With the other states of Eastern Europe, Romania maintains correct relations, but the cordiality that may have existed in the past has been superseded by wariness on the part of other leaders as the pathologies and idiosyncracies of the Ceausescu clan become more apparent. Erich Honecker in the GDR has refrained from criticizing the RCP leadership directly, but there are increasingly assertive statements in the East German press and in other fora that criticize the Romanians, directly or indirectly.[19] The same can be said for the Czechoslovak leadership which remains essentially pragmatic and thus alienated from the erratic behavior of Nicolae Ceausescu and his family and clan.[20] The Polish leaders, beset by massive problems of their own, comment on Romanian affairs cautiously and sparingly, clearly attempting to avoid controversy inside the Comecon and the Warsaw Pact at a time when Poland desperately needs economic aid and other forms of fraternal assistance.[21] Finally, relations between Bucharest and Sofia remain cordial, reflecting conscious efforts by both capitals to build a relationship of stability, security, and cooperation in a region previously characterized by considerable instability and conflict. Romanian-Albanian relations are only now developing after the hiatus of much of the Hoxha era, and the basic configurations thereof have yet to develop.[22]

During the last few years, a commonality of views has developed between the GDR, Hungary, and Romania on the issue of missile deployment and the stationing of advanced weaponry on the soil of other states. East Berlin, Budapest, and Bucharest all oppose such policies, and leaders in all three capitals expressed their views with a vehemence unfamiliar to the Soviets and to Western observers alike. But these commonalities are limited to a few issues and do not represent a real tendency towards a more general convergence or the establishment of informal alliances. Ceausescu's Romania is too far away from the others in most other matters to expect such development.[23]

A common thread that runs through much of Romanian foreign policy towards its "fraternal" associates in the socialist commonwealth is increasing isolationism in Bucharest and reluctance elsewhere in Eastern Europe to become too closely associated with the Ceausescu clan, whose behavior is widely perceived as irrational, illogical, and diametrically opposed to the basic trends of development now underway in all European communist-ruled systems. There is a certain amount of cynicism and disdain in this attitude, relegating Romania once again to the role of a banana republic, a Ruritania known mostly for its erratic and quixotic nature as a corrupt Balkan Operettenstaat of Madame Lupescu and the absentee landlords of the interwar period. Romania is increasingly isolated, because Nicolae Ceausescu considers this state superior to all others, and because those others consider it unworthy of the concert of modern socialist systems.

Relations with Other Socialist Systems

The RCP has maintained a vigorous foreign policy towards communist-ruled states and Marxist and revolutionary parties outside of Eastern Europe, and these relations have been solidified even during a period in which other foreign policy initiatives are in relative hiatus. This reflects Ceausescu's preoccupation with the notion that Romania is a developing system and thus should maintain special relations with others in this category. It is also a monument to Nicolae Ceausescu's self-perception of the RCP and himself as leaders and potential models for the revolutionaries of the Third World. Such a preoccupation has launched the General Secretary on a large number of visits to several countries ruled by local Marxists or communists, and to welcome to Bucharest even larger numbers of such leaders as well as the leaders of various revolutionary movements that classify themselves as "liberation fronts" and the like. There is little doubt that this area of activity remains a high priority for the General Secretary even at a time when the multitudes of political and socio-economic problems besetting Romania would indicate the need for policy priorities to be kept much closer to the home front.[24]

Throughout the entire Ceausescu era the RCP has been an ardent supporter of the North Vietnamese and their counterparts in the rest of Indochina. Romania provided much political support for Hanoi during the Vietnam War and in the aftermath of the unification of the country; a fair amount of material aid was also provided from the meager resources of the Romanian system. Support for Laos and Kampuchea was also a mixture of political and material aid. Throughout the Pol Pot regime, Ceausescu attempted to modify the irrational aspects of that regime, and, for reasons which probably had as much to do with *Romanian* interests as the rights of Cambodia, refused to support the Vietnam invasion of that unfortunate country. Throughout the entire period in which the Laotian communists exercised power, Bucharest remained a supporter, again in political and material terms. This kind of policy continues as Nicolae Ceausescu bills himself as a leader with much to offer to developing countries.[25]

Nicolae Ceausescu has maintained vigorous relations with Cuba and the regimes of Angola and Mozambique sponsored by Havana. Prior to the establishment of Marxists in power in these two African states Bucharest was one of the most important supporters of the national liberation movements operating in the colonial territories. In fact, it has always been Nicolae Ceausescu's position that all leftist liberation movements must be supported because they represent the forces of progress and anti-imperialism in a dangerous world. This outlook led to considerable Romanian support for the various liberation movements in Rhodesia prior to independence. There was also consistent and major support for the Marxist or Marxist-oriented movements of Southwest Africa and those forces fighting for independence inside South Africa. All in all, Bucharest's policy towards Marxist-leaning parties in power in the Third World is marked by a great deal of activism and material aid, designed to establish Romania as a reliable and active supporter and perhaps also a model of political and socio-economic development. In this regard, Romania has showed greater activism than her colleagues in the Warsaw Pact and Comecon, who often are mere auxiliaries for Soviet policy in the Third World.[26]

As Bucharest relates to the ruling Marxist or Marxist-oriented parties in Asia, Africa, and Latin America, it is clear that Nicolae Ceausescu considers these systems supremely important in both a political and socio-economic sense. In the latter area, these new states possess resources that are needed by the expanding but inefficient Romanian industries. By the same token, these systems are markets that can be utilized for export of Romanian industrial goods which would otherwise be unsalable on most open or developed markets. Politically, continued Romanian aid and support gives Bucharest an opportunity to enhance its influence way beyond her borders into areas that can normally be reached only by the major powers. Thus, an independent stance is achieved in the Third World, and a major foreign policy goal of the Ceausescu regime has been accomplished. Insofar as prestige abroad is a legitimizing device at home, such a success in leftist regimes in faraway places represents an added increment of legitimacy for the regime. And for Nicolae Ceausescu, personally, this is clearly a triumph of considerable proportions.[27]

Relations with the Capitalists:
Making the West Work for You

From the advent to power until the mid-1980s, Nicolae Ceausescu was a very active participant in the dialogue between East and West and one of the chief spokesmen of the notion that all states must coexist, regardless of political and socio-economic system. For twenty years the RCP General Secretary assiduously promoted bilateral relations with a great many states in Western Europe, North America, Latin America, and Asia for the purpose of expanded political and socio-economic influence and the benefits that such relations with the advanced capitalist states carry with them in the field of technology and advanced industrial processes. There is little doubt that these activities were also designed to enhance Romanian autonomy vis-a-vis the Soviet Union and the CPSU and thus establish Romania as an important international actor. This was an integrated effort for added policy leverage and the establishment of influence that vastly exceeded the real capabilities of this medium-sized state with modest resources. It was a serious effort of long-standing, and it was largely successful.[28]

In this prolonged quest, Nicolae Ceausescu pursued somewhat different tracks in his bilateral relations with the West European states. His relations with Latin Europe, particularly France and Italy, were conducted under the auspices of a shared culture, the heritage of Latinity, and the need for states of this heritage to act together for the protection of that heritage in a world increasingly dominated by the Anglo-Americans and the Russians. At the same time, Romania sought full access to the dynamic economies of these two major West European powers, and at times Bucharest was quite successful. But towards the middle of the 1980s, this effort began to sour as the leaders in Paris and Rome increasingly took issue with the dismal civil rights performance of the Ceausescu regime. At the present time, relations have cooled considerably, with little prospect for improvement as long as current repressive policies continue in Bucharest.[29]

Relations with West Germany were conducted on the basis of certain areas of shared interest, notably the need for these two states to establish an independent profile inside their respective alliances, and also for increased economic interaction. In addition, Bonn had (and still has) a vested interest in ensuring good treatment of the sizeable German minority and the continued granting of exit visas for those ethnic Germans who wish to emigrate. The Federal Republic was also clearly interested in reestablishing some of the former German influence in the Balkans, which was a major international factor in the period between the two world wars. All of these areas of common interest kept German-Romanian bilateral relations at a high level and in a relatively cordial state for close to two decades. Increasingly, however, Romanian efforts to profit further by the emigration of ethnic Germans through the imposition of extra taxes and corrupt extraction of resources owned by the German emigrants cooled these relations as well. During the second half of the 1980s, they reached a nadir that is not likely to improve much with current foreign and domestic policy practices as currently produced by the Ceausescu regime.[30]

Great Britain never played the same kind of role in Romania's foreign policy in Western Europe as did France, Italy, and the Federal Republic of Germany. Britain has less of an economic interest in the Balkans. Its industrial plant cannot provide goods and services that are superior to those offered by the major continental powers, and the latter have the advantage of location and access to markets. In addition it should be noted that Great Britain, during much of the Ceausescu era, has been ruled by conservatives whose ideological distance has been keenly perceived by Ceausescu. Thus, London's influence has been much less, and much less desired, by Bucharest.[31]

Nicolae Ceausescu has maintained cordial relations with the smaller states of Western Europe as well, but this is clearly of lesser importance to the rulers in Bucharest. The main motivation here seems to have been the need to be accepted as a major statesman in West European capitals. This may have been possible in years past, but the reputation of Romania in the 1980s has been so sullied by repression, economic irrationality, and the cult of the personality that few West Europeans take the Ceausescus and Petrescus seriously any longer. Thus, the quest for influence has largely failed among most of the statesmen and politically aware publics of the West.[32]

Romanian relations with the official structures of the West European states are supplemented by considerable contact with various political parties and movements there. Thus, the RCP has maintained constant contact with most of the communist parties of the area, at times with several such parties in those countries where splits have occurred. Furthermore, there is a considerable amount of activity pertaining to the leftist socialist parties that exist in a number of West European countries, and even the social democrats have been wooed on a rather regular basis. All of this is designed to show that the RCP is a trustworthy and active partner for all "progressive" elements under capitalism. The

Romanians clearly exhibit greater activism here than other East European communist parties.[33]

Romanian relations with the United States should be seen in a category different from that of other Western systems. As the global power representing the opposing Weltanschauung, the United States is technically the main enemy. At the same time it is clear that any autonomous foreign policy emanating from Bucharest depends to a considerable degree on the favorable reception that it may get in that global power. Nicolae Ceausescu has cleverly played up the notion of real foreign policy autonomy for his country and has, in turn, received a benevolent audience in Washington. The Congress of the United States has repeatedly granted Bucharest most favored nation treatment for Romanian export and there has been outspoken support for Ceausescu's foreign policy. Lawmakers and executives in the United States have been willing to disregard the obvious abuses that are routinely perpetuated in civil rights and in the treatment of ethnic minorities in return for Romanian autonomism, which is perceived to have positive ramifications inside the Soviet "bloc."

However, the sympathy for Ceausescu's Romania has worn very thin recently, and most favored nation treatment has been jeopardized on a number of occasions. In a fit of isolationism and defiance, Ceausescu has now ordered that Romania will forego such trading status with the United States because of American interference in the domestic affairs of Bucharest. This is but one of many signs that the clan considers itself outside and above any external considerations, even as such acts become economically costly and thus directly contribute to the decline of the standard of living.[34]

In retrospect it is clear that Nicolae Ceausescu managed to parlay the notion of Romanian autonomy and a national road to socialism and communism with great skill during the late 1960s and the decade of the 1970s. During the 1980s, however, the deteriorating conditions inside Romania and the increasingly repressive nature of the regime gradually isolated the country and made such success scarce and infrequent. At this point, Ceausescu is displaying even greater anti-Westernism, constantly hammering home the message that the West is bent upon destroying the achievements of socialism, and demanding constant and increased vigilance against such machinations. Particularly galling to the RCP leader is the spread of Western art and pop music to the youth of Romania who disdainfully reject Ceausescu's demands for greater attention to native art, music, and literature. This is a classic confrontation between an increasingly cosmopolitan youth culture, on the one hand, and a nativist, peasant-based set of values of national independence and superiority, on the other hand. The United States and the West in

general become the villains in this confrontation, and Ceausescu increasingly cuts out those avenues of contact that were established in
years past as an integral part of Romanian foreign policy. In this field,
too, Romania goes counter to prevailing trends in East-West relations.[35]

The Middle East: Ceausescu as Mediator

The General Secretary has taken a special interest in the Middle East,
where he has displayed a great deal of activity as a mediator between
the Arab states and Israel, and also in conflicts among the various states
of the region. There are a number of reasons for this high level of
activity. First of all, Nicolae Ceausescu's vision of himself as a great
statesman naturally pushes in the direction of involvement in one of
the world's premier troublespots, because this is, presumably, an area
in which his mediating skills can be put to the test for the greatest
amount of positive effect and publicity. Secondly, the Middle East contains
important economic resources that Romania requires, particularly oil;
furthermore, the economies of the region are still at a relatively low
level of development and thus offer prospects for greater involvement
by Romanian industry and construction trusts. Thirdly, the area is close
to the Balkans, and developments there are important for a number of
reasons that are related to this proximity. Successful Romanian involvement here would therefore carry greater weight internationally than any
other kind of foreign policy output emanating from Bucharest.

For almost two decades, Nicolae Ceausescu has been actively involved
in Middle Eastern affairs, travelling to the region or sending trusted
lieutenants, receiving the main political actors from all sides in the
Romanian capital, and displaying much initiative in international fora
such as the United Nations. As is well known, Ceausescu has maintained
good relations with Israel while the other states of Eastern Europe
followed the Soviet lead and broke such relations. Furthermore, the RCP
leader has managed to maintain considerable credibility in most of the
Arab states. This is indeed a masterpiece of diplomacy, and it will always
represent one of the highlights of the foreign policy conducted in the
"epoch of Ceausescuism."[36]

These successes notwithstanding, Romanian influence in the Middle
East has now been reduced significantly. Several reasons are immediately
apparent. First of all, the politics of the region have become excessively
complicated, thus establishing a mine field of contradictory claims and
demands through which few, if any, mediators can safely walk. Secondly,
the Middle East is now a premier area of big power political maneuvering,
and in this context Romania carries little clout and has become irrelevant.
Thirdly, the reduced prestige of Nicolae Ceausescu and his clan has

minimized the effectiveness of Romania as an actor anywhere, and particularly in a region as concerned with prestige, "face," and appearances as the Middle East. Finally, Ceausescu has become increasingly paranoid and inward-looking during the last few years, thus losing some of the verve and innovative capabilities that he earlier displayed in foreign policy. Taken together, these factors have pushed Bucharest into the role of spectator in this most troubled of regions. The success story of Romanian diplomacy is over.[37]

Principles of Foreign Policy Revisited

There emerges from this description a rather clear picture of the main principles of Romanian foreign policy. The first principle is and remains the safeguarding of national sovereignty. Despite realignment with the rest of Eastern Europe and the Soviet Union on some issues (partly out of economic necessity), Nicolae Ceausescu is a nationalist who views all of his political activity as subordinated to this premier goal. No effort will be spared, and no expense will be considered excessive, for the implementation of this principle.

The second principle is that Romanian power and prestige in the world must be safeguarded and enhanced. This can be implemented in a number of ways, through creative diplomacy and personal skill. In the end, the objective is to ensure that this prestige goes beyond real capability of power projection and real capability as measured by economic resources, military clout, or manpower. Such enhancement can only be achieved through manipulation, maneuverability, and the personal capabilities of the leadership, especially Nicolae Ceausescu.

Thirdly, the RCP General Secretary considers himself *the* representative of national communism in Eastern Europe and will undoubtedly continue to emphasize this point. As discussed above, nationalism remains a mainstay of Romanian politics under Ceausescu and will remain a guiding force even after Nicolae, after the clan itself has passed or been removed from the scene. The RCP leader demands recognition of this status in the councils of the Comecon and the Warsaw Pact. The rest of Eastern Europe has grown accustomed to these claims. They are now tolerated with sarcastic smiles, given the abysmal conditions in Romania, but they are not likely to produce policy that would respond to Ceausescu's claims.

Fourthly, the Ceausescu clan emphasizes the notion that Romania is a bridge between East and West, Moscow and Beijing, developing and developed countries, neutral and committed, and Arab and Jew in the Middle East. He also sees Romania as a spokesman for the interests of small and medium-sized states. This status of bridging the gaps that exist in the world, if accepted, would indeed add greatly to the prestige of Romania in the councils of nations. The various power blocs could certainly use such a mediator, despite the fact that the mediator is, at least formally, a member of one of those blocs. Unfortunately for the leaders in Bucharest, this status is not accepted by most players in the international arena, and the credibility of Nicolae Ceausescu continues to decline even as his claims to fame in this area grow louder. The result of this has been a gradual withdrawal of Romania from the hectic diplomatic pace of earlier years, but with a continued emphasis on Bucharest's role as a spokesman for the interests of the less well-developed political and socio-economic systems of the world. This is clearly one of the personal goals and emphases of the General Secretary himself, and as such it is not likely to be abandoned or even modified in scope and intensity.

The fifth major principle is the idea that foreign policy is an integral part of domestic politics and must serve the needs of the nation and its leaders, embodied in Nicolae Ceausescu and his close associates. Specific policies are designed to enhance the prestige of Romania and to improve its economic performance. Foreign policy is also important as a success that can help alleviate problems at home and offset poor performance in a number of areas. Ultimately, foreign policy is designed to lift Romania to its proper place internationally—a place she deserves because of superior achievements in all areas of human endeavor.

The sixth (and most important) principle is the utilization of foreign policy as a vehicle to solidify and expand the position of Nicolae Ceausescu and the clan in Romania itself. Romania, Ceausescu assumes, can only reach its full potential through the acts and inspiration of the Leader; hence, the status of the country in international affairs can only be achieved to its fullest through this leadership. It is clear that Romania continues to lose prestige due to its irrational and repressive behavior at home. The leadership figures around Nicolae Ceausescu cleverly shield him from this unpalatable fact, and through their sycophantic behavior they directly encourage more of the same. Under these conditions, Romania is becoming more and more isolated, more and more despised as an international actor. The successes scored in earlier years through active and innovative diplomacy and power brokering are being lost, undone. Nicolae Ceausescu and his clan live in a dream world, isolated from their own people, and now increasingly isolated from other states as well. Whether one measures this state of affairs as success or failure, it is certainly unique in a world of increasing interdependence.

Notes

1. An example of this is the granting of most favored nation status to Romania, despite the civil rights record of Bucharest. This status was finally rescinded this year. The State Department announcement was made on February 26, 1988 (see *Radio Free Europe Research,* Romanian SR/4, 4 March 1988, reported by Paul Gafton).

2. Nicolae Ceausescu continues this quest for international recognition, despite the diminished stature of his rule. See his opening speech to the RCP national party conference, in *Scinteia,* December 15, 1987.

3. Ceausescu continues to pursue an active policy in Asia and Africa, despite rising economic costs and declining political benefit. In April 1988, he traveled to Indonesia, Australia, Vietnam, and Mongolia. See *ibid.,* April 9, 1988.

4. At the twenty-seventh CPSU congress, Ceausescu waxed eloquent about the reform allegedly underway in Romania and Romania's economic achievements. See *Agerpres,* February 28, 1986.

5. See Ceausescu at the RCP national conference, in *Scinteia,* December 15, 1987.

6. The Romanians continue to criticize CMEA relations on this basis; see the speech by Romanian Prime Minister Constantin Dascalesu at the forty-third session of the CMEA, in *ibid.,* October 15, 1987.

7. Lately, Romania has had conflicts with both Bulgaria and Yugoslavia over air and water pollution allegedly stemming from Romanian industries. Bulgarian complaints were voiced in *Rabotnichesko Delo,* February 5, 1988; *Tanjug,* November 18, 1987, voiced similar concerns in Belgrade.

8. Lately, Ceausescu has made overtures to Erich Honecker to strengthen the position of these autonomist and anti-perestroika states; the Romanian Prime Minister visited East Berlin to discuss these issues in May 1988 (see *Scinteia,* June 1, 1988).

9. Nicolae Ceausescu at the RCP national conference, (*Scinteia,* December 15, 1987).

10. E.g. Ronald H. Linden, "Romanian Foreign Policy in the 1980s," in Daniel N. Nelson (ed.), *Romania in the 1980s* (Boulder, CO: Westview Press, 1987), ch. 8 (pp. 219–254).

11. For an excellent analysis, see Vladimir Socor, "The Soviet Presence in Romanian Industry," *Radio Free Europe Research,* Romanian SR/4, 29 May 1987.

12. Romania is still attempting to maintain an autonomous position in military matters. See the General Secretary's speech to the Military Council of the Warsaw Pact, printed in *Agerpres,* November 15, 1986.

13. Romania is also isolated in other matters such as human rights and economic reform. See, for example, Bucharest's position on human rights at the Conference on Security and Cooperation in Europe (SCE). Even the Soviets have criticized this; see reports from Vienna in *Financial Times,* June 14, 1988.

14. This criticism is now rather harsh; see, for example, *Rude Pravo,* June 24, 1988.

15. See, for example, Linden, "Romanian Foreign Policy in the 1980s."

16. Relations with China and North Korea have been cordial for a long time. See, for example, the account of a visit by a high level delegation to the two countries in December 1976. See *Scinteia,* December 23, 1976.

17. Ceausescu has reiterated his commitment to friendly relations with the states in the Balkans. See *ibid.,* December 15, 1987.

18. Ceausescu's sharpest attack on Hungary came at a recent RCP Central Committee meeting. His speech was published in *Agerpres,* June 28, 1988.

19. These references now tend to be veiled; in the past, the GDR criticized the Romanian autonomist stance outright or in private discussions between Honecker and Ceausescu. See *Scinteia,* February 7, 1977.

20. *Rude Pravo,* June 24, 1988.

21. In fact, in late 1985, Wojciech Jaruzelski, head of the Polish party, visited Romania to explore such cooperation. See *Scinteia,* November 23, 1985.

22. But environmental issues cloud relations with Bulgaria; see *Robotnichesko Delo,* February 5, 1988.

23. See recent discussions with the GDR on "autonomism," reported in *Scinteia,* June 1, 1988.

24. See, for example, the reports on the visit by Mengistur Haile-Meriam, Secretary General of the Ethiopian Workers' Party, to Romania, reported in *ibid.,* November 17, 18, 19, and 20, 1987.

25. Reports on Nicolae and Elena Ceausescu's recent visit to Vietnam showed continued strong support (*ibid.,* April 18, 19, and 20, 1988).

26. The Ceausescus visited a number of African countries in March 1988 (see *ibid.,* March 6 through 16, 1988). Romania's stature in these countries is severely diminished as the problems of economic development accumulate, and Bucharest has insufficient funds to help in a major way.

27. The General Secretary's view of his stature is fueled by the flattery heaped upon him by visiting dignitaries; see, for example, statements by Zaire's president Mobutu in *ibid.,* April 5, 1988.

28. For an overview, see Linden, "Romanian Foreign Policy in the 1980s."

29. On the cooling of Franco-Romanian relations, see *Le Matin,* January 18, 1984.

30. Relations with the Federal Republic are worsening because of Romanian policies towards the ethnic Germans in Romania. See *Süddeutsche Zeitung,* February 15, 1986.

31. These relations have cooled further; the Thatcher cabinet demonstratively cancelled recent visits to Romania for civil rights reasons. See *AFP,* July 4, 1988.

32. The smaller West European states now ridicule Ceausescu for his personality cult and his repressive policies. See, for example, a tape for Austrian television documenting the excesses of this in Romania (in the author's possession).

33. The General Secretary continues to emphasize this in his speeches, e.g. *Scinteia,* December 15, 1987. But many West European leftists are critical of his human rights policies. And others, such as the West German Social Democrats, have passed resolutions criticizing Ceausescu (*DPA,* July 3, 1988).

34. Most favored nation status was recently rescinded (*USIS,* February 27, 1988).

35. His anti-Westernism on this score is palpable; see *Scinteia*, December 15, 1987.

36. Recently, though, Ceausescu has associated himself more with the radical Arab states and movements. Particularly important are relations with the PLO. For reports of a relatively recent meeting between Ceausescu and Yasir Arafat, see *ibid.*, February 9 and 19, 1986.

37. This is clearly seen in actual prestige, despite the General Secretary's rhetoric (e.g. speech to the national conference of the RCP, in *ibid.*, December 15, 1987).

11

Romania, Perestroika, and Glasnost: The Maverick Beleaguered

The Romanian foreign policy stance is based upon the notion that Bucharest's quest for autonomy within the confines of the Warsaw Pact and the Comecon is acceptable to the leaders in the Kremlin, and, indirectly, to the other members of those international organizations. The Kremlin's forbearance, in turn, has been based upon the idea that the regime in Bucharest is so orthodox, indeed Stalinist, that there is virtually no danger of "rightist deviations" along the lines of Poland in 1980, or Czechoslovakia in 1968 (not to mention Hungary in 1956). Thus, the very orthodoxy of the Ceausescu leadership in matters such as party control, ideological expression, centralized planning and implementation in the economy, and control with the cultural sector traditionally helped the RCP as its leader attempted to fashion a distinctive foreign policy. After all, it was unlikely that such "deviations" in foreign affairs would lead to significant challenges to the party's authority at home. And even in foreign policy matters, the Romanian deviation was not serious, merely a nuisance (and, at times Romanian interests ran parallel to those of the Soviet Union in a number of areas of the world and fields of endeavor).

By the same token, Romanian relations with other socialist states and communist parties remained relatively cordial, or at least correct. True, there were occasional controversies with the Hungarians over the treatment of the ethnic Magyars of Transylvania, and the exchange on this subject occasionally became bitter. It was, nevertheless, kept within manageable limits, and occasional bilateral discussions helped alleviate the strains somewhat. Romanian foreign relations with other socialist states and parties, including those of the regional hegemon, were in relative equilibrium.[1]

The maintenance of equilibrium in the relationship between two or more units requires continuation of existing patterns, or the ability of one or more of the units to adjust to changes in the other units, or both. During the last three and a half years, the most important unit in the equation, the Soviet Union, has undergone considerable changes in many areas of socio-economic and political activity. These changes, in turn, have had an inevitable effect upon other "players," especially the states and ruling parties of Eastern Europe. Soviet-Romanian relations are no longer in equilibrium, and will not return to that state for a considerable period of time. Briefly put, the changes now underway in the regional hegemon have not been welcomed by the Bucharest leadership. On the contrary, Nicolae Ceausescu has made it quite clear that he sees no need to accept guidance from Moscow on specific issues embodies in the concepts of "glasnost" and "perestroika," particularly since these developments in the Soviet Union are country-specific in character and therefore non-transferable to other systems. Thus, the traditional Romanian emphasis on autonomy, "national roads" to socialism and communism, and non-interference in domestic affairs has been utilized to limit the effects of the massive changes now underway in the communist world. The result is considerable strain in the relationship, as will be seen below.[2]

The tension in Soviet-Romanian relations is further aggravated by the fact that the policies of Bucharest have also changed in a number of areas, particularly those that could be assumed under the notion of glasnost and perestroika. Briefly put, the Romanian regime has moved in the opposite direction of the Soviets (and a number of their counterparts in the rest of Eastern Europe) on issues such as economic reform, decentralization, and limited pluralism in political matters. The increasingly assertive stance of Nicolae Ceausescu and his close allies on these and other issues has added new elements of strain and disequilibrium.

This stance has also created considerable strain in some of the other foreign policy areas of Bucharest's activity. The most important of these is the relationship with Hungary. Here, the increasingly chauvinistic policies pursued by the Ceausescu clan have resulted in sharp criticism from Budapest and much of the outside world. Furthermore, thousands of Magyars (and several hundred Romanians as well) have left Romania and have been granted refugee status north of the border. These developments, which will be discussed in greater detail below, represent a potential danger point for Bucharest, particularly if the Kremlin should choose to use it a leverage for policy change in Romania.

Romania and Glasnost

Much has been written about the nature of glasnost, and there is no need to repeat it here. The notion that the political process must be opened up for greater debate has wrought important changes in the Soviet polity at all levels. Many topics hitherto "off limits" are now examined in considerable detail. Some of the most painful periods of Soviet history are discussed with astonishing openness. Open debate and criticism have invaded the political realm, and the press, television, and other media show this debate with astonishing frankness. This process is not yet a political revolution, because the monopoly of power by the communist party is being maintained, and the personnel changes that have taken place merely solidify the power of one element of that party, not the emergence (let alone acceptance) of alternative or competing centers of power. At the same time, there are now processes of change underway that may not be reversible; it is unlikely that the blossoming of political discourse can be halted or reversed without massive terror— in itself an unlikely development. And the dizzying speed of glasnost in the Soviet Union has had a considerable effect elsewhere in Eastern Europe, with few exceptions. Romania is, seemingly, one such exception.

From the very beginning, Nicolae Ceausescu rejected the notion that developments in the Soviet Union could (or should) have a direct effect upon the political, socio-economic, or cultural life of other socialist systems. The winds of change which were blowing modestly in the Soviet Union even before the advent of Mikhail Gorbachev were not welcome in Romania. At the RCP congress in November 1984, Nicolae Ceausescu was careful to emphasize the "Romanian way" and the need for all states to choose their national paths of development and their specific structures and procedures for political life.[3] The RCP General Secretary made similar statements at the CPSU congress in 1986, where he spent little time on developments in the host country but held forth in great detail about the achievements of Romania, which he described as massive and on target for the establishment of the "multilaterally developed society" and, subsequently, socialist society.[4] Throughout the following years Ceausescu's tone on this has become more and more assertive. He has repeated the well-known position that each system must develop its own mechanisms of political communication. Furthermore, the General Secretary is insistent on the notion that Romania has achieved an advanced level of political democracy, and this condition requires no change, only perfection of existing structures and processes. This attitude is further enhanced by a chorus of sycophantic advisers, writers, actors, and the ritualized party apparat, who sing the General Secretary's praises as the greatest communicator of all times, anywhere in the world. Under these circumstances, there is no reason to change the pattern or content of political discourse.[5]

Throughout the period since glasnost really accelerated in the Soviet Union, the Romanian leadership has become more and more insistent on the need for each system to develop along its own chosen path, without interference from others. Increasingly, too, the Romanians have asserted that the political, socio-economic, and cultural discourse found in Romania is superior to anything in existence in any other political system, the Soviet Union included. The writings about "socialist culture" now filling the press in this unfortunate country exceed anything seen before in terms of claims to achievements, popular enthusiasm, and the functioning of the political order. These claims clash dramatically with the frequent criticism launched by Nicolae Ceausescu and others against various forms of malfeasance on the part of individuals and groups in the RCP's leadership. They reflect the growing schizophrenia of Romanian political life under "mature Ceausescuism." But they also serve as an excuse for the dismissal of any *real* opening up of the political system to serious discussions (and thereby possibly serious reform). Glasnost simply is unnecessary in a system that already has perfected its communications capabilities beyond all others.[6]

Perestroika, Soviet-style, is also anathema to the Ceausescu clan. It should be noted that perestroika is always an integral part of the communist political order if by this concept we mean "reorganization"; communist systems are always noted for their frequent organizational tinkering with mechanisms and procedures in the quest of greater performance without *real* reform. *This* form of perestroika is part and parcel of the Ceausescu management style and has been for a number of years. Basically (and briefly put), Romanian perestroika has resulted in such concentration of power in the hands of a few individuals that even the most minute details are subject to direct intervention by the very top of the Ceausescu clan. The frequent recycling of individuals and structural components cannot hide this fundamental tendency in Romanian socio-economic management.[7]

This kind of perestroika is *not* what Mikhail Gorbachev has in mind for the Soviet Union. As discussed in great detail by Soviet policy makers and Western analysts, Gorbachev wants to restructure the Soviet economy and management system to produce greater efficiency, higher production, and more individual enterprise and entrepreneurship. This means *decentralization*, not concentration of power at the top. It also means that individuals will have greater opportunity to make decisions, criticize political authorities, and band together for the purpose of furthering their interests (presumably within the parameters of "democratic centralism"). Granted that perestroika as defined has not been implemented in the Soviet Union, but it is still a topic discussed in great detail every day in the press, or other media, and among important segments of the population. This process of discourse *itself* represents a significant element of change.[8]

Nicolae Ceausescu has expressly *rejected* this form of perestroika. The organizational centralization which was always present in Romania has been enhanced, not retracted. There is much less tolerance of divergent views than anywhere else in Eastern Europe (and much less than was the case in Romania itself at the beginning of the Ceausescu era). The notion of private enterprise is honored only on the black market and in the "third economy" as well as in the corruption of communist officials themselves. The idea of streamlining management and enhancing productivity through greater individual autonomy is fundamentally alien to the entire Ceausescu clan and specifically Nicolae and Elena Ceausescu. The ruling couple instead proclaim that *they* have the scientific answer to all questions of political and socio-economic management, and that others have no choice but to submit to these ideas. The General Secretary is much less amenable to criticism and much more likely to interfere, directly and erratically, in the procedures of subordinate organs and individuals. In short, there will be no Soviet-style perestroika in Romania under the Ceausescus. And should Mikhail Gorbachev fail in his quest for perestroika in the Soviet Union itself, the Romanian leadership is likely to proclaim *its* way as demonstrably superior, thus further postponing the possibility of real reform in this unfortunate country.

The conflicts between Bucharest and Moscow on the issues of glasnost and perestroika are more than mere Romanian assertions of autonomy and sovereignty. They are clashes of fundamentally opposed notions of social life, the nature of the political order, and the relations between ruler and ruled, between the economy and the polity. Ceausescuism is unique, and thus resistant to influences which now sweep the entire region. Whether or not it is impervious to such influences remains to be seen.

The attitude of the Ceausescu clan to the dramatic changes now underway elsewhere in the region is, in part, a result of the personalistic political order controlled by the clan, but it also reflects other, more broadly based, values and attitudes of Romanian political culture. Specifically, the Romanians tend to consider themselves different from the other peoples of the region. Furthermore, they also tend to look down upon the Russians and other Slavs; this is true for attitudes towards others as well, notably the Hungarians (but also most of the minorities inside Romania itself). These views are reciprocated by most of the other ethnic groups of the Balkans; in addition, many of the East Europeans located north of the Balkan region harbor traditional views of Romania as an "operetta" badly played by "un-serious" people in the tradition of irresponsible kings and Madame Lupescu of 1930s fame (or ill repute). Thus, there is a climate of ethnic relations based upon mutual contempt (or at least distrust) in this region. The maverick position of Romania during the last two decades on a number of issues of domestic and foreign policy has heightened general distrust of this country throughout the region, and there is clearly considerable ill feeling between Bucharest and Moscow on a number of issues. Specifically, Gorbachev and a number of other Soviet leaders and commentators consider the current regime and its policies in various areas an embarrassment to "scientific socialism" and have indicated this on a number of occasions.[9]

The attitudes prevailing throughout much of the "socialist common-wealth" about Romania and the Ceausescus are reciprocated by the Romanians themselves. In this respect, there is a certain congruence between the regime and the people; both official statements and popular attitudes among the ethnic Romanian masses reflect a high level of nationalism, at times even chauvinism in relations with other nations and their ethnic groups.[10] In fact, the Ceausescu regime has consciously fostered such attitudes as a mechanism for building mass support and legitimacy. Throughout much of the Ceausescu era, nationalism has been a mainstay of the clan's policies at home and abroad. Legions of historians, anthropologists, linguists, and literati have been mobilized to hammer home the messages of the Roman and Geto-Dacian heritage of the Romanian nation, the purity of this ethnic heritage, and, directly or indirectly, the superiority of the Romanians over all others in the region in cultural and scientific achievements. Since the celebrations of the century of Romanian independence in the 1970s, these claims have been exaggerated and unrealistic to the point of ridicule. During the last five or six years the Ceausescus have begun to refer to themselves as individuals who personify the glory and achievements of the Romanian nation as such. Thus, at the end of the 1980s, the cult of the nation has become the cult of the Ceausescu clan and ultimately the heads of the clan, Nicolae and Elena.[11]

Under these circumstances, it is no wonder that the RCP leadership rejects Soviet-style glasnost and perestroika. It is also entirely predictable that the direct or indirect criticism of Bucharest's policies emanating from the other capitals of Eastern Europe has created resentment and coun-terattacks from the Romania capital. It is also quite logical, if disturbing, that the views of the Ceausescus and their associates have produced specific policies towards non-Romanians that are clearly discriminating and, recently, conducive to considerable tension in the relations between Romania and some of her "fraternal allies," specifically Hungary.

A Troubled Relationship:
Hungary and Romania at Loggerheads

At the present time, the relations between Bucharest and Budapest are at their lowest point since the advent to power of the communists in the 1940s. During the last few years, the simmering conflict between these two "fraternal" leaderships has broken into overt recriminations and mutual changes of misconduct and unacceptable behavior. Much of the blame for this recent escalation must be put on the policies of the Ceausescu clan, but one cannot fully understand the nature of the contemporary conflict without an examination of the issues and events that preceded it.

Since 1948, a number of issues have bedeviled the relationship between Hungary and Romania. There was, first of all, the question of Transylvania, much of which had been in Hungary's possession for centuries, but was ceded to Romania at the end of World War II. This issue was debated in a number of fora, chief of which were history and anthropology. Each side claimed the right of heritage in Transylvania by arguing (a) that the Romanians had lived continuously in the mountains since the barbarian invasions overran Dacia Felix (Bucharest's version) or (b) that there was no evidence of such residence and that, in fact, the Magyars and Saxons represented historical continuity in settlement and culture (Budapest's view). This controversy, which was fought openly in academic publications, was conducted against the backdrop of considerable unhappiness in the Hungarian capital and elsewhere among the "orthodox" states of Eastern Europe over the Romanian stance on socialist and proletarian internationalism. This stance, in turn, was utilized by the Ceausescus as a device to bolster public support for the regime, a quest which reached its zenith in 1968 when General Secretary Ceausescu defiantly proclaimed the principle of sovereignty after the invasion of Czechoslovakia.[12]

Throughout the 1970s, the elements which constituted the conflict between Budapest and Bucharest did not change, but the level of the controversy rose to an occasional pitch, depending upon specific incidents and circumstances. Throughout the entire decade, Romanian nationalism was clearly on the rise, as the country went through prolonged celebrations of the contennary of its independence. Furthermore, Nicolae Ceausescu's nationalism became more and more pronounced and turned to chauvinism and personalized rule based upon exaggerated claims to Romanian superiority over others in all kinds of areas, especially culture and sociopolitical capabilities. These claims were made both in terms of ethnic groups residing on Romanian soil and in the more general context of Europe as a whole. Towards the end of the decade, Ceausescu was even openly discussing the notion that the cradle of civilization had been located on territory that now belongs to Romania.[13]

These chauvinistic claims clearly irritated others and helped raise the temperature in the dispute with Hungary over Transylvania to new heights. There were also specific policies that further aggravated already tense relations. Some of these policies were mere symbolic irritants, such as the renaming of cities with Romanian, even Dacian names, and the change in the name of the university at Cluj, which was one of the bastions of Hungarian culture in the area. But even such decisions had important political overtones and thus helped sour relations between these two ethnic groups on Romanian soil.[14]

More important were specific policies aimed against the Hungarians and other ethnic minorities. The emphasis on Romanian history, symbols, and language use represented a slap in the face for many non-Romanians with their own proud history (and their own traditions of chauvinism, directed against the Romanians). Romanian officialdom assiduously practiced these rules and added a few individual twists of their own. Unconfirmed reports indicated that birth certificates were falsified to alter the designated ethnic background of Hungarian-born infants, thus artificially increasing the number of "ethnic" Romanians and correspondingly decreasing the size of the Hungarian community. Countless examples of discrimination in education, the workplace, and other areas of interaction between individuals and groups of various ethnic backgrounds have been reported by emigres and samizdat publications.[15] And, throughout the Ceausescu era, the stridency of Romanian ideological indoctrination increased every year, producing a climate of chauvinism that was a major problem for non-Romanians.[16]

As discussed elsewhere,[17] the results of these policies were predictable. The ethnic Germans began to leave in large numbers, spurred by an agreement between Bonn and Bucharest which involved a considerable amount of economic aid. By the end of the 1980s, the German minority in Romania will be reduced to a relatively small number of individuals, many of whom are old and determined to end their lives in the Saxon land of Transylvania; younger individuals, by contrast, opt in increasing numbers for emigration to the Federal Republic. The eventual disappearance of the German minority from Romanian soil can be expected in the intermediate future.[18]

The Hungarians did not possess the option of emigration. Up to recent months, the Hungarian authorities would not accept those who escaped across the border, and on the Romanian side, controls were strict, in order to prevent such escapes. The motivations for such a policy were varied. The Romanian authorities did not wish to lose qualified labor; they were cognizant of the political problems *inside* the "socialist commonwealth" if such individual escapes became a mass exodus; they still adhered to the Ceausescu notion of socialist culture, in which all residents, regardless of ethnic background, would be socialized into the higher culture, represented by the "Ceausescu epoch." Nicolae Ceausescu himself constantly hammered home the notion that Romania *was* home to all ethnic groups, especially those who had resided on territory now belonging to Romania since the Middle Ages, and also repeatedly asserted that he rejected "efforts to instigate Romanian citizens of various nationalities to emigrate from their fatherland." (*Scinteia*, March 29, 1977).

This attitude prevailed until the early 1980s. At that point, other aspects of the "Ceausescu epoch" surfaced and took precedence over any other consideration or policy. The two most important elements of this "new thinking" were the construction of a new Bucharest and the "systematization" (sistematizare) of the countryside. Both of these ideas led to policies that had a profound effect upon inter-ethnic relations in Romania.

Destruction, Reconstruction, and Systematization: The Tangible Effects of Megalomania

Starting in the late 1970s, but accelerating throughout the decade of the 1980s, Nicolae Ceausescu embarked upon a program designed to leave his mark upon Romania well beyond his own life span (or that of the inner circle of the clan). This plan was manifested in the destruction of some of the oldest sectors of Bucharest and the construction of new, monumental buildings that would adequately represent the glory of the Ceausescu era. Subsequently, the General Secretary decided to launch a massive program of reorganization of the countryside, known as "systematization."

The former policy was unpopular in many segments of the population, whether ethnic Romanian or not. The latter approach of systematization is deeply resented by the Germans and particularly the Hungarians, and is widely perceived as directly discriminatory. The policies combined have raised ethnic tensions in Romania to a new pitch and have also produced a storm of external criticism.

"Systematization" is not a new concept in Romanian politics. During the early 1970s, the Ceausescu regime produced a number of plans designed to restructure settlement patterns, particularly in the countryside, in order to establish a more "scientific" relationship between raw materials, economic enterprises, and the residence of workers. The plans proposed were akin to similar attempts in the Soviet Union at a much earlier stage, and represented a long-standing notion that systematic planning of the location of these three crucial factors of production could result in much better economic performance. Some of the Romanian ideas on this subject were also derived from Nikita Khrushchev's aborted agrogorod scheme.[19]

As was often the case with Ceausescu's plans, implementation was lacking. While Romanian economic planners attempted to use some of

238   *Romania, Perestroika, and Glasnost*

the tenets of location theory for the placement of new factories, they did not embark upon significant *relocations* efforts. Thus, the settlement pattern which had developed all over the country for centuries continued in place. Then the General Secretary launched his controversial new plan for final systematization of much of the country, including areas with predominantly German and Hungarian population concentrations. The effects of this plan, if implemented, would be serious dislocation for large proportions of these minorities. Thus, the plan has been widely perceived as discriminatory and aimed primarily at these two ethnic groups. Whether or not this was the primary intention of the General Secretary's plan is not easily determined, but politically, it is perceptions that count, and these perceptions are rather clearcut, inside Romania and in the outside world. Nicolae Ceausescu has once again produced a scheme that is irrational, costly, and callous in its disregard for the human dislocation and suffering that it entails. It is bound to aggravate already tense relations with ethnic minorities in the country and with many important states abroad.

The plan, simply put, will entail three major efforts:

1. administrative merger and reallocation of thousands of villages;
2. the physical change, including actual demolition, of a number of villages or parts thereof;
3. significant population movement, of Germans and Hungarians out of areas of traditional residence and also of Romanians into such areas to an extent that far surpasses anything hitherto known in Romanian history under communist rule.

The result of the plan, if implemented, will mean the destruction of very large numbers of villages with German and Hungarian populations. The results of such a policy cannot be fully determined ahead of time, but they will be clearly disruptive and largely detrimental over the foreseeable future. A firestorm of criticism has had negligible effects upon the General Secretary and his close associates; in fact, much of this criticism has been dismissed as unwarranted external interference in domestic affairs or anti-system agitation at home. The leadership is clearly in no mood to accept criticism from any quarter as the clan removes itself further and further from domestic and external reality.[20]

As word spread about the plan, unrest in areas of heavy minority population concentrations resulted in outmigration of relatively large numbers, particularly Hungarians. Since 1986 several thousand Hungarians have left Romania and now constitute a significant economic and social problem for Budapest, whose leaders are pledged to help these unfortunate individuals and families. At the same time, increasing numbers of ethnic Romanians have also fled the country, and some of these have also ended up in Hungary; by now, the numbers extend to several hundred, and more are leaving every day. The Romanian refugees are not leaving because of ethnic discrimination, but because of the generally repressive nature of the system and its disregard for basic civil rights. That is the other side of the coin in the late 1980s: the RCP leadership discriminates against *everybody*.[21]

The nature of repression in Ceausescu's Romania is such that no other state in Eastern Europe can match it. This is true even if Albania is made part of the comparison, because post-Hoxha Albania has entered on a path of real, if cautious, liberalization. All around Romania there are tendencies towards regime acceptance of basic human rights, such as greater freedom of assembly, speech, and religion. This is not to say that these systems are now free in the Western sense of the word; on the contrary, they are still clearly autocratic systems, and there is still repression, both of groups and individuals. But the trend towards less repression and more rights is unmistakable all over Eastern Europe—except in Romania.

There are many and well-documented cases of discrimination and repression perpetuated upon religious believers, civil rights advocates, poets, writers, artists, workers who have protested economic decisions and the conditions in which they live, and academics who have advocated changes in the system.[22] There is no need to discuss these aspects further here. What *is* worthy of more detailed examination is the general *climate* of repression, which hangs over this unfortunate country as a cloak, hampering all aspects of human freedom, producing a tendency towards self-censorship, withdrawal, and atomization. These conditions are unique in Romania. They represent the greatest liability for any attempt to revitalize the system. At the same time, they also constitute Nicolae Ceausescu's greatest political success. Romania is calm, compared to Poland, Hungary, or Yugoslavia. It is the calm of despair.

The Nature of the Atomized Society

The Ceausescu regime has scored spectacular successes in its attempts to control a population of almost twenty-two million. There is relatively little unrest and few manifestations of popular discontent. The massive nationwide strikes that periodically paralyzed Poland during this decade have not found a counterpart in Romania; outbreaks of such activity in the latter country have been sporadic and limited to certain areas, thus more easily contained by the authorities and their agents of repression. Intellectual dissent tends to be limited to individuals or small groups, lacking the mass character of similar manifestations elsewhere.

Religious dissent is also sporadic and harshly repressed. From the standpoint of regime and system maintenance, this is indeed an impressive achievement.

Analysts have attempted to discover the reasons for this relative quietude in a country whose socio-economic conditions are abysmal and worsening at an alarming rate. One of the main reasons clearly is the use of nationalism and chauvinism as a legitimizing device. Briefly put, the Ceausescu regime has utilized the natural inclinations of the ethnic Romanian population towards strong feelings of ethnic superiority to buttress its own position in the masses. Thus, the emphasis on the glory of Romanian history, the Geto-Dacian heritage, the alleged achievements of Romanians in all fields of endeavor, and the thinly veiled expressions of animosity against other groups, particularly the Hungarians, have undoubtedly helped to maintain an element of support for the regime during the last two decades.[23]

This support is now clearly diminishing. The results of Ceausescu's economic policies are too apparent, too painful, too relevant for the daily lives of each individual trying to survive on Romanian territory, and no amount of symbolic gratification can offset these deficiencies. Increasingly, people of all ethnic groups must concentrate on the daily struggle for survival in a material sense. The economic hardships created by irrational economic policies represent a great equalizer, providing all individuals with the same handicap. The daily struggle becomes a preoccupation that sets all other concerns aside or relegates them to a secondary position. As discussed above, it becomes a control mechanism for the regime, because people are too preoccupied about mere survival to produce the energy necessary to challenge those who are ultimately responsible for the economic and social misery of the masses in the first place. Under these circumstances, a deceptive calm settles over the population, and the leadership can claim this quietude as legitimacy. In real terms, it is the kind of calm that produces conflict below the central level, with the potential for considerable destabilizing in the future.

At the present time, the frustrations of all Romanians, regardless of ethnic background, are focused in three separate but interrelated directions. First of all, the various ethnic groups engage in overt and covert recriminations against each other, attempting to blame each other for the multifaceted societal crisis and its escalation. There is little doubt that this tendency is being encouraged by the constant reiteration of Ceausescu of the claims to Romanian greatness and the incessant criticism of various forms of malfeasance at various levels of the party and the government and a corresponding disclaimer of responsibility by the General Secretary and his close associates. Furthermore, there is a great deal of Romanian chauvinism in the press and other elements of the media, and the tone is getting more nasty as time and the crisis progress. Here, then, is the systematic use of ethnic animosities as a mechanism for explaining the failures of the system, just as the same values and attitudes were used to produce whatever limited popular support the regime could claim in the past.[24]

Secondly, an increasing number of people focus their anger and resentment on the regime itself, although the expressions of these attitudes remain rather diffuse at the moment. There is little popular support for the leadership or the system for which it stands. Only those individuals who have been coopted into the bureaucracy or the leading circles of the RCP can be expected to support it directly; those who hope to experience such good fortune in the future represent another element of tacit support. The regime cleverly and intentionally coopts erratically, without any real discernible criteria for selection, thereby widening the circle of those who remain hopeful and thus supportive in some measure. This tactic suffices for now, but it is a weak reed indeed for the longer run.[25]

Thirdly, the most frequently used mechanism for dealing with the bleak and unpromising present and immediate future is withdrawal and atomization. Individuals have been reduced to a level of existence which does not carry with it any mechanism for solidarity with others, or kinship that goes beyond the immediate family. Atomization becomes the norm of existence, in which each individual must concentrate on mere survival, without opportunity for conspiratorial activity, designs on the existing order, or the development of counterelites. By the same token, there is also no opportunity for the leadership to produce any real collective spirit or willingness to sacrifice for a common "good." Thus, the constant demands by the leadership that further sacrifices are necessary fall on deaf ears. In many ways, the population is engaged in a form of massive (and passive) resistance to the regime and its policies. This resistance naturally reduces the possibility for improved production and ensures a worsening of social and economic conditions. Thus, the regime remains stable; overt opposition is minimal; and the political process continues with little interference. It is the stability of poverty, atomization, and political withdrawal. Only time will tell if this kind of decline in the standard of living as well as the public spirit can be sustained, or if it will result in the unravelling of the remainder of the societal fabric.

One might well argue that, in addition to documented violations of specific individual rights the Ceausescu regime has violated the most fundamental human right, namely the right to be a social animal, living with and interacting with others in a meaningful societal context.

Ultimately this will be the most significant indictment of the architects and executors of the Ceausescu epoch.

Notes

1. Ronald H. Linden, *Communist States and International Change* (London: Allen and Unwin, 1987); Aurel Braun, *Small-State Security in the Balkans* (Toronto, Canada: Studies in Russian and East European History, 1983).

2. E.g. Ceausescu's speech to the joint session of the RCP Central Committee and other leading political organs, November 28, 1988, in *Scinteia*, November 28 and 29, 1988.

3. *Ibid.*, November 19 and 20, 1984.

4. His speech was published in *ibid.*, February 28 and March 1, 1986.

5. E.g. articles on "socialist patriotism," such as one that appeared in *Era Socialista*, April 10, 1988.

6. Ceausescu at the November 1988 plenum, in *Scinteia*, November 29, 1988.

7. A recent example of such recycling was analyzed by Paul Gafton, *Radio Free Europe Research*, Romanian SR/14, 2 December 1988, (this personnel shuffle involved mostly high officials in government positions).

8. For an analysis of Gorbachev's program, see Thane Gustafson and Dawn Mann, "Gorbachev at the Helm," *Problems of Communism*, May-June, 1986, pp. 1–20.

9. Some of these differences occurred during Mikhail Gorbachev's visit to Romania in May 1987. See, for example, Anneli Ute Gabanyi, "Differences over Dinner," *Radio Free Europe Research*, Romanian SR/4, 29 May 1987.

10. One of the strongest expressions of this chauvinism and anti-Hungarianism came at an RCP Central Committee plenum in June 1988. See Ceausescu's speech, in *Scinteia*, June 29, 1988.

11. The pesonality cult seems to escalate every year. See, for example, articles honoring Nicolae Ceausescu on his seventieth birthday (*Saptamina*, November 30, 1979; *ibid.*, January 25, 1980; *Flacara*, January 24, 1986, *ibid.*, January 23, 1987; *Lumea*, January 22, 1988.

12. I have discussed this in my "The Communist party of Romania," in Stephen Fischer-Galati (ed.), *The Communist Parties of Eastern Europe* (New York, NY: Columbia University Press, 1979) ch. 7, esp. pp. 304–308.

13. E.g. *Flacara* on the "Dacian Imperial Milennium," (February 10, 1984). See also articles, clearly inspired by Ceausescu himself, linking him with this tradition (e.g. *Scinteia*, August 14, 15, and 16, 1986).

14. One of the best books on this subject is still Robert R. King, *Minorities under Communism* (Cambridge, MA: Harvard University Press, 1973), esp. ch. 8 (pp. 146–170).

15. Such policies have triggered a powerful reaction abroad. See, for example, statement by the West German Foreign Ministry on the rural resettlement plan, which is considered discriminating (*DPA*, August 18, 1988).

16. This chauvinism reached a peak at the June 1988 RCP Central Committee plenum; see *Scinteia*, June 29, 1988.

17. E.g. Trond Gilberg, *Modernization in Romania since World War II* (New York, NY: Praeger Publishers, 1975), esp. ch. 8.

18. *Ibid.*

19. For an interesting study of this program, see Steven Sampson, "Feldioara: The City Comes to the Peasant," *Dialectical Anthropology*, No. 4, 1979.

20. For the official Romanian perspective on "resettlement," see, for example, *Luceafarul*, July 16, 1988; *Scinteia Tineretului*, July 22, 1988; *Scinteia*, July 8, 1988.

21. Some of the Romanian refugees in Hungary are former party officials, who describe the repressive conditions in their homeland in graphic detail; e.g. the correspondent Pierro Benetazzo in *La Repubblica*, August 2, 1988.

22. Some of these repressions were meted out against individuals who claim to represent the "National Peasant Party;" see *Le Figaro*, January 7, 1987.

23. E.g. Crisula Stefanescu, "Patriotism as a Political Tool," *Radio Free Europe Research*, Romanian SR/6, 29 April 1988. See also Ceausescu at the RCP Central Committee plenum, in *Scinteia*, June 29, 1988.

24. *Ibid.*

25. For a discussion of the extent of the clan, see my "The Ship of State in Troubled Waters: The Relevance of Leadership Drift for Romania," (paper presented at the annual conference of the American Association for the Advancement of Slavic Studies, Boston, MA, November 1987) to be published by *Studies in Comparative Communism*, Spring 1989.

12

Romania—Aberrant or Typical?

Unique Elements

Romania and Ceausescu are examples of a political, socio-economic, and cultural system that has developed in special ways, so that today, towards the end of the 1980s, this political system has a number of unique features. Furthermore, the relationship between polity and society in Romania is constituted in a way not found elsewhere in Eastern Europe, perhaps anywhere in the communist-ruled world. It is worth our time to examine these unique features in some detail.

First of all, the amount and extent of centralized, indeed personalized, power in contemporary Romania is unique. Nicolae Ceausescu has gathered into his hands all the basic sources of power in the country, and his control of the information channels, the structures for decision-making, and the personnel involved in that process is beyond anything found anywhere else in the region, including the Soviet Union itself. Together with this unique concentration of power comes a personality cult which has been abandoned in the other East European systems (but may be rivalled by procedures elsewhere, such as North Korea). Nicolae Ceausescu is billed as the greatest human being in all areas of activity. He is surrounded by a rather large number of sycophantic court poets and scribes who make lucrative careers out of maintaining and expanding this personality cult. The General Secretary apparently believes all of this and has contributed significantly to the expansion of the myth by his own statements, decisions, and personnel selection. Furthermore, the personality cult has been extended to the rest of his family, especially wife Elena and favorite son Nicu, in a way that is unprecedented in the annals of European communism.

Secondly, the process of elite recruitment is unique in contemporary Romania. Recruitment to the top elite is almost exclusively on the basis of personal preference on the part of the first family. Preference is based upon kinship, marriage, or simply personal likes and dislikes. In this process, skills and capabilities are clearly secondary and may even be

245

counterproductive if they contribute to the General Secretary's highly developed sense of insecurity and threat to personal power. Thus, there is no regularized process of recruitment, and this means that important societal elites may remain excluded from the inner circles of power for considerable periods of time. When there finally is representation, the selected individuals must give up their group identity lest they be considered rivals and empire builders (should the latter occur, the individual in question would be removed post haste, thus eliminating even this meager access to power at the top).

Getting into the power circle is only half the battle; one must also stay there. Romania under Ceausescu is unique in the sense that "performance" as commonly defined in political and socio-economic matters is not established according to definable, non-personal criteria but rather depends upon the personal evaluation of the General Secretary and his inner circle (which includes his wife) at any one time. An individual recently recruited to an important position at the center may perform well according to his or her own perceptions, but this does not guarantee continuation in that position. In fact, too much success is likely to produce removal, officially under the auspices of "recycling of cadre," but in reality for the purpose of removing any chance that the successful individual may have for "empire-building." The result of all this is extreme cadre instability, loss of decision-making capability, and leadership drift.

The extent of leadership drift in contemporary Romania is indeed unique. Since there is no stability of cadre, and since few individuals can count on remaining in positions of power for any length of time, there is no incentive to show initiative in decision-making. Indeed, there is a considerable incentive *not* to exhibit such behavior, for fear of jealousy and retaliation, perhaps removal, by the top man himself. Decisions are simply not made, but rather held in abeyance until the General Secretary himself can act upon the problem at hand. In an increasingly complex society such as Romania it is clear that such attitudes and procedures simply reduce the decision-making process to a trickle, and a great many things simply will not get done. There is extreme rigidity at the top, and extreme drift and fluidity right below the pinnacle of power. The *extent* of this problem is unique in contemporary Romania, even though its existence is common to all communist-ruled systems in Eastern Europe.

Another phenomenon which is found throughout the region but exhibits its most advanced form in Romania is nepotism. There is an extraordinarily large number of relations from the Ceausescu and Petrescu families in top political and military positions in Romania today. Most of these individuals have no particular skills or qualifications other than their family lineage. The waste of valuable positions thus produced is unique. The amount of resentment and cynicism such a system produces among those who do have necessary skills is also unique in Romania. Taken together, these aspects represent the epitome of squandering badly needed assets. The deep crisis that Ceausescu's Romania is experiencing today is in no small measure the result of two decades of nepotism.

Corruption is not unique to Romania, but it is arguable that the amount and extent of it exceed whatever can be found elsewhere in the region. There is little doubt that corruption is beneficial to some extent in systems characterized by scarcities because it releases reserves that have been hoarded and thus mobilizes reserves necessary for increased economic and other societal activity. At the same time it is also clear that widespread and blatant corruption becomes counterproductive because it subverts performance based on skill and favors those who have access to scarce resources, often obtained illegally, and certainly outside of established procedures. The greatest cost of corruption is probably in the loss of public confidence. Widespread malfeasance of this nature leaves the man and woman in the street convinced that everybody is doing it, so it is time to get into the act. Public authorities therefore have no credibility. The losses that result from such attitudes are enormous, even if incalculable.

All of the elements discussed above produce a great deal of alienation, cynicism and withdrawal from politics in the general population. This is also not a unique Romanian phenomenon, but the extent of this alienation probably is, and the depth of resentment also exceeds that found elsewhere in the region. Only the small number of elites inside the clan can be enthusiastic about the present political and societal order, and many of these are, in fact, afraid of the capricious nature of the very apex of the power pyramid. Everybody else is alienated, and everybody is primarily concerned with the need to survive and attempt to maximize personal gain for the short run. There appears to be no overriding commitment to a broader goal or concept, such as "society" or "nation." Those individuals who do invoke such symbols tend to consider them in the context of another time, another political order, or, at the very least, another leadership. There is no other place in Eastern Europe where this particular form of political pathology has reached such depths.

Political pathology is a serious condition, but it is arguable that Romanian *society* is experiencing a crisis that goes beyond the political order and tends to rip apart the very fabric of that society. The socioeconomic and political crisis that seems to go on and on has begun to erode the sense of commonality that undergirds *all* collectives, regardless of specific manifestations. The average Romanian has become atomized, detached from his fellow citizens, concerned with his own little collectivity of family and perhaps a few friends. It is irrelevant to him what may happen elsewhere, to other people. There is no way that social science can measure the depth and breadth of this atomization, certainly not in a system as closely controlled as Ceausescu's Romania, but it is reflected in the arts, in literature, even in the political discourse (such as it is) that is found in the press. Above all, it is reflected in the faces of the silent masses trudging along the streets and country roads in search of food and purpose. No other system in Eastern Europe can show this level of atomization.

These factors, taken together, relegate Romania to a unique and unenviable position. The time-honored concept of "the sick man" can surely be utilized for a description of this political and societal system in the late 1980s. Romania is indeed unique, partly because some elements of this massive and multifaceted crisis are country-specific, and partly because the intensity and severity of other aspects are unmatched elsewhere in Eastern Europe, even if the same elements are present there.

Romania's Crisis as Part
of the Crisis of Ruling Communist Systems

Romania, as part of the interstate and ideological system of communism (or "Marxism-Leninism," which has been utilized as the official description for some time now), shares certain political and societal characteristics with the other states and parties of the region. The first of these is the increased emphasis on political, socio-economic, and cultural nationalism that now characterizes much of the behavior of the elites of Eastern Europe (undoubtedly with the approval of the general population and the nonpolitical societal elites of each country). Ceausescu's chauvinism may exceed the extent of national particularism found elsewhere, but it is part and parcel of the same trend that has been present in the region for a long period of time, and in an accelerated form during the decade of the 1980s.

The increased emphasis on nationalism has several ramifications, both domestic and external. In the local political and socio-economic environment, the political leadership increasingly attempts to legitimize its power and its programs by emphasizing the national nature of its rule. All of the capitals of the region now involve the history of their particular state as a guiding light for their own programs, and it is emphasized that political and socio-economic programs are conducted for the purpose of enhancing the *nation*, according to local conditions and needs. By the same token, each party leadership attempts to convey the message that

Moscow cannot and will not dictate developments in the East European states. This has made it possible for the various leaderships of the region to react in their own way to developments in the Soviet Union itself. Thus, the eight communist-ruled systems in Eastern Europe have reacted in a wide variety of ways to glasnost, perestroika, and other developments for change in the Soviet Union, ranging from low-key but still enthusiastic support in Hungary to overt rejection in Romania, with a considerable variety in between these extremes. Nationalism and national forms have become the key to contemporary political life in the East European "socialist commonwealth." In this respect, Romania is but an exaggerated form of the common trend of the entire region.[1]

Despite the fact that all East European systems are in a nationalist phase of development and consciousness, the fact remains that they are inside the Soviet security sphere, and will remain there for the foreseeable future. This undeniable fact of life has a direct and indirect impact upon the political and socio-economic behaviors of elite and mass alike. Politically, the presence of the Soviet Union as the regional hegemon sets certain parameters for domestic and foreign policy behavior, thus reducing the options that each elite has available to deal with the massive societal crises now confronting each state in the region. At times, these parameters are made quite clear by Soviet words and actions. At other times, the local elites realize on their own that they must refrain from certain kinds of acts and responses to problems in order to forestall Soviet displeasure or actions. A form of self-censorship develops, and it has a great deal to do with political choices in Eastern Europe even at a time when overt Soviet interference is at a low level of frequency and intensity.[2]

The mass public is also acutely aware of the Soviet presence in the region and in each political system. The average citizen may look largely towards the West for inspiration and even certain kinds of incentives and products, but deep down he or she knows that the systemic change that would be required for Eastern Europe to be like the West cannot be accomplished as long as the Kremlin acts as a control factor from the Baltic to the Black Sea. No matter how nationalistic the East Europeans have become, this is an undeniable and seemingly permanent feature of their lives.

Romania is also in the mainstream of the East European experience in terms of socio-economic and political performance. All of the states of the region are experiencing a considerable amount of trouble in agricultural production, the provision of consumer goods, the level of service in all kinds of areas, technology dissemination and diffusion, and in labor productivity. Furthermore, most of the systems are in the midst of an ossification process in the social structure, in which one of the main features of communist-ruled systems, upward social mobility, has been reduced to a trickle, and a certain amount of downward mobility can be found. The safety valve that such upward mobility always provided, then, has been shut off, and the citizenry of Eastern Europe finds itself in a situation in which socio-economic class is once again the factor that will largely determine the quality of their lives and the prospects for the future. Under these circumstances, consumption and amenities that can be enjoyed *inside* the class structure become even more important, and the pressure increases for better performance in this area. This is a particularly dangerous form of catch-22 because it requires the ability to provide goods and services *before* labor productivity will rise, while any rational economic analysis will demonstrate that production must surely rise before consumption. There is clearly no easy way out of this dilemma, and there may be no way out at all. This is indeed a bleak prospect that reduces all of the East European systems to a condition of perpetual crisis. The only real question, then, is the extent to which each system has the coping mechanisms necessary to weather such constant crises.[3]

The crises facing the societies of Eastern Europe are brought about by faulty policies, inadequate performance, and mass apathy, but one of the main reasons for their persistence can be found in the ossified structures of the political order, particularly the communist parties, the governmental bodies, and the planning agencies. The communist parties of the region have changed little in terms of organization during the last few decades. The principles of personnel selection have also remained rather static, thus ensuring the recruitment of similar people over time. The decision-making procedures have focused on the principles of democratic centralism, "the upward flow of personnel and the downward flow of power and authority." Control is maintained over other political structures through the principles of "overlapping membership and interlocking directorates." The top leaderships of most of the parties in Eastern Europe are old and conservative. There is a definite need for rejuvenation.

All of these characteristics have remained while society as such has changed dramatically. It therefore stands to reason that changes must take place in the governing structures, too, and that "new blood" must be inserted into the top leadership bodies. Various steps have been taken to open up the decision-making structures to new entrants, new ideas, expert advice, and individuals with the skills needed in the last quarter of the twentieth century. The process of rejuvenation is therefore underway in the parties of the region, utilizing many of the same principles. The RCP is also engaged in rejuvenation and the recycling of personnel, and as such is found in the general trend of Eastern

Europe. But, as discussed in detail above, the principles utilized for this process in Romania are unique, and uniquely ineffective.[4]

It is no secret that the political systems of Eastern Europe are beset by serious problems of mass discontent and alienation among the masses. This is such a common phenomenon that the serious analyst may well argue that this condition is endemic to communist systems. Other analysts (and also the reform-oriented leaders in Eastern Europe) maintain that the current level of alienation is related to faulty practices and policies, and as such they can be remedied. This is more than an academic distinction, because it carries within itself the key to solutions, be they partial or fundamental. In any case, there is widespread agreement in Eastern Europe that changes are necessary in order to remove or at least alleviate the level of mass apathy and alienation. There is also considerable agreement about the *direction* of these changes. Basically, it is felt that the system must be made more open, must permit a wider range of opinions and proposed solutions. Furthermore, it should allow for more meaningful participation by wider segments of the population and, above all, more substantive participation by the societal elites that have hitherto been largely excluded from the actual decision-making process. Increased participation along these lines should produce greater mass commitment and thus increase production and the output of goods and services. The improvement in material conditions resulting from this revitalization process in turn will help mobilize even greater segments of the population. Thus, the developmental spiral will go upwards, not downwards as it has for a number of years.[5]

Romania is part of the East European problem of mass alienation and apathy. The Ceausescu regime also agrees with its counterparts elsewhere that change must take place. But the congruence between Romania and the rest of the region ends here. Ceausescu is determined to revitalize the citizenry (and thereby the entire system) through increased levels of modernization, exhortation, and indoctrination, not broadened participation. He redefines the diet rather than providing more food. He lectures the masses on the need to readjust their values rather than providing more services. He preaches organic unity rather than the value of diversification, pluralism, heterogeneity. Nicolae Ceausescu therefore is not part of the solution; he is, in large measure, the problem.

Romania as a Laboratory of Politics

While it is clear that Romania provides the analyst with a unique case and also a case in which many commonalities are found with other communist-ruled political and socio-economic systems, this country also tells us something important about the nature of politics anywhere, regardless of particular organizational and structural features of a specific system. Specifically, Ceausescu's Romania illustrates the sources of power, authority, legitimacy, and the relationship between the individual and the collectivity, between society and polity, in a way that is highly informative precisely because it is such a unique case.

Contemporary Romania is characterized by extreme centralization of power—not a new observation, but nevertheless an important one, because this concentration of power is unique in modern systems and draws upon sources that are no longer commonly utilized in our day and age. Power in Romania is derived from the ability of one individual to gather into his own hands the crucial organizational ties that keep modern society together and moving. Specifically, Nicolae Ceausescu controls the flow of personnel, the criteria for measuring performance, the mechanisms of recruitment and termination, and the rotation of personnel throughout the vast supervisory system that represents the communist party. He also controls the most important coordinating bodies that gather information, dissect it, and utilize it for the recommendation of policy. Through this coordinating capacity the General Secretary is the only individual who has access to *all* of the information and has the opportunity to participate in *all* of the deliberations, if he chooses to do so. Finally, Ceausescu has retained (indeed expanded) his capability to examine and judge performance. This right is fundamental because it provides the leader with the ability to change personnel and judge individuals, thereby constantly maintaining the flow of personnel throughout the system. It has often been said that whosoever controls the nomenklatura in communist systems also controls the system itself. This is clearly true in other kinds of polities as well.

Ceausescu's Romania also provides us with a graphic illustration of the fact that those who determine the political agenda determine the actual operation of the system itself. The extent to which the General Secretary controls the areas of discussion and the mechanisms utilized for this discussion is unique, but it is still a part of the general political science lesson discussed above. Furthermore, the RCP leader has managed to establish the right to change that agenda, gradually or suddenly, in part or fundamentally. True, the agenda is still inside the parameters of "Marxism-Leninism," but even that concept is continuously reinterpreted by Nicolae Ceausescu. Only "the Leader" knows what the basic elements of this doctrine are at any one time.

Contemporary Romania is further illustrative of the adage that power flows from control over the means of coercion. The armed forces and the security policy have remained under the personal control of the General Secretary, and mechanisms have been instituted to ensure the continuation and expansion of this control. The amount of supervision is particularly significant in the case of the police, and here it may indeed be reciprocated by support for the existing order, because the personnel of this crucial instrument have few skills other than coercive capabilities and would not do well in a different system.

The sources of power discussed above are typical for the successful maintenance of the leadership's position in any political system. There are two other sources which greatly enhance the power of any leader, namely authority and legitimacy. Authority, I take it, is the right accorded to the leader or leaders by the politically active and aware public, to make binding decisions; legitimacy is the acceptance by that public (however defined) of the decisions made.[6] In contemporary Romania, authority and legitimacy are largely lacking for substantial parts of the public, the societal elites, and also parts of the political elite.

Authority as defined was once an important part of the Ceausescu regime and a prime element of its support and maintenance mechanism in society. When Nicolae Ceausescu came to power in 1965, he was a consensus candidate with support from the most important elements of the RCP elite because it was believed that he would be a moderate leader, possibly controllable by the "old guard" who had formed around Gheorghe Gheorghiu-Dej. Elements of the technical, managerial, and artistic intelligentsia saw in the new leader an individual who might move Romania out of the Stalinist legacy and provide a more moderate political and socio-economic climate. The general population, always skeptical, assumed that the succession to the "old man" Gheorghiu-Dej probably would be no worse, and as such this attitude represented a form of grudging authority granted by default.

Nicolae Ceausescu dramatically expanded his sources of authority through a continuation of skill, luck, and actual policy during the next few years. His emphasis on nationalism, national sovereignty, and political and socio-economic autonomy made his rule palatable, indeed acceptable, to widening strata of the societal elites and the general population. The RCP leader was "doing the right thing" by standing up to the Russians. His emphasis on the organic link between society and polity smacked of old-fashioned Romanian populism and the accepted notion of rule by "the man on horseback." The party's control over the arts, literature, and other forms of expression was not yet fully consolidated, and there was some autonomy for the technocrats and the managers. The standard of living remained low, but there was a sense of progress, of hope. Authority, or the right to rule, was there because it appeared that the right decisions were made, and the regime appeared to leave people alone to pursue their individual needs and desires. With a long tradition of parochialism and subject attitudes, it was not difficult for most

Romanians, regardless of civil status, occupation, or residence, to accept the notion that Nicolae Ceausescu could and should rule. This was, indeed, a form of political authority.

There was also a measure of political legitimacy during the early years of Ceausescu's rule. Many elements of society accepted some of his policies, particularly the nationalistic elements; elites and the mass public alike felt that this notion was indeed *their* notion also. The emphasis on rapid socio-economic development through continued high investments and ongoing stress on the heavy and extractive industries represented a continuation of established policies and as such reconstituted the status quo. Some of the technical and managerial elites, in fact, assumed greater participation for themselves in the specific formulation and execution of such policies and therefore supported them.

Beginning in 1971, and continuing to the present time, Nicolae Ceausescu launched a series of policies that gradually reduced his authority and legitimacy to the point where few individuals or groups in contemporary Romania can be said to accord either of these presumably crucial elements of regime maintenance. The ideological campaign alienated the artistic intelligentsia and elements of the general population; the excessive speed of socio-economic development and the irrational decisions made in economic planning reduced support among the technical and managerial elites to a minimum; the personality cult, nepotism, and blatant display of personal power turned many in the RCP hierarchy away from the support they had hitherto provided. Increasing numbers of individuals of all strata began to question the right of this individual to make binding decisions. Support for actual policies dwindled as the socio-economic performance of the system deteriorated, and the Ceausescu leadership responded to each year's failures with increased production quotas, personnel changes, and various schemes designed to skim revenue from the increasingly pauperized population. This process of gradual loss of both authority and legitimacy continued for a decade and a half, and it has accelerated during the last three years, since the middle of the 1980s.

Now, in the latter half of the 1980s, the Ceausescu regime survives with a minimum of authority and legitimacy. This is a phenomenon of considerable interest to political scientists because it demonstrates that a political system can survive for a period of time despite the virtual loss of these key ingredients. Every year in which the General Secretary and his clan remain in power, indeed *increase* that personal power, while losing authority and legitimacy, is a case study of the ingredients necessary for power and the capability of regimes to exist in spite of theories and hypotheses advanced about the nature of politics. The Romanian aberration can only be explained in the context of this deviation from established theories carefully constructed.

The Ceausescu regime survives because of the *nature* of its power. There are several ingredients involved, one of which is unpredictability. The clan rules by controlling the political agenda, by personnel selection and personnel management, by defining the criteria of performance, and by supervising the execution of policy. In all of these areas, Nicolae Ceausescu constantly changes the parameters within which policy and personnel operate, and he also changes the agenda and criteria of performance to such an extent that no one can predict inputs or outputs. The process of decision-making is likewise personalized and unpredictable in the extreme. Under these circumstances, no counterelites can form in opposition to a specific set of policies, because there are no such identifiable sets. Opposition can only form against the *nature of rule.* This is a much more difficult process, which requires greater coordinating capability, stamina, and willingness to take risks. Above all, it requires time. But if much time elapses in the formation of counterelites, the risks of preventative action by the existing leadership are also magnified. Thus, the political leadership can survive through unpredictability, differential remuneration and elite recruitment, and preemptive policy moves designed to remove issues around which opposition may effectively form. Authority and legitimacy are not required as long as unpredictability keeps all individuals and groups outside the clan itself off balance, subject to "divide and rule" tactics.

Ceausescu's Romania demonstrates that a regime can maintain itself for a considerable period of time as long as the elements of coercion remain loyal to the regime. When arbitrary use of coercion becomes the system, potential or actual counterelites are reduced by fear, and recruitment to such elites is much more difficult. Coupled with arbitrariness is unpredictability. The regime's coercive elements may strike for no apparent reason, thus keeping the general population as well as societal elites outside of the clan perpetually off balance. The other side of the policy of unpredictable coercion is unpredictable rewards; no one knows if tomorrow might not bring an invitation to join the inner circle of the ruling elite, with all the perquisites that this entails in a system such as Ceausescu's Romania. Individuals are faced with the awful choice of staying in opposition, getting organized, and thus becoming extremely vulnerable, on the one hand, or simply keeping quiet for fear that they may be betrayed by their colleagues, or alternatively, getting rewarded by the unpredictable clan, especially the General Secretary himself. These conditions are so severe for coalition formation that the alienation of large numbers of individuals must be fundamental, and the circumstances of life must be truly desperate for any coalition to form.

What is defined as "desperate" varies greatly from system to system, from one political culture to the next. The Ceausescu clan is itself a product of Romanian political culture, and thus this leadership knows instinctively, or in some other way, what the breaking point of tolerance may be at any one time. Repression can be relieved, additional goods and services provided on a temporary basis, troublemakers may be expelled, arrested, intimidated, or promoted (thereby silenced), and other ameliorative moves can be made to stave off revolts based on the absence of authority and legitimacy. The crisis deepens, but the regime survives.

The regime's control over the forces of coercion can be maintained much more easily if those elements are made up of individuals lacking in skills and professionalism, because unskilled individuals must stay with the regime that provides them with privileges. An alternative regime would not necessarily provide such perquisites, and the lack of professional skills would severely hamper any economic or social prospect for such individuals. In fact, a different elite may attempt to legitimize itself in the general population and in selected societal elites by punishing the representatives of coercion. All of these factors tend to make the least professional elements the most loyal to a repressive regime. The main thing is to make sure that the public and the military are made up of such unskilled and poorly professionalized individuals, and to prevent the process of professionalization from taking place inside these apparats. In this respect, the Ceausescu clan has been highly successful in the police, less so in the military (but even in the latter apparat professionalism can be manipulated through frequent personnel changes and personnel corruption).

A regime can survive without authority and legitimacy provided that the socio-economic conditions are so serious that individuals are primarily concerned with physical survival and thus are unable to effectively form groups that can act politically. Contemporary Romania is now in such a condition, as discussed in considerable detail above. Most of the energy that is left in individuals after hard work in outmoded factories, over-crowded offices, or poor collective or state farms is expended in a search for food and essential services, oftentimes to no avail. Thus, people are pauperized, but the regime is more secure. This is the security of crisis, provided the crisis is deep enough and comprehensive enough to reduce the masses and the non-clan elites to a scramble for survival. This is the success of minimal performance.

We can now begin to reconceptualize the notions of power and performance. While it is generally true that a regime's power is enhanced through political and socio-economic performance (as defined in the literature),[7] contemporary Romania shows that power can also be enhanced through non-performance or poor performance in the same areas of activity. The level of such performance must be low enough so that the population is consumed by its quest for survival and possible personal enhancement, rather than collective needs and wishes. Thus, low performance in these sectors becomes superior *political* performance, because it reduces or eliminates any organized challenge to those in charge of the political order. If we accept these notions, Nicolae Ceausescu is not a failure (as many are wont to conclude nowadays) but a startling success. His power (and that of the clan) increases while the condition of society deteriorates. The political analyst must begin to discuss the question of whether or not such power, such a *political* success, can be maintained at the expense of society, indefinitely, or alternatively, where the "breaking point" may be found. At the present time, the Ceausescu clan appears to be firm in the saddle precisely because of the poor performance of the system in all fields other than that of enhancement of the clan. Our research agenda must now include those questions that take this seeming anomaly into account and force us to ask again about the relationship of power, authority, and legitimacy in Romania, in communist-ruled systems, and in all political systems.

Notes

1. See Gilberg and Aspaturian, *The Soviet and East European Party Congresses* (manuscript prepared for the U.S. Government, 1987), esp. pp. 242–257.

2. For an overview of this relationship, see J. F. Brown, *Eastern Europe and Communist Rule*, ch. 2 (pp. 30–62).

3. The other East European states are responding by opening up their political and socio-economic systems to greater participation and discussion, but not Romania. See Nicolae Ceausescu's speech to the recent RCP national congress in *Scinteia*, December 17, 1987.

4. The most recent of these personnel shuffles took place in early June 1988, when Constantin Olteanu took over the post of ideological chief from Constantin Mitea (*Radio Free Europe Research*, Romanian SR/8, 23 June 1988) and later that month, when Prime Minister Constantin Dascalescu, First Deputy Prime Minister Gheorghe Oprea, Deputy Prime Minister Stefan Andrei, Stefan Birlea, Chairman of the State Planning Committee, Ilie Vaduva, Minister of Foreign Trade and International Cooperation, and Tudor Postelnicu, Minister of Internal Affairs, were admonished by the PEC, and in some cases "censured" (Dascalescu was admonished, but Oprea, Andrei, and Postelnicu had "votes of censure" passed on them). Andrei and Postelnicu are alternate members of the PEC, and Dascalescu a full member. These admonitions and punishments came because of irregularities in foreign contracts and environmental pollution problems, but such irregularities

are commonplace, and the purge thus probably represented another capricious Ceausescu housecleaning.

5. J. F. Brown, *Eastern Europe and Communist Rule*, ch. 4 (pp. 113–158).

6. For standard definitions, see, for example, Karl W. Deutsch, *Politics and Government*, pp. 13–15, and 212–214.

7. *Ibid.*, pp. 156–157 and 205–206.

Romania and Western Scholarship: A Bibliographic Essay

Romanian studies in North America and Western Europe constitutes a small but growing field of scholarship in history, political science, economics, and, to a lesser degree, literature. The smallness of the field is somewhat puzzling, though, because Romania represents a fascinating example of the interplay between old and new, West and East, communism and traditional nationalism, and between the institutional mechanisms of Marxist-Leninist systems and personalized political rule.

During the last few decades, notable contributions to the study of the peculiar path of Romanian history have been made by R. W. Seton-Watson, David Mitrany, Keith Hitchins, Ghita Ionescu, Stephen Fischer-Galati, Ken Jowitt, and a number of Romanian scholars such as Andrei Otetea, Stefan Pascu, Constantin Giurescu, and others. All these authors have discussed the relationship of emerging nationalism, religion, and the struggle for autonomy in a geographical area dominated by multinational empires. From the mass of material they have processed and analyzed there emerges the notion of an ethnic group that maintained a form of national consciousness throughout long years of suppression by others, a group that entered the eighteenth-century European scene as a national movement in Transylvania and the Principalities and that reached its goal of a national state in the nineteenth century. This literature is also clear on the basic features of economic development, the social and political consequences of underdevelopment, the nature of political power, and the traditions of personalized leadership, all very important topics in our generation.[1]

The Romanian Communist Party has been the driving force of development in all fields in that country for four decades. Western scholarship has therefore focused upon the party, and a number of good books and articles have been produced on this topic. The best are written by Michael Shafir, Robert King, Ghita Ionescu, and Vlad Tismaneanu. These studies show the cracks and fissures of the party and its determination to act as the chief modernizing agent of a whole society as the nation struggles to move ahead from a position of relative under-development. The books by Shafir and Ionescu that put this saga into the now broadly based socio-economic and cultural contexts of Romanian society make for fascinating reading.[2]

Romania is an integral part of the Balkans, and a number of scholars have put Romania into the comparative context of the peninsula as a whole in terms of political, socio-economic, and cultural development. John Lampe has looked at Romania from the vantage point of the historian, and George W. Hoffman from that of the economist. A number of other scholars have examined nationalism and ethnicity in the same fashion. The result of this comparative scholarship is a broad understanding of the concepts of regionalism and cultural zones.[3]

Economic development is, of course, an integral part of the general societal development, and there is a considerable literature on this subject. Among the most important are works by John M. Montias and Marvin Jackson, as well as those by a number of Romanian scholars (again, written prior to the onset of Ceausescu's obscurantist fixation during the last decade or so). These works focus on the nature of economic organization and production and on the political implications of the special features of that development. A recent study by Dionisie Ghermani examines Ceausescu's disastrous economic policies and predicts a bleak future for this richly endowed country.[4]

The works of Montias, Jackson, Ghermani, and other students of Romanian economic development delineate the essential features of Marxism-Leninism in Romanian planning and implementation and point out the national peculiarities, as well as the personal idiosyncrasies of Nicolae Ceausescu and his close associates, commonly known as his "clan." The literature on economic development in the socialist period is impressive in its scope and depth.

Developments in religion, arts, literature, and other cultural areas have been discussed by a number of scholars, creating a small but potent body of literature. Anneli Ute Gabanyi has been a prolific analyst of cultural policy and developments. The best research on religion in Romanian history and politics is produced by Earl Pope, who has shown the intimate connection between religion and nationalism in this Balkan country. Some Romanian scholarship on literature, art, and literary criticism is also of value.[5]

During the last twenty-three years, Romania has experienced massive political and socio-economic dislocations as a result of the increasingly erratic leadership of Nicolae Ceausescu and his clan. Personalized leadership is clearly more important in Romania than in any other system in contemporary Eastern Europe, and a considerable literature has developed on Ceausescu and, to some extent, his wife Elena. Among the *many* biographies on this topic, the best is the monograph by Mary Ellen Fischer, which points out both the personal and societal context of Ceausescu's policies and helps us understand the peculiar configuration of factors that produced the "Romanian enigma" in our decade.[6]

The complexities of Romanian politics cannot be understood without reference to the societal groups and elites with claims to political influence, if not power. In this context, the military represents an important interest group and a major element of support for the current regime. Without it, Ceausescu clearly could not survive in power; with its support, the dictatorship may remain intact for a considerable period of time, despite the abysmal conditions created by failed policies. The military is also a major factor in foreign policy and security matters, again serving as one of the pillars of the "Ceausescu era."

There is clearly a need for Western examinations of this critical structure of Romanian politics. This need is met, in part, in the works of Walter Bacon, who has provided insightful analyses of the military in its dual capacity as pressure group and support mechanism for the Ceausescu regime. Ivan Volgyes and Dale Herspring have explored the role of Romania's military within the Warsaw Pact in their work on the reliability of the armies of the Southern Tier.[7]

The evolution of local politics and the emergence of new socio-economic and cultural forms at the regional and local levels are discussed in a number of good studies published during the last two decades, particularly the works by John Cole, Steven Sampson, Daniel Nelson, Gail Kligman, and Katherine Verdery. Their painstaking research has shed more light on the complexities of Romanian society as it moves through the stages of modernization; but they also underscore the importance of traditional forms and behavior patterns even now, in the twilight of the twentieth century.[8]

Romanian foreign policy has been examined in some detail, because in many ways it represents the most interesting facet of Romanian politics. It is here that Ceausescu has been the most active and had the greatest success, which has brought Bucharest to a position of influence in the world far beyond that normally attributed to medium-sized powers. But it is also in the arena of foreign policy that the "fall from grace" has been the most spectacular, as the irrational domestic policies of the Ceausescu clan and the regime's dismal civil rights record finally alienated most governments of the world.

A number of scholars have contributed to our understanding of Romanian foreign policy. Aurel Braun and Ronald Linden have produced important works on this subject, and Christopher Jones, Teresa Rakowska-Harmstone, and others have examined Romanian policy in the more general context of Warsaw Pact security issues.[9]

From this growing body of literature, several fundamental concepts emerge—concepts that have remained constant over time and have profoundly affected the contemporary political order. One of these concepts is nationalism, which has helped Romanians maintain their group cohesiveness in the face of centuries of adversity and foreign domination. It has shaped political life even under communist rule and has reached a dominant position, albeit in a perverted form, under Nicolae Ceausescu and the clan. Whatever the aftermath of the demise of this clan in the future, nationalism will remain a major force in Romanian life for years to come.

The literature discussed above also deals, directly or indirectly, with political culture that has been shaped by the experiences of centuries and largely determines the way in which individuals and groups in Romanian society relate to each other and to political authority. The basic aspects of this culture have set the parameters for all political activity in contemporary Romania; these activities, in turn, help mold the culture itself in an ongoing process. No serious study of the contemporary era and no predictions about the Romanian political future can ignore this crucial aspect.

Most of the literature also examines Romania's economic underdevelopment and its effects upon all aspects of societal life, including political behavior. The quest for economic growth has produced an obsession with "catching up" to the more advanced societies of the East and West, with profound effects upon decision-making and goal-setting. The quest has now become counterproductive, threatening the very foundations of society and the physical survival of unknown numbers of people. Romania has become a "laboratory" where the irrational decisions of regimes are tested against the traditional quietude of a population used to deprivation and rapacious rule. This "laboratory" tests the endurance of an entire people, as well as the notion that mismanagement and misrule will eventually result in popular protests, perhaps even a change in the regime itself. Where is the threshold of such politicization? How far can this tolerance go? All scholars studying Romania must attempt to answer these questions.

Nationalism has also shaped Romanian foreign policy, for the quest for autonomy and maximum possible sovereignty is directly related to nationalism (which has clearly become chauvinism in the last decade). Thus, economic development and autarky are manifestations of the same fundamental force. And Nicolae Ceausescu himself represents a personalized but potent expression of this nationalism as he moves from one disastrous decision to another. The literature discusses this either as a separate element in more specialized studies or as part of a larger analysis.

One of the most pressing issues to arise from the chauvinistic policies of the Ceausescu era is the question of interethnic relations in Romania, particularly the treatment of the ethnic Hungarians in Transylvania and elsewhere. This issue has now become an international problem, adding to the massive dilemmas facing Soviet leadership as it struggles with the effects of glasnost and perestroika at home and in the "front yard" of Eastern Europe. The conflict between Budapest and Bucharest on the treatment of ethnic Hungarians in Romania only adds to the instability of Eastern Europe.

This is not a new issue. There is a considerable literature on the problems of ethnicity and interethnic conflict, as witnessed by the lengthy bibliography on this subject completed by C. Carter Bentley. On Romania specifically, the best conceptual study is still Robert R. King's work on minorities in the Balkans.[10]

This book has expanded upon the existing literature in two primary ways. First, it has updated matters discussed elsewhere and put them into the context of the contemporary era. Second, it has attempted to provide a systematic interpretation of the basic aspects of Romanian politics and examine their relationship with nationalism as an independent and dependent variable. It also has investigated the importance of nationalism in Romanian domestic and foreign policy.

This book has also discussed policy-making and policy outcomes, especially in regard to establishing authority, legitimacy, and power. A number of scholars have defined "legitimacy" as the right to rule that is accorded the regime by the population.[11] "Authority" and "power" have been defined as the capability to persuade and to make decisions that are enforceable by various means.[12] Policies are typically made in the context of procedures, institutions, and structures. Does the policy-making process function the same way in countries with personalized power, such as Romania? If not, what are the consequences? This book has offered a systematic examination of these and related questions in an effort to determine if Romania is typical of communist-ruled systems, or alternatively, *sui generis*.

Notes

1. R. W. Seton-Watson, *A History of the Roumanians* (Cambridge, England: Cambridge University Press, 1934). David Mitrany, *The Land and Peasant in Rumania* (New York, NY: Greenwood Press, 1968; first edition by Gale University Press, 1930). Keith Hitchins, *Orthodoxy and Nationality: Andreiu Saguna and the Rumanians of Transylvania, 1846–1873* (Cambridge, MA: Harvard University Press, 1977); *The Rumanian National Movement in Transylvania, 1780–1849* (Cambridge, MA: Harvard University Press, 1969). Ghita Ionescu, *Communism in Rumania,*

1944–1962 (London: Oxford University Press, 1964). Stephen Fischer-Galati, *The New Rumania: From People's Democracy to Socialist Republic* (Cambridge, MA: The MIT Press, 1967); *Twentieth Century Rumania* (New York, NY: Columbia University Press, 1965); *The Socialist Republic of Rumania* (Baltimore: The Johns Hopkins Press, 1969). Kenneth Jowitt, *Revolutionary Breakthroughs and National Development: The Case of Rumania, 1944–1965* (Berkeley, CA: University of California Press, 1971). Andrei Otetea, et al., *Marea Rascoala a Taranilor Din 1907* (Bucharest: Editura Academiei Republicii Socialiste Romania, 1967). Miron Constantinescu, et al., *Istoria Romaniei* (Bucharest: Editura Didactica Si Pedagogica, 1969). Stefan Pascu, *Marea Adunare Nationala de la Alba Iulia* (Cluj: Universitatea Babes-Bolyai, 1968). Dinu Giurescu, *Illustrated History of the Rumanian People* (Bucharest: Editura Sport-Turism, 1981).

2. Michael Shafir, *Rumania: Politics, Economics, and Society* (Boulder, CO: Lynne Rienner Publishers, 1985). Robert R. King, *History of the Rumanian Communist Party* (Stanford, CA: Hoover Institution Press, 1980). Ionescu, *Communism in Rumania, 1944–1962.* Vladimir Tismaneanu, "Ceausescu's Socialism," *Problems of Communism*, Vol. XXXIV, January–February, 1985.

3. John R. Lampe and Marvin R. Jackson, *Balkan Economic History, 1550–1950: From Imperial Borderlands to Developing Nations* (Bloomington, IN: Indiana University Press, 1982). George W. Hoffman, *The Balkans in Transition* (Westport, CT: Greenwood Press, 1983; original edition, 1963).

4. John M. Montias, *Economic Development in Communist Rumania* (Cambridge, MA: The MIT Press, 1967). Marvin R. Jackson, *National Accounts and the Estimation of Gross Domestic Product and Its Growth Rate for Romania* (New York, NY: World Bank, 1985). Dionisie Ghermani, "Rumäniens Reformverdrossenheit–Keine Ansätze von Neuerung," in Rolf Schlüter (ed.), *Wirtschaftsreformen im Ostblock in den 80er Jahren* (Paderborn: Ferdinand Schöninger, 1988).

5. Earl Pope, "The Contemporary Religious Situation in Rumania" (paper presented at the Second World Congress for Soviet and East European Studies, Garmisch, West Germany, 1980). Anneli Ute Gabanyi, *Partei und Literatur in Rumänien Seit 1945* (Oldenbourg: Untersuchungen Zur Gegenwartskunde Südusteuropas, 1975).

6. Mary Ellen Fischer, *Nicolae Ceausescu: A Political Biography* (Boulder, CO: Lynne Rienner Publishers, 1988).

7. Ivan Volgyes and Dale R. Herspring, *The Political Reliability of the Warsaw Pact Armies: The Southern Tier* (Durham, NC: Duke University Press, 1984). Walter M. Bacon, Jr., "The Military and the Party in Romania," in Ivan Volgyes and Dale R. Herspring (eds.), *Civil-Military Relations in Communist Systems* (Boulder, CO: Westview Press, 1978).

8. Gail Kligman, *Calus: Symbolic Transformation in Rumanian Ritual* (Chicago, IL: Chicago University Press, 1981). Daniel N. Nelson, *Democratic Centralism in Romania: A Study of Local Communist Parties* (Boulder, CO: East European Quarterly, 1980); *Elite-Mass Relations in Communist Systems* (London and New York: St. Martin's Press, 1987). Steven L. Sampson, *National Integration Through Socialist Planning: An Anthropological Study of a Romanian New Town* (Boulder, CO: East European Monographs, 1984). John Cole, "Familial Dynamics in a

Rumanian Village," *Dialectical Anthropology,* 1, 1976; "Family, Farm, and Factory: Rural Workers in Contemporary Romania," in Daniel N. Nelson (ed.), *Romania in the 1980s* (Boulder, CO: Westview Press, 1981). Katherine Verdery, *Transylvanian Villagers* (Berkeley, CA: University of California Press, 1983).

9. Ronald H. Linden, *Bear and Foxes: The International Relations of the East European States, 1965–1969* (Boulder, CO: East European Quarterly, 1979); *Communist States and International Change: Yugoslavia and Romania in Comparative Perspective* (London: Allen and Unwin, 1987). Aurel Braun, *Small-state Security in the Balkans* (Toronto, Canada: Studies in Russian and East European History, 1983). Christopher D. Jones, *Soviet Influence in Eastern Europe: Political Autonomy and the Warsaw Pact* (New York, NY: Praeger Publishers, 1981). Teresa Rakowska-Harmstone (ed.), *Communism in Eastern Europe* (Bloomington, IN: Indiana University Press, 1984).

10. C. Carter Bentley, *Ethnicity and Nationality: A Bibliographic Guide* (Seattle, WA: University of Washington Press, 1981). Robert R. King, *Minorities Under Communism: Nationalities as a Source of Tension Among Balkan States* (Cambridge, MA: Harvard University Press, 1973).

11. Karl W. Deutsch, *Politics and Government: How People Decide Their Fate* (Boston, MA: Houghton Mifflin Company, 1980). Carl J. Friedrich, *Man and His Government* (New York, NY: McGraw-Hill, 1963).

12. *Ibid.*

Epilogue: The Death of Personalized Dictatorship

During the dramatic month of December 1989, Romania joined the ranks of other East European states in casting off the yoke of communist power and thus setting course for an uncertain future. The Romanian case was particularly dramatic, as could be predicted given the nature of the Ceausescu regime, with its "rule by clan," its nepotism, its repressive stance on all matters of ideology and human rights, and its utter disregard for the emerging pluralism in modern society that had been accommodated, at least in part, in the other socialist systems of the region even before the demise of the communist order. In Romania, the explosion of popular wrath, together with the military's change from oppressor to agent of liberation, swept away the most centralized and seemingly monolithic regime of all of European communism. But such regimes leave legacies that may prove harder to dislodge than the leaders themselves.

The Romanian revolution was made possible by a convergence of forces, as discussed in chapter 9. First, it required the willingness of countless individuals to literally risk their lives for change. Second, the refusal by factions of the armed forces to massacre their fellow citizens turned the tables in a fluid situation. Third, some badly needed early leadership was provided by elements of the military hierarchy who, together with some reform-oriented groups and individuals both inside the party and out, had long contemplated the need for action. Finally, external factors and the knowledge that the Soviet Union would no longer intervene to shore up repressive regimes changed the psychological and emotional parameters in which the masses and potential leaders functioned, thus setting the stage for political action that would have been unthinkable a few weeks earlier.

By the fall of 1989, it had become clear to many Romanians that the Ceausescu clan was an anachronism, a relic of the past in a place and time when history was being shaped with astonishing speed and thoroughness. This perception was pervasive in the technical and managerial intelligentsia (in fact, it had long existed in those circles), and it had begun to permeate important sectors of the military leadership, as well. The latter were becoming aware of their increasing responsibilities to the nation as a whole, not merely to the dictator and his entourage, and this idealistic notion was coupled with intense dissatisfaction with the evident favoritism shown by the Ceausescus to the Securitate and the clan itself. Here was a clear illustration of the negative side of clan rule: Although a clan founded on the basis of personal relationships creates maximum solidarity *inside* the clan, by the same token it produces intense resentment in groups outside this hallowed circle. As a result, when external elements are called upon to support the few at the top, there is no real incentive to do so, but reasons abound to take actions designed to reduce or eliminate the clan. A clan rules totally; it also falls totally.

The perceptions discussed above have long represented the views of the forward-looking individuals in Romanian society, who realized that the Ceausescu regime was devastating for the prospects of rejuvenation, be it economic or psychological, after the eventual death of the dictator. The direct exploitation of economic resources for the benefit of the clan was serious but probably not completely debilitating. But in the persistence of irrational economic decision-making that drove Romania further and further towards chaos, intelligent observers saw the specter of permanent damage to industrial infrastructures, agricultural capabilities, and technological skills. Furthermore, the blanket of fear, paranoia, and insecurity draped over the population by the extensive informant system may have destroyed the entrepreneurial spirit of the population, and the widespread corruption and moral ambivalence nurtured by years of economic scarcity will remain for a considerable period to come. The crippling effects of these trends accumulated rapidly during the last few years of the Ceausescu era, lending an urgency to the thoughts and fears of the progressive thinkers. When circumstances were right, their ideas were translated into action in a great sweep of *Götterdämmerung*, a reckoning with those who had ruled as eastern potentates for so long.

The opportune moment for such a reckoning cannot be predicted with any certainty. Although it may be possible to establish a series of contingency plans that could be activated as the moment arises, it is not clear that this was the case in Romania. Rather, a series of historic events occurred over a relatively short period of time, culminating in the now famous mass rally in Bucharest that turned into a frenetic rejection of Nicolae Ceausescu, his clan, and his policies. The most important of these preparatory events have been discussed in considerable detail in the press and other media and need no further elaboration here. They include the repressive measures ordered against Laszlo Tökes in Timisoara (and the reaction of the people of that city, which showed that Romanians and Hungarians alike supported the outspoken cler-gyman); the brutal initial suppression of the demonstrations in the city itself; and, finally, the eruption of unrest elsewhere, leading to the flight, capture, and eventual execution of the dictator and his chief co-culprit. The absence of Nicolae Ceausescu from Romania just one week prior to these momentous events may have provided conspirators with an opportunity, but these circumstances are still cloaked in secrecy and may never be fully revealed. Suffice it to say that the arrogance of this man, as demonstrated by his departure for Iran at a time of great unrest, was matched only by his utter inability to understand the masses as they shouted him down at his last rally. The surprised expression on the general secretary's face as he finally grasped the fact that the slogans chanted were not the canned panegyrics of yesterday but expressions of intense hatred for him and his regime will forever illustrate the chasm between potentate and people. This marked the beginning of what can be properly termed a people's revolution.

It behooves us to examine the "breakpoints" in a people's life, when passive submission and fear give way to hope and, ultimately, popular uprisings—a topic that scholars have long discussed. The Romanian example is, in fact, a particularly apt one because it involves a traditionally quiescent population that for centuries endured harsh repression, inter-spersed with violent outbursts of popular wrath (the so-called jacqueries, the latest of which occurred in 1907 in the bloodiest peasant revolt in modern European history). The events of December 1989 show, again, the capacity of a desperate population to act forcefully, even to the point of sacrificing life and limb, when conditions become intolerable. And it is clear, too, that the Romanian situation in that month had reached such a point—economically, politically, and spiritually.

Economically, the situation had clearly reached a crisis. The population faced another winter with little or no heat, very scarce food supplies, and a continued governmental emphasis on the export industry that would, once again, shortchange domestic services and consumer goods. The crisis in the health sector, discussed in previous chapters, was bound to worsen since little had been done to repair the crumbling infrastructure. And the school system had been reduced to a minimum in terms of hours taught and subjects learned. The economic quality of life, therefore, was deteriorating rapidly, with no prospect for improvement or even a halt to the downward slide.

The most important crisis, however, was spiritual, in the collective psyche of the population. The widespread fear of the Securitate and of one's neighbors, friends, and perhaps even family destroyed the civic spirit, atomized the population, and created individuals who lived unto themselves, in a vacuum. A society without traditional bonds is no longer a society; it is merely a collection of individuals who happen to reside in a certain place. In one sense, the "desocialization" of Romania was a major success for the Ceausescu regime because it reduced the chances for any organized opposition to develop while the clan was still in charge. But it also produced a situation in which there was no bond between the ruler and ruled, merely despair and a deep-seated hatred ready to flare at the earliest opportunity. Ironically, the Romanian population was ultimately united when this despair and hatred could be focused upon a common enemy—the ruling elite. The only element missing was a trigger mechanism, an event that would galvanize the masses to *collective* acts of courage and revenge rather than individual cowardice and submission.

That trigger mechanism was the brutality of the security forces as they suppressed the initial demonstrations in Timisoara. Torture, mass killings, and the symbolism of a dead child offered as an arrogant warning against any further challenges to the clan and its strong-arm Securitate combined to ignite the rage of the people. They also helped turn the regular army against the regime in a decisive move that made the success of the revolution possible. Thus, popular outrage and an army that made a dramatic decision at the crucial time were the key ingredients of the people's revolution in Romania.

But all of these factors would have been useless if external circumstances had been unfavorable. In the past, reform-oriented forces in Eastern Europe were always held in check by the possibility of intervention by Soviet forces, be they political or military, to prop up repressive regimes. With the advent of Gorbachev, however, there emerged a Soviet policy that encouraged changes in the various states of the region. In fact, Gorbachev made it clear that the Soviet Union would like to act as a catalyst for such change everywhere. This meant that the political situation of the ruling elites in Eastern Europe would become untenable unless they produced reform, quickly and thoroughly. It turned out that none of the communist leaders in the region could do this successfully, and they were eventually swept away.

In this context, Romania appeared to stand alone. Nicolae Ceausescu had successfully insulated his nation from Soviet influence; he had followed a draconian policy of autarky that would, presumably, eliminate any dependence upon the outside world; finally, through the mechanisms of fear, repression, brutality, and depoliticization he had forced the population into complete submission, to the point that it appeared the revolution of 1989 would leave Romania untouched. It looked like a brilliant, if demented, plan.

In the end, Ceausescu was wrong. In an age of instant communications, no one can fully insulate or isolate an entire population from the truth and the rush of events. One by one, the icons of communism were smashed. Day by day, then hour by hour, the tide of history washed over Eastern Europe and produced its own cleansing, a "chistka" that will change history forever. Word of this momentous revolution soon reached Romania. The public learned that even Erich Honecker had lost control in East Germany, which was particularly significant because Ceausescu and Honecker had established a relationship based upon their mutual rejection of Soviet-style glasnost and perestroika, assuming instead that they could rule as before in their autonomous stances. In Czechoslovakia, too, repression had been dispelled by the massive outpouring of popular will. Thus, the two hard-line states with which Ceausescu identified had experienced the full force of change. Why, then, not here, in Romania? At once, the psychological climate changed, the unthinkable became feasible, and thought became action.

The Legacies of Ceausescuism

All political systems carry legacies that inevitably influence the characteristics and behavior of both the system itself and the main actors in it. This is particularly true in Romania, which lived under Ceausescuism for a quarter of a century and suffered the most thoroughgoing repression of any communist-ruled state in Eastern Europe. (In fact, it probably rivaled that during the height of Stalinist obsession in the Soviet Union during the 1930s.) These legacies are troubling and represent clear danger signals for the future of Romania. In my opinion, they are as follows:

The Legacy of Mass Depoliticization

Throughout the quarter century of Ceausescuism, the masses in Romania gradually became depoliticized. This meant that the average man and woman ceased to take an interest in public affiars, withdrew from activities in this realm, and focused almost exclusively upon private matters. There was a collective shrinking of horizons and a privatization of thoughts and concerns. Any understanding of the political process as a set of interactions for choice was lost. It was replaced by the realization, bolstered by daily experience, that the government's power was total and that it was perpetrated upon people, without any participation by the masses. The ruler had wishes, and the wishes became instant realities. There was no process, no unfolding, no give-and-take.

This legacy will create major problems for Romania in the future. The masses, now thrust upon the political scene, demand instant solutions; what is more, they demand *full* solutions and complete gratification of their demands, just as the dictator did in the past. There is, as yet, no real understanding that there must be give-and-take, compromises, disappointments, and a willingness to accept losses along the way.

The solution calls for broad-based civic education, but Romania is a country with no tradition of democratic pluralism, no mechanisms (as yet) to foster such attitudes, and no reserve of legitimacy for the *institutions* of the system. In fact, the existing political institutions must be torn down, and new structures must be erected to establish the beginnings of institutional and procedural legitimacy. Furthermore, this must be undertaken quickly since there are no other sources of legitimacy available. The process of governance must then be given time to unfold so that the population will understand that here, finally, is a system that exists to serve the national interests, a system that is more than a personal instrument for the ruler and the top political and socio-economic elite. Without such developments, Romania is likely to experience mass rule (perhaps even mob rule) and prolonged stalemate and instability. This, in turn, would eliminate any chance of economic improvement, and continued poor economic conditions might help pave the way for more uprisings, more chaos, and, eventually, the emergence of another strong-man or clique.

The Legacy of Fear

One of the most pervasive traits of Romanian society during the Ceausescu era was the sense of fear that gripped much of the population. This was not merely a fear of officialdom and authorities but a fear of other people—neighbors, friends, work associates, and even relatives. This kind of legacy cannot be erased merely because the common enemy is gone; the unity produced by the shared hatred of Ceausescuism and its system of rule is not sustainable now that the focal point has been removed. This is already borne out by events since the demise of the Ceausescu clan.

The legacy of fear is fueled by the legacy of suspicion and the tendency to focus on personal needs or the needs of the immediate family. Suspicion is a natural concomitant of fear, and it undermines the prospects for building the trust that is essential for the survival of a pluralistic and functioning Romania. At the same time, the tendency to satisfy personal needs at the expense of a common spirit of collective achievement persists. This could be expected after years of extreme material scarcity and insecurity, but it must be overcome in order to establish and nurture a new civic spirit. To make matters worse, it is clear that economic conditions will continue to deteriorate as a workable political system evolves. In the meantime, a willingness to sacrifice for future improvement must be fostered, but the legacies of fear, suspicion, and parochialism will make this difficult. Thus, the future of the new Romania hangs in the balance on this issue.

The Legacy of Corrupt Bureaucracies

Most serious analyses of Romanian politics and society cite the alarming level of corruption, both public and private, that exists in the system. There can be no doubt that this has been widespread among all sectors of society, especially in the bureaucracy at every level. This, in turn, has created a pervasive attitude in the general population that no political figures can be trusted; rather, they must be bribed if any kind of action is to be undertaken. Furthermore, the population has no sense of "administrative efficacy" (if we define this as a belief that bureaucrats can be expected to treat people fairly and equitably on the merits of the case at hand), and this attitude is likely to persist for a long time in wide segments of the population. In fact, trust in officials may be the scarcest commodity of all; it must be earned by the bureaucrats and taught to the people. Until this task is accomplished, policy implementation will be difficult, further endangering the performance of those who must administer the new order.

The Legacy of Authoritarianism

The most enduring of all legacies in contemporary Romania is that of authoritarianism. Authoritarianism may take many forms, from the Ceausescu version and previous modes of communist rule to the military and royal dictatorships of the interwar period. There was also the period of populist and authoritarian rule by the Iron Guard, the League of the Archangel Michael, and other movements that claimed to govern in the name of the people, against bureaucrats and those who represented "part of the whole" rather than "all of the people." These legacies reject the notions of pluralist democracy, in which compromise and partial solutions represent the norm rather than the exception. However, authoritarian tradition does allow for one element of populist rule, namely "mob rule," in which masses of alienated individuals take to the streets in the pursuit of *complete* demands. And from this authoritarian-populist legacy also arises the likelihood of another strongman emerging to set things straight, "clean up the mess," and make binding decisions. The certainty of autocratic rule can be attractive in comparison to the seemingly constant chaos of political pluralism, with its incessant pulling and hauling, its compromises, and its horse-trading.

Under present circumstances, this tradition may well appeal to many Romanians as a way out of chaos and uncertainty. It is fairly certain that a new strongman, should he emerge, will not be a communist, but he may rule in many ways that are familiar to those who lived through the Ceausescu era, albeit without the obvious excesses of that period. Such a regime would alienate a large number of the intelligentsia, but it might be welcomed by important factions of the peasantry and the working class. But, almost by definition, the regime of such a ruler would produce polarization, instability, and stalemate, possibly followed by renewed bloodshed. These are, indeed, troubling prospects.

The Legacy of Class and Regional Differences

The post-Ceausescu order is afflicted with a number of problems that preceded the communist regime but were exacerbated by the rule of that party. The rapid industrialization of the country initially provided a vehicle for massive upward social mobility, and it had a beneficial effect upon the structure of socio-economic classes in Romanian society. This process has now slowed down, and its positive side effects have been reduced. But more importantly, the process has deepened the differences between the city and the countryside, where the least educated, least enterprising, and least productive members of society are left behind as others participate in the modernization process. The importance of education and technical knowledge has created a further schism in society, between those who possess these skills and those who do not. This, in turn, has reinforced the traditional differences between intellectuals and artists, on the one hand, and all other social strata, on the other. This distinction was made clear in early February 1990 as Silviu Brucan, one of the leading members of the Salvation Front, discussed the role of intellectuals as leaders of the nation. Such distinctions, although real, are not welcome among the workers and peasants, who suffered more than others during the Ceausescu regime and now demand their place in the political order.

Regional differences were also accentuated during the Ceausescu era due to the uneven development of the various counties. This then fueled the regional rivalries that have been so much a part of Romanian history. The distinction between the capital city and the rest of the country was also reinforced; in fact, the excessive centralization of power under Nicolae and Elena Ceausescu widened the chasm between Bucharest and other places. This is a dangerous legacy at a time when central authority is severely eroded and may be difficult to restore in an unsettled political situation.

The Legacy of Ethnic Heterogeneity

The nationality policies of the Ceausescu regime left Romania with another legacy that will yield problems of considerable magnitude in the future. A mainstay of Nicolae Ceausescu's policies was his emphasis on Romanian ethno-chauvinism, which glorified (and falsified) the history and accomplishments of the Romanian nation, often at the expense of the other ethnic groups in the country. The policies that emanated from this outlook were clearly discriminatory, especially in the case of the ethnic Hungarians whose suffering has been described by a number of authors. Other groups suffered as well from this excessive emphasis on the real and alleged achievements of the Romanians.

The bitterness that developed over time in response to these policies fanned already existing hatreds. The euphoria of revolution cannot mask this underlying problem, and it is likely that the aftermath of the momentous year 1989 will see a resurfacing of old ethnic animosities. This will take two forms: First, the minorities (particularly the Hungarians) may act out their resentment against the treatment meted out to them by the Romanians, and, second, the fluid political situation may foster a chauvinistic policy on the part of a leadership attempting to establish its own legitimacy in the ethnic Romanian population. These differences between groups will surely affect the political and social life at the regional and local levels, as well. With central authority still weak, such developments could become seriously destabilizing, further enhancing the possibility that a strongman will surface in the ensuing chaos.

The Legacy of Pervasive Bureaucratic Ceausescuism

Perhaps the most debilitating legacy of all stems from the way in which the Ceausescu clan, a relatively small and homogeneous group at the top, spread its tentacles throughout all of Romanian society with a vice grip on the process of appointment to public office, overlapping memberships, and interlocking dictatorships. After a quarter century of rule, all officials are, in a sense, "Ceausescuites," in that they owe their positions to the old order. They are also used to the procedures of autocracy and unrestrained power; such power was exercised upon these officials, and they, in turn, invoked their version of it upon the people. The mind-set that developed as a result of such practices cannot be changed overnight. At the same time, the new political leadership, whatever its form, cannot dismantle the old bureaucratic order instantly but must utilize its representatives to rebuild Romania while exercising political control over them. This is a massive and difficult undertaking, and its success is not ensured. Should it fail, there would be an increased tendency toward the restoration of autocracy, one that is devoid of the obvious excesses of Ceausescuism. The alienation of progressive elements in the technical and managerial intelligentsia that would result might well accelerate existing controversies in the various ruling bodies. A political stalemate is therefore a real possibility.

The Legacy of an Outmoded Industrial Infrastructure

Regardless of who they are, the individuals and groups that ultimately assume the positions of power in Romania must deal with an industrial infrastructure that is outmoded, run-down, and beset with serious managerial deficiencies. Furthermore, the working class is relatively unproductive—a group whose work ethics were formed in the years of Stalinism and Ceausescuism. It will be a Herculean task to deal with all of these economic problems at a time of relative political instability. Yet, it is quite clear that economic reform is a sine qua non for the survival of *any* future political system in Romania. The prospects of success are not particularly good in the short or even intermediate run.

The Legacy of a Creative People

Most of the legacies of the Ceausescu era are negative, but one source of optimism for the future remains. The Romanians (as well as the ethnic minorities residing on Romanian soil) are a creative people with considerable resilience. They have endured repression and rapaciousness before, and they have emerged from the excesses of oppressive regimes with renewed energy. The Ceausescu clan exaggerated the achievements of the Romanians to an extent that made them the laughingstock of Europe, but such nonsense should not obscure the fact that there *are* considerable achievements to celebrate in science, art, literature, and even in some fields of economic endeavor. The creativity and spirit that produced such results under difficult conditions represent real assets as the political process moves fitfully towards new forms, new procedures, and new leadership. One must fervently hope that the spirit will rise to this new and massive challenge.

The achievements of the Romanians do not extend to the political realm, partly because few opportunities were available in this arena. The people, oppressed by foreign and domestic rulers and focused instead upon their villages and families, left matters of power to others and erected firm barriers between themselves and the ruling elite. What is now needed is a new civic spirit with a focus on the *national* level and *all* of society. Creating such a civic consciousness will require all of the positive elements of the people's legacy.

Whither Romania?

As daily events overtake the ability of even the actors themselves to absorb them, analysts everywhere are attempting to draw a coherent picture of the sweeping changes in recent months and of the political order that will follow. This is an extraordinarily difficult task under present conditions, and any conclusions at this stage must be tentative. But a systematic examination of Romanian political culture, traditions, and the legacies of the Ceausescu era allows us to make certain predictions, with a reasonable expectation of fulfillment. The following observations are in order:

1. There will be a prolonged period of political and social instability as Romania gropes for a new formula of power, participation, and pluralism. "Prolonged" in this context means a number of years, not months; even early elections will not solve the problem. In fact, the elections to be held later this year (1990) are likely to enhance such instability because the changes now emerging in society will be directly reflected in the legislative and executive branches of the new political order. And given their divergent agendas and their unwillingness to compromise, the many political parties now surfacing will tend to cancel each other. Consequently, administrative order must be restored long before political stability is achieved. One can therefore expect that much governance will be done via administrative decree. This, in turn, will spark opposition in the political parties, in interest groups, and in the masses themselves, although this may be partly offset by authoritarian tendencies in all of these groups. Further controversy will arise from the convictions of the technical and managerial intelligentsia that they must now be given a major share of power. It is also likely that they will look upon the chaotic political process with some disdain, possibly leading to an attempt to establish an oligarchy of technocrats. Such an effort would clearly raise the level of conflict in the system, increasing the likelihood of political stalemate.

2. Whatever the results of the political process, the economic crisis will continue for a number of years. There is no need to elaborate upon the political ramifications; suffice it to say that economic chaos will make Romania very difficult to rule. Furthermore, such a situation will likely stimulate increasing pressures for "law and order," thus paving the way for authoritarian elements to rise to the top of the fluid political order. Under these circumstances, the armed forces, whose credibility was vastly enhanced by their role in the revolution, may step in to restore some semblance of order and some aspect of predictability in political and socio-economic life. But the military leadership cannot single-handedly run the country, so an alliance may be made with the technocrats and the managers for this purpose.

3. Joint rule by the military and technocratic factions would not preclude a limited form of pluralism. Political parties will run candidates for elections. A legislative process will produce laws and regulations. The masses of the population will have opportunities to participate politically, and they will use them, at times in the streets—in demonstrations, rallies, and other forms of mass behavior. But these sectors of political power will only *share* this commodity with the military-technocratic alliance, they will not control it. Thus, a form of pluralism *below* the pinnacle of autocratic power will emerge. After several years in this mode, Romania may indeed develop a type of pluralism as we know it in the West but certainly not in the immediate future.

4. The communist *party* will cease to exercise power and influence, but *communists* will continue to play an important role in their individual capacities. Despite the obvious discredit of the Ceausescus and the clan, communists cannot be totally excluded from political power in Romania in the 1990s. These communists will be hemmed in by formal and informal restrictions, but they will have an influence, in part because their mind-set is shared by others who are not tainted by party membership. Such a legacy, though understandable, remains a real liability because it hinders the development of the public trust in political institutions and processes that is so desperately needed.

5. Romanian democracy, should it develop, will be different from that in West Europe or the United States. In the euphoria spawned by recent events, some Western analysts and many policy-makers have a tendency to forget that the traditions and cultures of other countries are very different from those in our own Anglo-American or West European contexts. There is little chance that structures, procedures, and institutions in post-revolutionary Romania will match ours in functional terms. Political cultures emerge slowly, and we must be prepared to wait for "democracy" as we know it to develop anywhere in Eastern Europe, especially in Romania. But let us also acknowledge that virtually *any* system will be more humane, more just, and eventually more efficient than that of the Ceausescus. In that light, the Romanian revolution was an event of hope, ripe with possibilities for the future.

At the present time the structure of political power in Romania remains fluid, but at the end of January 1990 the following structure had emerged. These individuals occupied top positions in the newly constituted political bodies of Romania:

Council of the National Salvation Front

Executive Bureau

President	Ion Iliescu
First Vice President	Dumitru Mazilu
Vice Presidents	Cazimir Ionescu
	Carol Kiraly
Secretary	Dan Marţian
Members	Bogdan Teodoriu
	Vasile Neacşa
	Silviu Brucan
	Gheorghe Manole
	Ion Caramitru
	Nicolae Radu

Council of Ministers

Prime Minister	Petre Roman
Deputy Prime Ministers	Mihail Drăgănescu
	Gelu Voican-Voiculescu
Ministers	
Agriculture and the Food Industry	Ştefan Nicolae
Chemical and Petrochemical Industry	Gheorghe Caranfil
Culture	Andrei Pleşu
Education	Mihai Şora
Electrical Engineering, Electronics, and Computer Science	Anton Vătăşescu
Energy	Adrian Georgescu
Foreign Affairs	Sergiu Celac
Foreign Trade	Nicolae M. Nicolae
Geology	Ioan Folea
Health	Dan Enăchescu
Internal Affairs	Lt.-Gen. Mihai Chitac
Justice	Teofil Pop
Labor and Social Care	Mihnea Maremeliuc
Light Industry	Constantin Popescu
Machine-Building Industry	Ioan Aurel
Metallurgical Industry	Ioan Chesa
Mining	Nicolae Dicu
National Defense	Army General Nicolae Militaru

National Economy — Col.-Gen. Atanase Victor Stănculescu

Oil — Victor Mureşan

Post and Telecommunications — Stelian Pintilie

Sports — Mircea Angelescu

Transportation — Corneliu Burada

Tourism — (Acting) Mihail Lupoi

Water, Forestry Management, and the Environment — Simion Hîncu

CHAIRMEN OF OTHER NATIONAL OR CENTRAL BODIES

General Police Inspectorate — Lt.-Gen. Ioan Jean Moldoveanu (Deputy Minister of Internal Affairs)

Romanian Radio and Television — Aurel Dragoş Munteanu

ROMPRESS (Romanian Official Press Agency) — Neagu Udroiu (Director General)

National Commission for Standards and Quality — Mihail Victor Buracu (Minister Secretary of State)

National Commission for Town and Territorial Planning — Şerban Popescu-Criveanu (Minister Secretary of State)

National Commission for the Control of the Nuclear Activities — Olariu Stefan Alexandru (Minister Secretary of State)

Bucharest Institute for Nuclear Physics — Gheorghe Pascovici (Director General) (Minister Secretary of State)

National Commission for Statistics — Petru Pepelea (Minister Secretary of State)

National Commission for Labor Safety — Virgil Iga (Minister Secretary of State)

Romanian Bank for Foreign Trade — Vasile Voloşeniuc*

It is upon the shoulders of these individuals that the matter of political transformation now falls with uncertain prospects for the future.

---

*Source: Radio Free Europe Research, January 21, 1990.

Index

Vlad Tepes, 51, 175
Voican-Voiculescu, Gelu, 279
Voitec, Stafan, 84
Voloşeniuc, Vasile, 280

Wallachia, 25, 27, 28, 44
Warsaw Pact, 57, 173, 181, 196, 203, 215, 216, 217, 219, 224, 229
West Germany. *See* Federal Republic of Germany
Winter, Richard, 84

Women, 66, 90, 92, 125
Work ethic, 12, 158
Work force, 146(table), 147(tables), 155. *See also* Human resources; Occupational categories
World War II, 46–47, 163

Yugoslavia, 7, 12, 47, 212, 213, 216, 226(n7), 239

"Zionists," 48